HTML Web Publishing 6-in-1

by Todd Stauffer

A Division of Macmillan Computer Publishing
201 West 103rd Street, Indianapolis, Indiana 46290 USA

Acknowledgments

The author would like to thank the hard-working team at Que for helping to make this project happen so quickly and gracefully, including Jane Brownlow, Mark Cierzniak, Kate Givens, and Henly Wolin. Of course, there are many other important people whose names I don't ever learn—like, for instance, the folks down in accounting. Kudos to them, too.

Personally, I'd like to thank Donna Ladd, who, along with being the best editor I've ever had, is also my best friend and travel partner. Thanks for the support and understanding during the book crunch.

Trademark Acknowledgments

All terms mentioned in this book that are known to be or are suspected of being trademarks or service marks have been appropriately capitalized. Que Corporation cannot attest to the accuracy of this information. Use of a term in this book should not be regarded as affecting the validity of any trademark or service mark.

President
Roland Elgey

Senior Vice President/Publishing
Don Fowley

Publisher
Joseph B. Wikert

Publishing Director
Karen Reinisch

Manager of Publishing Operations
Linda H. Buehler

General Manager
Joe Muldoon

Director of Editorial Services
Carla Hall

Managing Editor
Thomas F. Hayes

Director of Acquisitions
Cheryl D. Willoughby

Acquisitions Editor
Jane Brownlow

Product Director
Henly Wolin

Production Editor
Kate Givens

Editors
Elizabeth Barrett
Judith Goode
Rebecca M. Mounts

Product Marketing Manager
Kourtnaye Sturgeon

Assistant Product Marketing Manager
Gretchen Schlesinger

Technical Editors
Tony Schafer
Sunil Hazari

Media Development Specialist
David Garratt

Acquisitions Coordinator
Michelle R. Newcomb

Software Relations Coordinator
Susan D. Gallagher

Editorial Assistant
Jennifer L. Chisolm

Book Designers
Kim Scott
Glenn Larsen

Cover Designer
Jay Corpus

Production Team
Maribeth Echard
DiMonique Ford
Nicole Ruessler
Julie Searls

Indexer
Tina Trettin

Composed in *Helvetica* and *Palatino* by Que Corporation.

Contents

Part II: Web Graphics and Animation   101

Part VI: Web Publishing Tools 371

We'd Like to Hear from You!

Que Corporation has a long-standing reputation for high-quality books and products. To ensure your continued satisfaction, we also understand the importance of customer service and support.

Tech Support

If you need assistance with the information in this book, please access Macmillan Computer Publishing's online Knowledge Base at:

http://www.superlibrary.com/general/support

Our most Frequently Asked Questions are answered there. If you do not find the answer to your questions on our Web site, you may contact Macmillan Technical Support by phone at **317/581-3833** or via e-mail at **support@mcp.com**.

Also be sure to visit Que's Desktop Applications and Operating Systems team Web resource center for all the latest information, enhancements, errata, downloads, and more:

http://www.quecorp.com/desktop_os/

Orders, Catalogs, and Customer Service

To order other Que or Macmillan Computer Publishing books, catalogs, or products, please contact our Customer Service Department:

Phone: 800/858-7674

Fax: 800/882-8583

Or visit our online bookstore:

http://www.mcp.com/

Comments and Suggestions

We want you to let us know what you like or dislike most about this book or other Que products. Your comments will help us to continue publishing the best books available on computer topics in today's market.

Henly Wolin
Product Development Specialist
Que Corporation
201 West 103rd Street, 4B
Indianapolis, Indiana 46290 USA
Fax: 317/581-4663
E-mail: **hwolin@que.mcp.com**

Please be sure to include the book's title and author as well as your name and your phone or fax number.

We will carefully review your comments and share them with the author. Please note that due to the high volume of mail we receive, we may not be able to reply to every message.

Thank you for choosing Que!

About the Author

Todd Stauffer is a magazine writer, host of the Peak Computing Radio Hour in Denver, CO, and cohost of the television show "Disk Doctors," airing nationally on JEC Knowledge TV. He's the author of *HTML by Example, Using HTML 3.2 2nd Edition, Using the Internet with Your Mac,* and four other titles. In addition, he has coauthored five titles, all of which have been published by Que Corporation.

Todd's articles have appeared in local and national magazines including *The Inside Line, WebSight Magazine,* and *Windows Magazine.* He writes a regular column for *Peak Computing Magazine* called "On the Internet," available weekly on the Web at **http://peak-computing.com**. He also serves as an expert television guest on "Jones Technology Update" and the "Computer Zone" and gives occasional seminars along Colorado's Front Range. His story "Mac vs. PC: Sometimes it's War" won Peak Computing Online a "Hot Site" award from *USA Today*.

Todd has also worked as a freelance advertising writer, technical writer, and magazine editor, all in consumer-oriented computing. Outside of computing, he currently freelances as a car reviewer for the *Colorado Springs Gazette Telegraph* and as a travel writer/photographer for various publications.

http://members.aol.com/tstauffer/

Introduction

One of the most exciting things you can do with your computer is become your own Web publisher—if you've ever had something you just needed to say, or some reason to put together your own corner of the Web. If you're a writer, editor, hobbyist, or businessperson, you've probably seen that there's an advantage to being on the Web. Well, go for it.

If you've ever worked in a word processing program, you're ready and qualified to learn the HyperText Markup Language (HTML). It's not difficult at all. Even though Web pages these days are still constructed of little codes, it's getting easier and easier to create and publish exciting pages on the Web. That's why we've put together this new approach to HTML—*HTML Web Publishing 6-in-1*.

Aside from covering the latest standards and talking about current technology, this book is focused on quickly getting you up to speed on all the basic HTML commands. Then, the text takes you much further into other exciting areas like multimedia, scripting and Web programming, and even Dynamic HTML.

Who Should Read This Book

Just about anyone who appreciates a no-nonsense, step-by-step approach to learning a new computer topic should read *HTML Web Publishing 6-in-1*. This book focuses on getting things done quickly by breaking the learning process up into short, quick lessons. Within each of its six parts, the text has been broken into small, easily digested chunks to make learning HTML and associated subjects very easy.

In fact, it should take very little time at all. You may notice that this book is fairly substantial. But here's a little secret—it's not even all about HTML! This text is filled with other aspects of creating content for the Web. Topics get as complicated as actual JavaScript programming and as approachable as quick reviews of the latest Web editors. Hopefully, most everything you'll need to know to become a Web page specialist is right here in this text.

The only qualification you need to read this book is a passing relationship with the World Wide Web. If you've ever "surfed" using Netscape Navigator, Internet Explorer, or a similar program—and the concept of the Web made sense to you—then you're ready to begin participating from the other side. Welcome to the world of Web content creation.

How This Book Is Organized

HTML Web Publishing 6-in-1 is divided into six parts:

- **Part I: Creating Web Pages**   Almost every Web page has some basic elements in common. Here, you'll learn what an HTML tag is and which tags are required on every HTML document. You'll also learn how to create a basic page and save it for display on the World Wide Web.

- **Part II: Web Graphics and Animation**   After creating a basic Web page, you're ready to spruce it up with all kinds of goodies—from portraits and photos to animations, presentations, and even digital video. If you're a movie-maker, photo album aficionado, or you're responsible for getting your products or services on the Web, here's where you'll create the visuals.

- **Part III: Enhancing Web Pages**   This part gets you quickly up to speed on the very latest in HTML. I mean the *very* latest. Not just tables, forms, and frames but stuff even some experts don't get yet—like HTML style sheets. Best of all, it makes perfect sense.

- **Part IV: Scripting**   For some folks, this is the guts of the book. You may not be one of those people, but that's all right. Check out this part anyway. Even a few of the examples and tricks might prove useful and fun on your Web pages. And, best of all, scripting gives you amazing freedom to gather data from your users and create exciting, dynamic content.

- **Part V: Dynamic HTML**   Speaking of dynamic content, here's the next level of Web content creation. Now, Web pages act less like the printed variety and more like animated presentations created in programs like Microsoft PowerPoint. Add animation, special effects, colors, and even dynamic content directly to your Web pages. This is getting exciting.

- **Part VI: Web Publishing Tools**   Throughout most of this book, you focus on the most basic tools for creating Web pages—a text editor and a good graphics program. But, in this part, you'll look at many of the tools designed to make the job easier. Most of these programs are great once you already know the basics. And, if you've worked straight through the book, you *will* know the basics.

Each part is divided into several lessons. Because each of the lessons takes only 10 minutes or less to complete, you'll quickly master the skills you need. In addition, the straightforward, easy-to-understand explanations and numbered lists within each lesson guide you quickly and easily to your goal of mastering HTML.

Conventions Used in This Book

The following icons are included throughout the text to help you quickly identify particular types of information.

TIP   **Tip Icons**   mark shortcuts and hints for saving time and creating HTML documents more efficiently.

Term Icons   point out easy-to-follow definitions that you'll need to know in order to understand HTML and related topics.

Caution Icons   mark information that's intended to help you avoid making mistakes and losing time or data.

CAUTION

In addition to the special icons, you'll find these conventions used throughout the text:

On-screen text	On-screen text appears in bold type.
What you type	Information you need to type also appears in bold.
Items you select	Items you need to select or keys you need to press also appear in bold type.

xxi

`<code>`	Special HTML tags (or codes). The brackets are part of the HTML command.
`Computer output`	Long sections of computer text appear in a monospace font.
➡	This character indicates code that should be typed as one line. When you see this character, you will know to type the code as one line, even though the dimensions of the book don't allow this.

Errata and frequently asked questions will be posted on my Web site at **http://members.aol.com/tstauffer/** on the World Wide Web. Feel free to drop by if you have any questions or concerns about the text. Enjoy!

Creating Web Pages

What Is HTML?

1

In this lesson, you learn what the HyperText Markup Language (HTML) is, how it works, and where HTML is used. You also learn what applications you can use to create HTML documents.

The HyperText Markup Language

The HyperText Markup Language (HTML) is a series of standard codes and conventions designed to create pages and emphasize text for display in programs like Web browsers. HTML is the basis of the World Wide Web, a global service of the Internet. The Web is the most graphical of all Internet services, allowing users to create their own *Web pages*.

TERM   **Web Page**   A single HTML document, regardless of its length. A Web *site* is a number of pages linked together and controlled by a particular individual or organization.

Although the scope and importance of HTML has changed somewhat over the past few years, its basic purpose is still the same. HTML is designed to create attractive, *multimedia*, electronic publications, specifically for the World Wide Web.

TERM   **Multimedia**   Digital images, movies, sounds, and specialized presentations like those created with Microsoft PowerPoint or Macromedia Director. HTML is capable of including a number of different types of **multimedia** files in a Web page.

It's important to note, however, that HTML is not programming. (*Programming* means creating scripts or applications using complicated computer languages like C++ or Java.) Instead, creating Web pages is more often referred to as "authoring," simply to make the distinction between creating computer applications (which can be exceedingly difficult) and creating Web pages, which tends to be much easier.

Hypertext and Hyperlinks

One of the keys to HTML—and, by extension, a key to the way the Web works—is its support of hypertext links. Using special commands in HTML, a Web author can change certain text to make it "clickable." When the user clicks hypertext, shown in Figure 1.1, her Web browser generally responds by loading a new Web page.

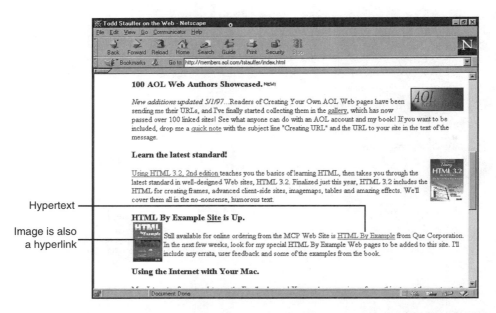

Figure 1.1 Hypertext links usually appear on a Web page in a different color and underlined.

But not all links are necessarily text—images can also be "clickable." In that case, it's more appropriate to call the link a hyperlink, but it's not terribly important. The terms are basically interchangeable.

What's more important is recognizing what a big part hyperlinks play in the world of HTML creation and the World Wide Web. Nearly every page on the Web, ultimately, is in some way linked to every other page. On a smaller scale, hyperlinks make it important for you to consider the organization of your site. They also make it possible for your Web page to take part in a larger world of related pages.

But how is it possible to link to all these pages? Every page on the Web (and most other Internet resources) has a special address that uniquely identifies it. Those addresses are called *Uniform Resource Locators (URLs)*.

TIP   **How Do You Say That?**   This text will be much easier to read if you say URL like the name "Earl."

Uniform Resource Locators

Most Internet services have some sort of addressing scheme, so you can find a particular resource easily. For each service, these addresses tend to be a bit different.

For instance, you would send an e-mail message to my America Online account using the address **tstauffer@aol.com** in an e-mail application. To access the AOL public FTP site (where you might download the AOL software application), on the other hand, you would enter the following address in the FTP application you are using: **ftp.aol.com**.

The World Wide Web also has its own addressing scheme, but it's slightly more advanced than the schemes of its predecessors. Not only is the Web newer, but its addresses have to be more sophisticated because of the Web's unique ability to access all of the different Internet services.

URLs are these special addresses. They follow a format like this:

protocol://internet_address/path/filename.ext

or

protocol:internet_address

An example of an URL to access a Web document would be:

http://www.microsoft.com/windows/index.html

Look at that address carefully. According to the format for an URL, **http://** would be the protocol and **www.microsoft.com** is the address of Microsoft's Web server computer. That's followed by a backslash (/) to suggest that a path statement is coming next.

The *path statement* tells you that you're looking at the document **index.html**, located in the directory **windows**.

Path Statements   If you're familiar with DOS, Windows, or UNIX, you will probably recognize path statements straight away. Mac OS users and others simply need to realize that a path statement offers a "path" to a specific file on the server computer's hard drive. A Web browser needs to know in exactly which directories and subdirectories (folders and subfolders) a file can be found, so a path statement is a standard part of any URL.

There are two basic advantages to the URL.

- First, it allows you to indicate explicitly the type of Internet service involved. HTTP, for instance, indicates the HyperText Transfer Protocol—the basic protocol for transferring Web documents. You'll look at this part of the URL in a moment.
- Second, the URL system of addressing gives every single document, program, and file on the Internet its own, particular address.

The Different Protocols for URLs

HTTP is the protocol most often used by Web browsers to access HTML pages. Table 1.1 shows some of the other protocols that can be part of an URL.

Table 1.1   Possible Protocols for an URL

Protocol	Accesses...
http://	HTML documents
https://	Some "secure" HTML documents
file://	HTML documents on your hard drive
ftp://	FTP sites and files

Protocol	Accesses...
gopher://	Gopher menus and documents
news://	UseNet newsgroups on a particular news server
news:	UseNet newsgroups
mailto:	E-mail messages
telnet:	Remote Telnet (login) session

By entering one of these protocols, followed by an Internet server address and a path statement, you can access nearly any document, directory, file, or program available on the Internet or on your own hard drive.

CAUTION

mailto:, news:, telnet: These protocols have slightly different requirements to create an URL. *mailto:* is followed by a simple e-mail address, *news:* is followed by just the newsgroup name and *telnet:* is followed by just a server address (no path statement).

Where Is HTML Used?

Aside from the World Wide Web (which is overwhelmingly the major use of HTML), HTML is beginning to become popular in other parts of the Internet as well. For instance:

- Some e-mail programs have begun to support certain commands in HTML.
- Some of the Internet's UseNet discussion groups also support HTML, although not all do.
- Some programs and operating systems are beginning to use HTML to format their online help documents.
- Companies often use HTML to create *intranets,* or Internet-like networks within their companies, for posting announcements, product information, and other important documents.

Generally, these are more limited uses of HTML—perhaps a few codes are used to change regular text into italic or to include a clickable hyperlink to an interesting Web site. For Web authors, HTML tends to get rather involved, since there are a lot of interesting commands available for Web pages and sites.

In other applications (like the e-mail program in Figure 1.2), limited HTML support is generally built into the program.

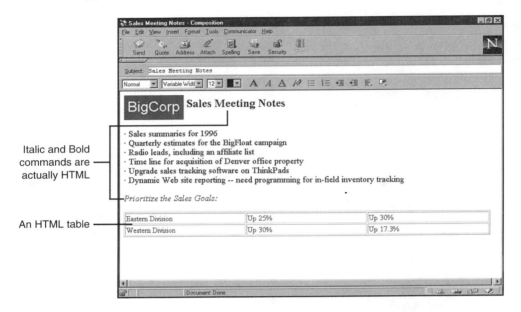

Italic and Bold commands are actually HTML

An HTML table

Figure 1.2   Some e-mail programs are now beginning to allow users to send HTML-enhanced e-mail messages to one another.

So how is it that HTML is able to travel through e-mail and UseNet just as it does over the Web? Part of the reason is the fact that HTML is text-based—in fact, every HTML document is nothing more than a plain text document. There are no images or multimedia in an HTML document. Instead, the document *points* to the image files, which must be individually available alongside the HTML document.

So, when a viewer (like a Web browser) reads the HTML document, it will also read instructions for loading and positioning any images or multimedia files that you've decided to include. To create an HTML document, then, all you really need are the same tools you'd use to create a plain text document.

What Type of Editor Should You Use?

There are many different HTML and Web editing programs available, like Netscape Composer or Microsoft FrontPage Express, which are designed to make creating Web pages easier. These programs work a little like an HTML-enabled e-mail program: They hide the HTML codes from the Web author. This can be useful, in some cases, once you understand quite a bit about HTML.

TIP   **Special Tools**   These specialized Web editing programs, like FrontPage Express or Composer, are discussed in Part VI, "Web Publishing Tools."

Unfortunately, the world of HTML is still at a point where learning the individual codes is important—even if you often take advantage of the convenience of a Web editor. At times, you'll find that advanced commands—things like dynamic HTML, scripting, and multimedia plug-ins—aren't even built into a typical Web editor, because the specifications move so quickly. In that case, it's important to fall back on editing the HTML document by hand:

- For most of the lessons in this book, a simple *ASCII* text editor will suffice.
- For Windows users, the built-in text editor NotePad should work fine.
- For Mac OS users, SimpleText or the freeware program BBEdit Lite (**http://www.barebones.com/**) is a good choice.
- UNIX users pick their editor of choice: VI, Emacs, or anything similar.

TERM   **ASCII**   A standard set of text characters that can be transmitted between any number of operating systems and read without translation. Most programs that call themselves "text editors" save and load documents in ASCII text.

In this lesson, you learned what HTML is and where it's used. You also learned what type of program you should use to create HTML documents. In the next lesson, you'll learn the basic design rules for a Web page.

Design Considerations

2

In this lesson, you learn the basic design rules for organizing and creating your Web pages.

Organize Your Document

HTML was originally envisioned as a way to put scientific and academic papers on the Internet for anyone to read. Some of those roots are still apparent in the methodical way in which a document can be organized. Some of the commands in HTML are designed for such organization, so you'll want to consider them as you plan your pages:

Title   Each HTML document has a title specified in its code.

Headings   There are optional headings, ranging in six different sizes, that you can use to set off different parts of your document.

Paragraphs   The main text of your Web page can be divided into a series of paragraphs using the HTML paragraph command. The words within these paragraphs can then be aligned in certain ways, forced to use particular font styles (like bold or italic), and other options.

Horizontal Lines   Horizontal lines can be used to visually break up related parts of an HTML document into sections.

Lists   HTML supports the creation of three basics types of lists: numbered, bullet, and definition lists (with both a term and a description of that term).

Tables   More advanced HTML allows you to create tables that hold data in a way that's similar to a spreadsheet application such as Microsoft Excel. Text, hyperlinks, and images can be arranged in rows and columns for easy viewing.

Figure 2.1 shows you how these organizing elements can be put together to create an interesting, easy-to-read Web page.

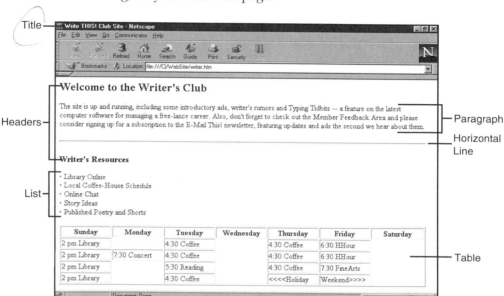

Figure 2.1 Many of HTML's commands are designed to help you organize your page.

Clearly, these commands don't take into account the rather visual nature of the Web—those parts (like graphics and clickable buttons) are important, too, and it's always important to remember that you're designing Web pages to be read on a computer screen.

Chunking Text

Technically, a Web page can be any length that you desire—a really long page forces your user to scroll in their Web browser (so he can see contents that don't fit on the screen). And while this is possible, it's not always desirable. If you want to keep your readers interested, it's best to *chunk* the text on your page, so that the pages aren't terribly long and they aren't filled with paragraph after paragraph of boring text.

Chunking This isn't exactly an official HTML term, but it does describe a process for document creation. This book, for instance, uses chunking to break up the text. Flip through and notice that there are never more than three or four paragraphs before a figure, tip, or other callout appears. On a Web page, you should try to break up paragraphs of text with images, horizontal lines, headings, and lists.

Part of this chunking theory also suggests that you should consider the fact that your readers are looking at your Web pages on a computer screen. It's important, then, to make this as comfortable a prospect as possible. That means creating pages that don't take up much more than a single screen, but use hyperlinks to lead the reader to the information they're interested in seeing. A good example of this is shown in Figure 2.2.

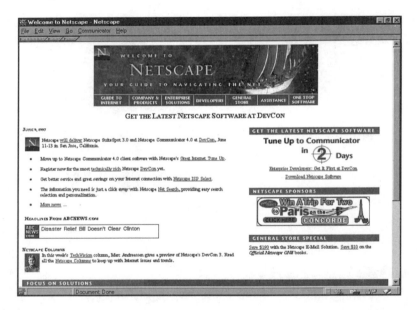

Figure 2.2 Whenever possible, design your pages so they only take up about one screen and use hyperlinks to move users to new pages.

The Bandwidth Issue

Another important thing to remember about Web pages is that everything you post on the Web has to be downloaded by the folks who visit your site. Web browsers go through a three-step process:

1. When a user's Web browser encounters a new Web page, it begins by bringing the page over the Internet to that user's computer.
2. Then it brings all of the associated graphics and multimedia files.
3. As that is happening, the browser does its best to display what has already arrived and format it correctly. But, this process takes time.

In fact, it can take too much time if you're not careful. That's another reason why you should ensure that your pages aren't too long, that they include hyperlinks to pages with more information, and that they're well organized. Your users will thank you—especially the ones with slower modem-based connections to the Internet.

Fortunately, the text within a Web page (along with the HTML markup commands) doesn't really take that long to transfer. Images and multimedia files take considerably more time. So, when you're thinking about and designing your Web pages, try to remember that the fewer graphics you include, the better. A well-designed *index page*, like the one shown in Figure 2.3, will load quickly while allowing users to make their own decisions about what to read next.

 TERM   **Index Page**   The first page of a Web site—it generally serves to introduce the reader to the site, give the "latest news" about the site, and serve as a hyperlinked table of contents. The index page is sometimes called the *home page*.

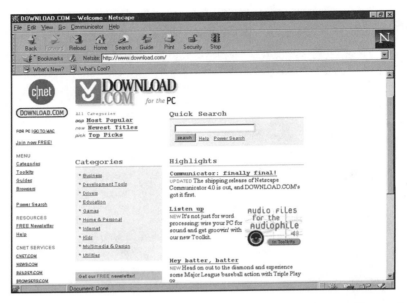

Figure 2.3 A short page with a few, small graphics can be both appealing and quick to display in the user's Web browser.

In this lesson, you learned some of the basic design considerations for creating Web pages. In the next lesson, you'll create a template to help you build all your HTML documents.

Creating an
HTML Template

In this lesson, you learn how to create a template for your Web pages and how to test the pages you create.

Starting an HTML Document

You've already learned this—all you need is a text editor. In Windows 95, that's Notepad or WordPad. For Macintosh users, SimpleText is the perfect HTML editor. UNIX users can opt for VI or Emacs. Basically, all you need to remember is that HTML pages, while they include the .HTM or .HTML file extensions, are simply ASCII text files. Any program that generates ASCII text files will work fine as an HTML editor—even a word processor such as WordPerfect or Microsoft Word.

TIP **Save as ASCII** If you create an HTML page in a word processor, don't forget to use the Save As command to save it as an ASCII text file.

Add Document Tags

The first HTML tags you'll learn are the document tags. These are the tags that are required for every HTML page you create. They define the different parts of the document.

TERM **Tags** Most HTML commands are referred to as tags, since you're "tagging"—or marking—certain text with a particular behavior. For instance, in: `<i>this is italic text</i>` the `<i>` and `</i>` commands, *tag* the enclosed text as italic. (Notice that the slash marks the difference between an opening and closing tag; `<I>` is an opening tag and `</I>` is a closing tag.

Like a magazine article, an HTML document has two distinct parts—a head and a body. The head of the HTML document is where you enter the title of the page.

To create the head portion of your HTML document, type the following in your text editor:

```
<HEAD>



</HEAD>
```

This section will eventually tell the Web browser what special information should be made available about this page, and what it should call the document in the title bar of the browser window.

If you've got a head, then you'll need a body, right? The body is where you'll do most of your work—you'll enter text, headlines, graphics, and all your other Web goodies. To add the body section, start after the </HEAD> tag, and enter the following:

```
<BODY>



</BODY>
```

Between these two tags, you'll eventually enter the rest of the text and graphics for your Web page.

There's one last thing you need to consider. In order that all Web browsers understand that this is an HTML document (remember that you're saving it as ASCII text, so the browser could be confused), you need to add some tags on each side of the head and body tags you've created. Above the first <HEAD> tag, you need to enter the following:

```
<HTML>
```

and after the last </BODY> tag, type the following:

```
</HTML>
```

Now, at least as far as our Web browser is concerned, you have a complete Web document!

The Comment Tag

There's one other tag to discuss in this chapter, called the comment tag. This tag is fairly unique, in that it's actually used to make the Web browser ignore anything the tag contains. That can be text, hypertext links, image links, even small scripts and programs.

CAUTION

Don't Comment Old HTML   It's best to delete obsolete links and tags from your documents, rather than just using the comment tag. Some browsers will display certain tags even if they are "commented out."

For now, you'll use the comment tag to hide text. The point in hiding the text is that it allows you to create a private message that is intended to remind you of something or to help those who view the raw HTML document to understand what you're doing. That's why it's called the comment tag. For instance:

```
<!--This is a comment that won't display in a browser-->
```

The comment tag is a bit different from other tags, in that it contains text, but doesn't have an opening and closing tag. Instead, the text for your comment is enclosed in a single tag that begins with <!-- and ends with -->.

Generally, you'll use the comment tag for your own benefit—perhaps to mark a point in a particular HTML document where you need to remember to update some text, or perhaps to explain a particularly confusing part of your page. Because it's fairly easy for anyone to view your raw HTML document, you might also use the comment tag to create a copyright message or give information about yourself.

Create an HTML Template

Now, take what you know and create a template. By saving this template as a generic text file, you'll have a quick way to create new HTML files—simply load the template and use the **File**, **Save As** command to save it as your new Web page.

1. Start by entering the following in a blank text file:

```
<HTML>
<HEAD>
<TITLE>Enter Title Here</TITLE>
<!--Designed By Todd Stauffer-->
<!--Last updated 10/12-->
</HEAD>
<BODY>

</BODY>
</HTML>
```

2. Next, save this as an ASCII text file called **TEMPLATE.HTML** (or **TEMPLATE.HTM** if you're using DOS or Windows 3.1).

Now, whenever you're ready to create a new HTML document, simply load TEMPLATE.HTML into your text editor and use the **File**, **Save As** command to rename it.

Naming Your Files

We've already mentioned that file extensions are an important part of all the file names you use for your Web site. Because other Web browsers may rely on the file extension to know what sort of document or file it is, you'll need to include the appropriate extensions with all your Web site files.

Your Web site will almost always begin with a file called **index.html**. Most Web server software programs will automatically load this page if the URL of your site is accessed without a specific path and file reference. For example, entering this URL in your browser:

http://www.sun.com/

actually results in the URL **http://www.sun.com/index.html** being loaded in your browser. Your Web site's first page should be designed with this in mind. If you plan to offer only Netscape-enhanced pages, for instance, you'll want to let your users know this on the index.html page.

 TIP   **Know Your Operating System**   Remember that it's important to know what operating system your Web server uses. Some of the suggestions in this section for styles of file names will not be helpful if you're using a DOS-based server, since names are limited to the 8.3 format.

Testing Your Page

You'll need a Web browser to check on the appearance of your Web page as you create it. All Web browsers should have the ability to load local pages from your hard drive, just as they can load HTML pages across the Web. Check the menu of your Web browser, as shown in Figure 3.1 (if it's a graphical browser), for a command like File, Open File.

Figure 3.1   Click **Choose File** to load an HTML document from your hard drive.

To test an HTML document in your Web browser:

1. Use the **File**, **Save** command to save any changes you've made to the HTML document in your text editor.

2. Switch to your Web browser, then choose the **File**, **Open File** command to open the file in your browser.

    The document should appear in your Web browser. Check it for problems, typos, and other issues.

3. Switch back to your text editor and make any changes that are necessary, or continue working on the page.

In this lesson, you created an HTML template and learned how to test your creations. In the next lesson, you'll learn about putting your Web pages online.

Putting Your
Pages Online

*In this lesson, you learn the basics of saving files on the Web
and accessing them using URLs.*

Finding a Web Server

Before you can display your HTML pages on the Web, you'll need access to a
Web server. This may already be taken care of for you, especially if you work
with an Information Systems (IS) department in a larger corporation. If this is
the case when you want to update the site, you'll just need to know how and
where to send your HTML files. Otherwise, you'll need to make some arrange-
ments on your own.

 TIP **Free Space?**   If you already have Internet access through an Internet
Service Provider (ISP), you may already have Web storage space available to
you. Ask your ISP for information on saving HTML documents to your Web
space.

What Is a Web Server?

A Web server is simply a computer with an Internet connection that runs
software designed to send out HTML pages and other file formats (such as
multimedia files). The server computer should have a relatively high-speed
connection to the Internet (faster than any available modem connections, for
instance) and be powerful enough to deal with a number of simultaneous
connections from the Internet.

Web server software generally requires a fairly robust operating system (like UNIX, Windows NT, or OS/2), although software is available for other versions of Microsoft Windows, and the Macintosh OS is a very popular choice for Web server computers.

Dealing with an ISP

For any sort of connection to the Internet, you'll probably need to deal with an Internet service provider. These companies offer dial-up and special high-speed connections to the Internet, as well as generally offering Web and other types of Internet servers for your use.

 TIP **Looking for a Provider for Your Web Page?**   With your Web browser, you can access lists of ISPs around the country (and world) at **http:// thelist.com** or **http://www.yahoo.com/Business_and_Economy/ Companies/Internet_Services/Web_Presence_Providers/**—which includes a listing of free Web page providers. You might also check with your current ISP for Web deals, since many popular online services offer free or cheap Web space.

For the typical smaller Web site, you'll want to buy space on the ISP's Web site. Generally, this will give you an URL that begins with the name of the ISP's host computer, but points to a special directory for your HTML pages, as follows:

> **http://www.isp.com/***username*/**index.html**

With most Web server programs, the default page that is first loaded is named index.html, so that's the name you'll use for the first page you'd like to present to users when they access your Web site.

Uploading Web Pages

Once you've decided on an ISP, you're ready to create your HTML pages and upload them to the server. To do all this correctly, though, you'll probably need to ask a few questions:

- **What is my site's default URL?**   This should be something like the ISP's host address and a directory for your username. For instance, if your username is **jsmith** and your ISP's Web server is **www.webco.net** then the default URL for your site might be **http://www.webcom.net/jsmith/**.

Different ISPs will organize this in different ways, so you'll need to make sure you get this right.

TIP **Your Own Domain** Many ISPs will give you the option, at an increased price, of creating your own domain name for your site. Then users could access your site at http://www.*yourname*.com/.

- **How do I upload files to my site's directory?** You should get instructions for accessing your Web site's directory on the Web server computer using either FTP or a UNIX shell account. We'll discuss this more in the section, "Updating Your Web Site," in this lesson.
- **Are there any limitations to the names I can give my files?** The operating system in use by the Web server may not be instantly obvious to you. If this is the case, you'll want to ask if there is a certain file name length or a certain format for naming files you need to follow.

TIP **How to Name Files** When in doubt, use the DOS 8.3 file name convention in the style *filename.ext* where *filename* can be no more than eight letters, and *.ext* is a three-letter file name extension, such as **.htm**.

- **Can I create subdirectories within my main Web site directory?** Most Web servers will give you this capability, but some will not allow you to do so.
- **What support is offered for CGI programming?** Some servers won't allow you to add CGI scripts to your Web site for processing forms or adding other interactive features. At the same time some will, but require you to pay extra or pay to have the provider write those scripts (regardless of your ability). If you plan a highly interactive site, then you should ask about CGI support.

Organizing a Web Site

The most important thing to remember when organizing a Web site is how the server computer you're using will differ from the computer you use to create Web pages. This is because you'll need to know the exact path to HTML pages and multimedia files you use in creating your Web page. As we've seen before, an URL requires both a server name and a path statement to the file. This includes files that you've placed on your own Web server—so while you're creating your Web pages, you'll need to know where your files will eventually be.

Although there are a number of different ways to arrange a Web site, there are some rules of thumb to keep in mind. For the most part, any organization you create for your Web site files should be designed to make updating your pages easy in the future. If you have to move all your files around every time you change something on a Web page, you'll also be forced to change all the hypertext links on many other pages—and that can be incredibly time-consuming.

Types of Organization

Here are a couple of different types of organization for Web sites:

- **Single-directory sites**   Smaller sites (with just a few HTML pages and graphics) can often get by with a single directory on the Web server. All your graphics and HTML pages are in this one directory. One of the biggest advantages of this system is that links to local files and graphics require no special path statements.

- **Directory by function**   One way to organize more complicated sites is to put each section of related Web pages in the same directory. For instance, in your main directory you might offer only your first (index) page and its associated graphics. For a business site, then, you'd have subdirectories for About the Business, Product Information, Technical Support, and so on. In each of these subdirectories, you'd include all the related HTML files and the graphics for those pages.

- **Directory by file type**   Some people prefer to create subdirectories according to the type of file as opposed to the content of the page. Your main directory may have only the index page of your site. Other subdirectories might be Graphics, Web Pages, Downloadable Files, and so on. The main advantage in organizing this way is that files generally have to be replaced only once. If you use a graphic on a number of different pages, for instance, you replace it once in the Graphics subdirectory, and all the HTML pages that access this graphic will use the new one.

- **Hybrid**   The best way to organize a large site might be a hybrid of the last two preceding methods. Creating separate subdirectories for non-recurring items (such as individual Web pages in each category) while creating other subdirectories for items used multiple times (such as graphics) lets you get at all the files in an efficient way. A hybrid organization is shown in Figure 4.1.

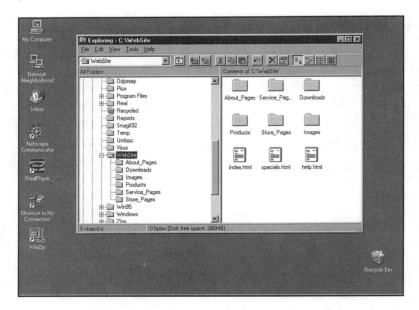

Figure 4.1   In this hybrid site (displayed in Windows Explorer), different functions are organized into different folders, but a single image folder is also used for image file types.

Naming Your Files

You've already seen that file extensions are an important part of all the file names you use for your Web site. Because other Web browsers may rely on the file extension to know what sort of document or file it is, you'll need to include the appropriate extensions with all your Web site files.

Your Web site will almost always begin with a file called index.html. Most Web server software programs will automatically load this page if the URL of your site is accessed without a specific path and file reference. For example, entering this URL in your browser:

http://www.sun.com/

actually results in the URL **http://www.sun.com/index.html** being loaded in your browser. Your Web site's first page (whether it's a "front door" page or the first page of your site) should be designed with this in mind. If you plan to offer only Netscape-enhanced pages, for instance, you'll want to let your users know this on the index.html page.

The other consideration for naming your files is the organization you plan to use for your site. If you're using a single-directory organization, your file names should be as unique as possible, and graphics and other files should probably have names that relate to associated Web pages. For instance:

> about_company.html
>
> about_header.jpeg
>
> about_ceo_photo.jpeg

When possible, these names will help you determine which files are associated with which HTML pages when you go to update those files.

For graphics and other files that show up on multiple pages, you might want to come up with a memorable prefix, like gen_ or site just so you can easily replace these universal files when necessary.

Updating Your Web Site

If you organize your site well, updating the site is simply a matter of replacing an outdated file with a new file using the same file name.

You'll need to check with your company's Information Systems contact or your ISP to figure out exactly how you'll update files. With an ISP, you can generally use an FTP program to *put* new files in your directory organization on the Web site, as shown in Figure 4.2. You might instead be required to use a UNIX-based shell account for your uploading. In either case, it's a fairly simple process:

1. Your Web space provider will require you to enter a username and password to gain access to the Web server, whether by FTP or shell account. Generally, you will point your FTP program to the Web server itself (for instance, www.isp.com), unless the provider has created a *mirror site* to avoid direct access to the Web server.

Mirror Site An exact replica of a Web server's hard disk, which is kept separate for security reasons. For instance, you might not be able to directly access your company's Web site files...but you can change a mirror of that Web server, and your changes will be handled by knowledgeable Internet specialists. Many companies prefer to isolate their Web servers from their corporate network so that important data is impossible to access from outside the company.

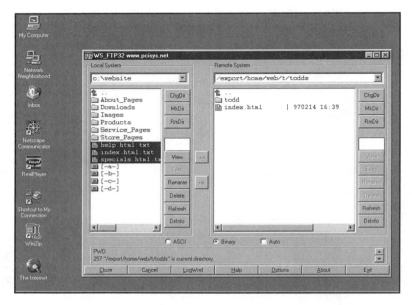

Figure 4.2 An FTP client program is being used to transfer Web site files from a hard drive to the Web server computer.

2. After clearing the security procedure, you'll most likely be in your personal Web site's main directory. (If not, you'll need to use the cd command in UNIX or otherwise change directories in your FTP program.)

3. From that point, you can update files using the Put command—simply upload the updated files with the same names as the outdated files. In nearly every case, the old files will simply be overwritten. If you're using new files, upload them using the same names and paths that your Web page links use to refer to them.

TIP **Prototype Your Site** It's a good idea to maintain a folder or directory on your own hard drive that is as identical as possible to the Web site you make available on a server—so you can test your organization and file names.

In this lesson, you learned how to organize, name, and upload your HTML documents to your Web server. In the next lesson, you'll learn about the document head and HTML tags.

HTML Tags and the Document Head

5

In this lesson, you learn more about how HTML tags work and what tags are appropriate for the head of your document.

Types of Tags

There are two basic types of tags: containers and empty tags. As the name implies, containers are designed to hold something—usually text or other HTML commands.

An example of a very basic HTML page might be:

```
<H1>Hello!</H1><HR>
```

The result of these tags and text is shown in Figure 5.1.

Most of HTML involves placing items inside containers, which have an opening tag and a closing tag. In the example, notice that the command for a horizontal line (<HR>) has only one tag—it's not a container (it's an *empty* tag). But the heading tag, in this case <H1>, needs an </H1> on the other side of the item to end the formatting code. The text item "Hello!" is inside this <H1></H1> container, and that tells the browser to make it appear with the level-1 heading font and size.

 Empty Tag A tag that doesn't act on anything. Empty tags usually perform a very specific task on their own, without focusing on specific text. <HR> creates a horizontal rule (a line), for example, but it doesn't act on any specific text the way that <H1></H1> does.

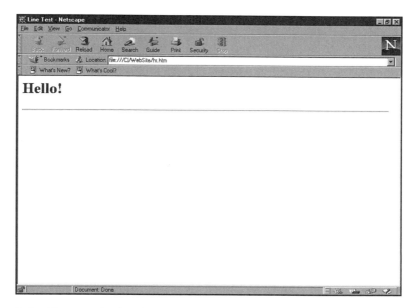

Figure 5.1   Here are the header and horizontal line tags as viewed in a Web browser.

Keep the following points in mind when you're working with tags:

- For HTML containers, every opening tag must have a corresponding closing tag. Closing tags are the same as opening tags, except that they have a forward slash (/) in front of them. For example, the opening tag for *italics* is <I>, and the closing tag is </I>.

- You don't have to put spaces between HTML codes, nor do you have to use carriage returns. In the example, the Web browser puts a carriage return after a heading container and another one before the horizontal line. If you want to specify your own spacing, you need to know some further HTML codes. For now, let the browser do its work.

TIP   **Extra Spaces Ignored**   In fact, browsers often ignore extra spaces or returns. That can be a good thing, because it allows you to use returns to make your HTML document easier to read, without affecting how it will look in a browser. But this behavior can also be a bit frustrating, since HTML doesn't work with spaces and returns the same way a typical word processing program does.

- Many HTML tags also have special *attributes* that affect the way that tag displays. Attributes can also be used to give the Web browser additional information, like where to find a particular image file. For instance, the <BODY> tag can have the attribute BACKGROUND which tells the Web browser what image to load for the background of a Web page, like <BODY BACKGROUND="bricks.gif">.

- After you've begun an HTML document, you can keep adding to it and revising it. Just hit the **Reload** key of your browser to test your changes.

With the concept of tags under your belt, you're ready to look specifically at the tags in your document's head section.

The Document Head

As the name implies, the head section of any HTML document precedes the main information (or the *body*) of the Web page. The tag <HEAD> and closing tag </HEAD> surround the contents of the head section. Text contained between the <HEAD> and </HEAD> tags points to general information about the file and is not displayed as part of the document text itself.

The <HEAD> container may hold a number of different elements, including:

- <TITLE> Describes the document's name.
- <BASE> The original URL of the document.
- <META> Embeds any additional information.

Only the <TITLE> element is required. The rest are optional and often do not appear in basic HTML constructions. In fact, even complex pages require only the <TITLE> for full World Wide Web functioning.

But it's important to know how all of these tags work because they can help you produce a richer, more sophisticated Web site.

Your Web Page's Title

It's as simple as it sounds—the <TITLE> element names your document, like the title of this book, its chapters, or even the section headers. Every HTML document you create should include a title—and only one title—within the <HEAD> element. Effective use of the <TITLE> and </TITLE> tags results in a descriptive and stimulating sentence that sums up the document content in a concise manner.

TIP **Choose Great Titles** The title of any HTML document does not assign a file name to that page. Instead, it's used to give the browser window a title when the page is viewed. Your title is also used when your readers create a Web browser bookmark to your page, or when a search engine catalogs your site. So, make sure it's a great title that encourages people to visit your page!

Figure 5.2 shows the title on the home page for Power Computing (**http://www.powercc.com/**). The <TITLE> of the document is written in HTML as follows:

```
<TITLE>Welcome to Power Computing</TITLE>
```

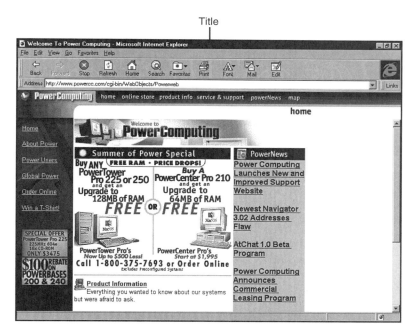

Figure 5.2 HTML codes (like bold or italics) will not work since the <TITLE> is shown in the browser window's title bar.

Creating an effective title for your HTML document isn't exactly a technical skill, but it can affect the success of your page on the World Wide Web. You construct an HTML document to send a message to the world, but this solitary message is competing for attention with millions and millions of other pages. The title of your document is one of several elements responsible for attracting an audience and should be given some serious consideration.

Consider the good and not-so-good titles that you come across when surfing the Net. Here are some simple suggestions:

- **Avoid generic titles**   Say exactly what your site does, what the page is about and why it's interesting. Remember that any page title might be used as a bookmark or entry in a search engine like Infoseek or Lycos.
- **Avoid catchy slogans**   Company names don't always help, either, unless they're very familiar. Remember that your title should indicate the nature of the service or the purpose of the page.
- **No more than 60 characters**   HTML does not limit the length of the TITLE element. However, before you rush off to give your Web pages endlessly descriptive names, keep in mind that the space where the title is displayed (either the viewer's title bar or window label) is limited.

The <BASE> Tag

File paths and URLs can get a little complicated, and they tend to be a stumbling block for new Web page designers. The <BASE> tag, however, can be used to make this process a bit more palatable.

Since the <BASE> tag is tied up with creating hyperlinks, it's discussed more in depth in Part I, Lesson 10, "Understanding Links and URLs."

The <META> Tag

Put simply, the <META> element takes care of everything else you could ever want to say about your document, including indexing and cataloguing information. Think of <META> as the library catalog card for your Web site—by using this tag, you can present Web search engines (like Yahoo! and Excite) with keywords and a description of your content. That makes your page easier to find for people who have similar interests.

If present, the <META> option must include the CONTENT attribute as well as either the NAME or HTTP-EQUIV attribute—but never both.

<META> can even be used to automatically load new Web pages, as discussed in Part I, Lesson 11, "Adding HTML Links."

<META> can also be used to help Web search engines like WebCrawler and Yahoo! figure out things about your page. There are two fairly common <META> tags that search *robots* look for:

```
<META NAME="description" CONTENT="Write your description here">
<META name="keywords" content="Write your keywords here, in
➡a comma separated list">
```

Robots Often called "bots," robots are small computer programs designed to move around on the Web looking for interesting pages to catalog. Some of them are designed to read and store the description and keywords you enter for your page.

The first <META> tag is used by robots to describe your site in the Web directory's listing. For the CONTENT attribute, descriptions should be between 50 and 200 words, depending on the search robot (shorter is probably best). An example might be:

```
<META NAME="description" CONTENT="Virtual writer's group
➡for Colorado, including job listings, tips, advice and
➡discussion.">
```

The other <META> tag is for keywords that you want the search robot to associate with your site. The idea is, if a user enters these keywords at a major search engine, it's more likely to present your page as an alternative. Here's a sample, again for my page:

```
<META NAME="keywords" content="writers, writer, free-lance,
➡ for hire, articles, submissions, postings, want ads, Colorado
➡writer">
```

In this lesson, you learned about the HTML tags in the head of your document, including <TITLE> and <META> tags. In the next lesson, you'll begin adding text to the body of your document.

Entering Body Text

In this lesson, you learn how to begin entering text in the body of your HTML document.

The Body Section

The body section of all HTML documents is defined by the <BODY> container element. It has an opening tag, <BODY>, to show where your information starts; and a closing tag, </BODY>, that indicates where the data ends. Inside the body you find text, hyperlinks, headings, graphics, image maps, forms, tables, and everything else your users actually see.

Figure 6.1 shows how the body tags look in a Web page.

The sample HTML code is Listing 6.1 shows where the body fits in the overall Web page structure. Note that it's embedded inside the <HTML> opening and closing tags, which means it's a substructure of <HTML> itself. Almost everything else in your document is contained in the body and thus fits inside the <BODY> </BODY> tags.

Listing 6.1   Sample HTML Body Element

```
<HTML>
<HEAD>
<TITLE>Write This!</TITLE>
</HEAD>
<BODY>
<H1>Welcome to the Write This! Writer's Group</H1>
...actual content of page
</BODY>
</HTML>
```

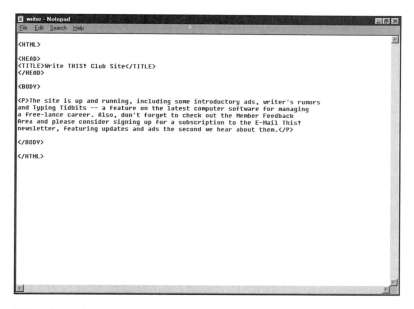

Figure 6.1   Using the template you created in Lesson 4, you can add text to your page between the <BODY> tags.

Entering Paragraph Text

As mentioned earlier, all the text that will be displayed on your Web page should come between the <BODY> and </BODY> tags. The body tags are container tags that tell a Web browser what parts of the HTML document should be displayed in the browser window.

We've seen that you can just type text into an HTML document and it will be displayed in the browser. Technically, though, most of the text you type should be in another container tag: the <P> (paragraph) tag. This tag is used to show a Web browser what text in your document constitutes a paragraph. For the most part, Web browsers ignore more than one space between words and will ignore returns that you add to your HTML file while you're creating it.

In order to give the appearance of paragraphs, then, you have to use the paragraph container tag. The paragraph tag uses the following format:

```
<P>Here is the text for my paragraph. It doesn't matter
➡ how long it is, how
many spaces are between the words or when I decide to hit
➡ the return key. It
will create a new paragraph only when I end the tag and
➡ begin with another one.
</P>

<P> Here's the next paragraph. </P>
```

CAUTION

The <P> Container Although it is technically a container tag, the </P> tag is not required at the ends of paragraphs by most browsers. This tends to cause a little confusion. Many people end up using <P> as an empty tag, assuming that it's designed to insert a line break at the end of paragraphs (or even to create multiple blank lines). That's not its purpose. Using <P> as a container, as shown previously, gets the most reliable results in all different types of browsers.

The paragraph container tells the Web browser that all of the text between the on and off tags is in a single paragraph. When you start another paragraph, the Web browser will drop down a line between the two.

Here's that same example, except now it has some extra spaces. Remember, spaces and returns almost never affect the way the text will be displayed on the screen. In a paragraph container, the browser will ignore more than one space and any returns.

```
<P>Here is the text for my paragraph.
It doesn't matter how long it is, how many spaces are
➡ between the words
or when I decide to hit the return key. It will create a new
➡ paragraph
only when I end the tag and begin with another one. </P>

<P> Here's the next paragraph. </P>
```

Both this example and the previous example will be displayed in the Web browser in exactly the same way, as shown in Figure 6.2.

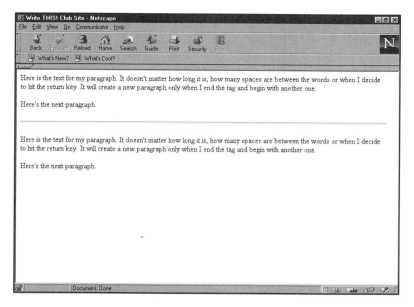

Figure 6.2   Here are both paragraphs shown in a Web browser. Notice that hitting the Return key when entering text has no effect on how paragraph text is rendered.

The *
* Tag for Line Breaks

But what if you want to decide where a line is going to end? Consider the example of entering an address in a Web document, as follows:

```
<P>
Richard Smith
14234 Main Street
Anycity, ST 00001
</P>
```

It looks about right when you type it into your text editor. However, when it displays in a Web browser, it looks like Figure 6.3.

You already know what the problem is: Web browsers ignore extra spaces and returns. But if you put each of those lines in its own paragraph container, you'd end up with a space between each line—and that would look wrong, too.

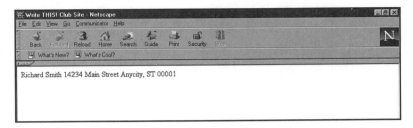

Figure 6.3 It's difficult to line up text in a paragraph container.

The answer is the empty tag <BR>, which forces a line return in your Web document. (The "BR" in the tag stands for "break.") Properly formatted, the address would look like this:

```
<P>
Richard Smith<BR>
14234 Main Street<BR>
Anycity, ST 00001<BR>
</P>
```

And it would look just right in a Web browser, as shown in Figure 6.4.

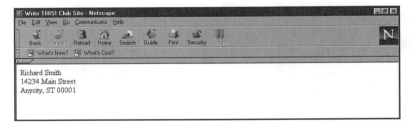

Figure 6.4 This address is rendered correctly using the <BR> tag.

**Only One
 Is Legal** Although Netscape's browsers tend to recognize more than one <BR> tag for creating additional line breaks, the HTML standard doesn't recognize this method. The accepted way to add space in an HTML document is using the <PRE> container, as discussed in Part I, Lesson 8, "Headings, Lines, and Paragraph Styles."

CAUTION

In this lesson, you learned how to enter text between the <BODY> tags for display on your Web page. In the next lesson, you'll learn how to change the style of paragraph text.

Adding Text Styles

In this lesson, you learn how to change the styling and emphasis of text in your HTML document.

Physical Styles

If you've used almost any word processor, you'll instantly recognize HTML's physical style elements. Physical styles emphasize your Web page's plain text with boldface, italic, and underlining. These container tags are absolute, which means that every Web browser displays the physical style elements in exactly the same manner.

Although some browsers may have limitations on how they can display logical text styles—such as Lynx, which is a text-only browser—there is no other way for a browser to interpret a physical style. Bold is bold. Italic is italic. Logical styles (covered in the next section) may be flexible, but physical ones are not.

Table 7.1 contains some descriptions of physical styles.

Table 7.1   Physical Styles and Their Meanings

Container	Meaning
`<B>  </B>`	Boldface (where possible)
`<I>  </I>`	Italic
`<TT>  </TT>`	Monospaced typewriter font
`<U>  </U>`	Underlined
`<SUB>  </SUB>`	Subscript
`<SUP>  </SUP>`	Superscript

Adding a physical style to your Web page is simple. The key is selecting the text that will be contained by the style tags. The contained text is what will be styled in the Web browser:

1. Enter text in your HTML document.

2. Place the cursor at the beginning of the text you'd like to style. Type the opening tag for the style you'd like to apply to this text.

3. Move the cursor to the end of the text you want to style.

4. Type the closing tag for the style you're applying to this text. Listing 7.1 is an example of some physical styles added to the example Web page:

Listing 7.1   Example Physical Styles

```
<P><U>Site News!</U></P>
<P>The site is up and running, including some<B>introductory ads</B>,
<I>writer's rumors</I> and <TT>Typing Tidbits</TT> -- a feature on the
➥latest computer software for managing a freelance career. Also, don't
➥forget to check out the <I>Member Feedback Area</I> and please
➥consider signing up for a subscription to the <TT>E-Mail This!</TT>
➥newsletter,featuring updates and ads the second we hear about
➥them.</P>
```

Figure 7.1 shows how these physical styles are rendered in a Web browser.

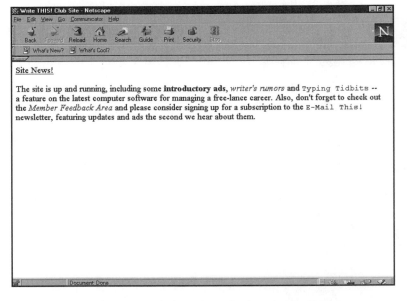

Figure 7.1   Browsers do not vary in how they display physical styles.

Logical Styles

In Lesson 6, you learned that the paragraph container doesn't just create space between paragraphs of text—it actually defines the enclosed text as something called a "paragraph." That's an important distinction, because it means a paragraph is actually a *logical style* in HTML.

 Logical Style An HTML style that can be rendered by the Web browser in any way that it chooses. Although most browsers tend to render paragraph text in a way that seems to make sense (single-spaced with a blank line between the paragraph and the next container), paragraphs could be rendered in other ways—all green text with a flush right margin, for instance—if the browser programmer decided it was necessary.

Each logical character style has an opening and a closing tag that form a container for the inserted text. Table 7.2 shows descriptions of logical styles.

Table 7.2 Logical Styles and Their Meanings

Style	Description
<EM>	Emphasized text
<STRONG>	Strongly emphasized text
<CITE>	Text in a citation
<CODE>	Text representing an HTML element sample
<DFN>	Text in a definition
<SAMP>	Text in an output sample, similar to code
<KBD>	Text representing a keyboard key
<VAR>	Text defining a variable or value

One of the interesting points about logical styles is that, no matter how you use them, your Web users can view them more or less the way they want. All they have to do is configure their browsers to display each logical style in a particular way.

For instance, if a reader likes emphasized text to be in a 24-point Times Roman font, all of the text in <EM> containers will be displayed as 24-point Times Roman (if her browser allows her to change how <EM> is rendered).

TIP   **How Styles Work**   With physical HTML styles, a browser will usually render them if it's capable or ignore the styles if it can't render them (like some text-only browsers can't render italic). With logical styles, the style will always be rendered—within the limits of the browser.

The fact is, <EM> is usually rendered as italicized text and <STRONG> is generally shown as bold text. The point is, these tags *could* be rendered as something else. That often makes them a better choice, since some Web browsers (like those for the Windows CE OS, WebTV, text-only terminals, and similar devices) find it useful to render text in some way other than italic or bold.

Listing 7.2 shows the same example as Listing 7.1, but it uses logical styles instead of physical ones. The results are pictured in Figure 7.2.

Listing 7.2   Logical Styles

```
<P><STRONG>Site News!</STRONG></P>
<P>The site is up and running, including some <STRONG>introductory
➥ads</STRONG>, <EM>writer's rumors</EM> and Typing Tidbits -- a feature
➥on the latest computer software for managing a free-lance career.
➥Also, don't forget to check out the <EM>Member Feedback Area</EM> and
➥please consider signing up for a subscription to the <SAMP>E-Mail
➥This!</SAMP> newsletter, featuring updates and ads the second we hear
➥about them.</P>
```

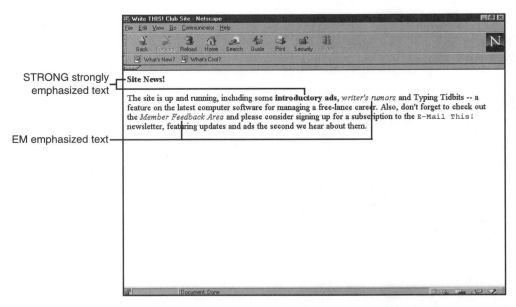

Figure 7.2   In a typical browser, logical styles are rendered in a way that's similar to physical styles.

Font Size and Color

The <FONT> container gives you control over how large or small text looks on-screen and what color it will be. For the SIZE attribute, the *value* is either an actual text size (one through seven) or relative to the normal size of the body text (from +4 down to -4).

```
<FONT SIZE=value>
```

For example, the following creates a "drop-cap" effect:

```
<FONT SIZE=7>W<FONT SIZE=3>elcome!<BR>
```

That size change is shown in Figure 7.3. To change the entire document's basic font size, use the HTML 3.2 empty tag **<BASEFONT SIZE=value>** shortly after the <BODY> tag in your document. Again, the *value* can range from one through seven (the standard browser text size is three).

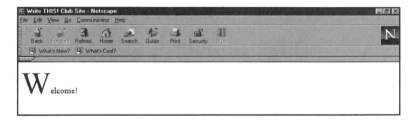

Figure 7.3 The <Font> container can be used to change the size of certain text.

It's also possible to change the color of individual words (or sentences, paragraphs, and so on) with a quick addition to the <FONT> container tag: the COLOR attribute. Here's how it works:

```
<FONT COLOR=RED>This text is red.</FONT>
```

In this lesson, you learned how to change the emphasis and style of text in an HTML document. In the next lesson, you'll learn how to add headings and change the styling of entire paragraphs of text.

Headings, Lines, and Paragraph Styles

In this lesson, you learn how to add headings, dividing lines, and new paragraph styles to your HTML documents.

Add Headings

Heading tags are containers, and unlike many other HTML tags, they double as paragraph tags. Ranging from level 1 to level 6, headings allow you to create different levels of emphasized headlines to help you organize your documents. Here's an example; see Figure 8.1 for the results.

```
<H1>Header Level One is the largest for headlines or page
➧titles</H1>
<H2>Level Two is a little smaller for major subheads</H2>
<H3>Level Three is again smaller, for minor subheads</H3>
<P>This is regular text.</P>
<H4>Level Four is about the same size as regular text, but
➧emphasized</H4>
<H5>Level Five: again emphasized, but smaller than regular
➧text</H5>
<H6>Level Six is generally the smallest heading</H6>
```

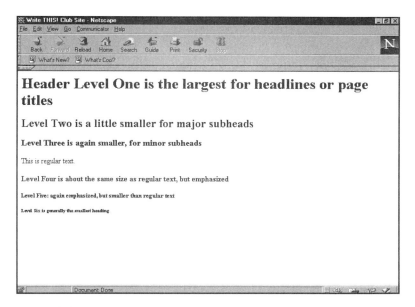

Figure 8.1 HTML Heading tags at work. Notice that the fourth entry is regular text between <P> and </P> tags.

You cannot include a Heading tag on the same line as regular text, even if you close the Heading tag and continue with unaltered text. A Heading tag has the same effect as a <P>, in that it creates a new line after its "off" tag. The following:

```
<H1>This is a heading</H1> And this is plain text.
```

offers the same results as:

```
<H2>This is also a heading</H2>
<P>And this is plain text.</P>
```

In both cases, the Web browser will place the header text and plain text on different lines, with the header text appearing larger and the plain text appearing "normal" in size.

The following listing shows an example of headings in action; Figure 8.2 shows how headings look in a browser:

```
<H1>Site News!</H1>
<P>The site is up and running, including some <STRONG>introductory
➥ads</STRONG>, <EM>writer's rumors</EM> and <TT>Typing Tidbits</TT>
```

```
➥-- a feature on the latest computer software for managing a
➥freelance career. Also, don't forget to check out the <EM>Member
➥Feedback Area</EM> and please consider signing up for a
➥subscription to the <STRONG>E-Mail This!</STRONG> newsletter,
➥featuring updates and ads the second we hear about them.</P>
<H2>Writer's Rumors</H2>
<P>We've recently gotten wind of a new start-up in Fort Collins,
➥expected to reach out to teens in the area with dine-on-a-dime
➥restaurant reviews, local music news, special teen-night-out
➥features and Teen Night club reviews. The grapevine tells us the
➥monthly will be taking on free-lance talent from the Denver and
➥Boulder pool, including younger adults.</P>
```

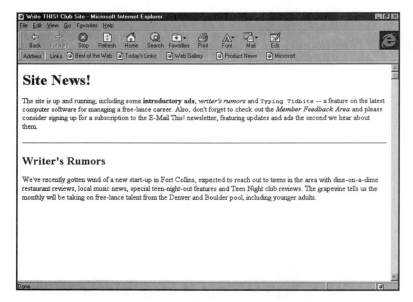

Figure 8.2 Headings make a page look more organized—like a good magazine article or business report.

Horizontal Lines

The <HR> tag places a shadowed line across the width of the Web browser's window. If the reader changes the size of the window, the line resizes to match. The <HR> tag is an empty tag and does not require a closing element for functioning. It stands for horizontal rule, which is just another way of saying a horizontal line.

Horizontal rules insert a paragraph break before and after the line. The <HR> tag can be added anywhere in a document, although it always appears on its own line, as shown in Figure 8.3:

```
<HR>
<H2>Writer's Rumors</H2>
```

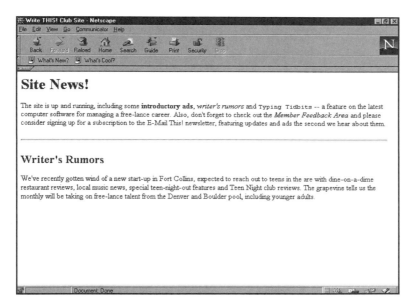

Figure 8.3   Horizontal rules make their own space on the page, like headings and paragraphs.

The HTML 3.2 specification provides additional attributes for horizontal rules. These give you control over the weight of the line, its length, and the location of the hard rule within the browser's window. You can also drop the "etched" look of the line in favor of a solid black rule. Table 8.1 lists the <HR> parameters and what they do.

Table 8.1   Style Attributes to *<HR>*

Attribute	Description
SIZE=#	Sets thickness of horizontal line
WIDTH=#	Sets width as a measure of pixels or percentage of viewer window's width

Attribute	Description
ALIGN=direction	Allows line to be justified left, center, or right within the viewer window
NOSHADE	Changes appearance of horizontal line to be solid black with no "etched" effect

You can add any of these attributes by typing them into the <HR> tag before adding the closing bracket (>). An example would be:

```
<HR SIZE=2 WIDTH=75% ALIGN=CENTER NOSHADE>
```

Paragraph Styles

If you want to put information on the Web and you already have it in a non-HTML document, you don't have to spend your time retyping. Instead, you can use HTML's preformatted text container tags <PRE></PRE>. This container lets you keep the original formatting of the text, and even regular keyboard-entered returns as line breaks, without the <BR> tag. Other containers, like <BLOCKQUOTE>, give you extra control over the appearance on your text.

The *<PRE></PRE>* Container

The preformatted text element, represented by the tags <PRE> and </PRE>, supports blank spaces and lets other tags or links (like the bold and strong text styles and anchors) modify the text. The one catch is that WWW browsers normally render preformatted text in a plain, monospaced font, such as Courier.

Using the <PRE></PRE> container, text is rendered in exactly the way you type it. It's not easy to do the following without the <PRE> tags and have it still look like Figure 8.4:

```
<PRE>
Whose woods these are I think I know,
   His house is in the village though.
He will not see me stopping here
   To watch his woods fill up with snow.
</PRE>
```

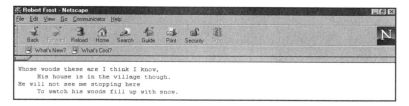

Figure 8.4 Using the <PRE></PRE> container, you can line up text using spaces and Returns.

Preformatted text is excellent for items like programming code examples that you want to indent and format appropriately. <PRE></PRE> tags also enable you to align text by padding it with spaces for table creation. However, because those tables will appear in monospaced font, you may prefer to spend the extra time constructing standard HTML table blocks.

Using <PRE> for Tables

One use for <PRE> is creating a primitive table. The key to making this work correctly is alignment. Realize that each space taken up by an HTML tag (like <B>) will not appear in the browser's display, so you'll need to compensate.

CAUTION

<PRE> **Alignment** You may be tempted to use <B> or another emphasis tag for the column heads in your table. Realize, however, that it is nearly impossible to align columns so that they will appear correctly in every browser when one row is bold and other rows are plain text. Different browsers make bold text a fraction wider than regular text, so that the row becomes increasingly misaligned. Even if it looks good in your browser, chances are it won't work in all of them.

To create a simple table:

1. Open your template and enter the following listing (or a similar table) between the <Body> tags.

```
<HR>
<H2>Average Free-Lance Rates (Per Hour) by Region</H2>
<PRE>

Region     Newspapers  Magazines  Business  Advertising

NorthWest    $40        $50        $75       $100
NorthEast    $35        $45        $70       $95
SouthEast    $30        $40        $65       $90
SouthWest    $25        $35        $55       $75
</PRE>
```

2. You may need to play with the spacing a bit to line everything up. Save the HTML document, then use the **Open File** command in your browser to proof it. Keep playing with it until it looks right.

TIP **No Tab in** `<PRE>` If you use a more advanced text editor or word processor, fight the urge to use the Tab key to align `<PRE>` elements. Use the spacebar instead.

The *<BLOCKQUOTE>* Container

If you want an entire paragraph of indented text, the `<BLOCKQUOTE>` container performs this function. Unlike `<PRE>`, `<BLOCKQUOTE>` does not keep any line feeds already present in your text nor does it allow consecutive blank spaces. What it does provide is a uniform indented format.

It's okay to throw other HTML tags in the `<BLOCKQUOTE>` container, too, such as text styles and line breaks. Here's an example of a blockquote; Figure 8.5 shows how the the indented text appears in a browser:

```
<H1>Site News!</H1>
<BLOCKQUOTE>The site is up and running, including some
➡<STRONG>introductory ads</STRONG>, <EM>writer's rumors</EM> and
➡<TT>Typing Tidbits</TT> -- a feature on the latest computer
➡software for managing a free-lance career. Also, don't forget to
➡check out the <EM>Member Feedback Area</EM> and please consider
➡signing up for a subscription to the <STRONG>E-Mail This!</STRONG>
➡newsletter, featuring updates and ads the second we hear about
➡them.</BLOCKQUOTE>
```

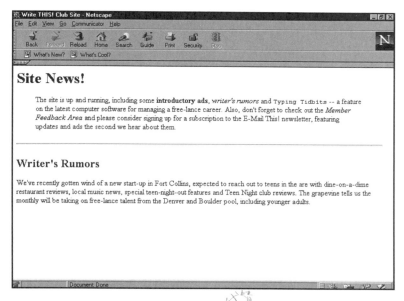

Figure 8.5 The <BLOCKQUOTE> container is a substitute for <P> that indents an entire paragraph.

<BLOCKQUOTE> text uses the regular body text font (the same style featured throughout the rest of your HTML document) as well as an even indentation from the left margin.

The *<ADDRESS></ADDRESS>* Container

The <ADDRESS></ADDRESS> container is used to create paragraph-like text, specially formatted to stand out as the address listing or line for your Web page. In most browsers, the <ADDRESS></ADDRESS> container is displayed as an italicized paragraph—but, as with any logical style, browsers are free to display address text any way they want to.

An example of <ADDRESS> might be:

```
<ADDRESS>This site last updated 6/12 by tstauffer@aol.com</ADDRESS>
```

Traditionally, the <ADDRESS></ADDRESS> container is used toward the end of a Web page to give information like:

- When the page was last updated.
- Who should be contacted concerning the page (usually the Webmaster's e-mail address).

- What the URL for this page is.
- Phone numbers or physical addresses for the company or association.

Most of these elements aren't vital to your page's contents, but they're nice additions to consider. An example of a full address might be:

```
<ADDRESS>
This page last updated 6/12 at 9:08pm.<BR>
Contact tstauffer@aol.com with corrections or problems.<BR>
MyCorp<BR>
132 W. Highland St.<BR>
Richville, CA 91000<BR>
714-777-1200<BR>
</ADDRESS>
```

Notice the use of <BR> to insert line breaks within an <ADDRESS> container. This address is shown in Figure 8.6.

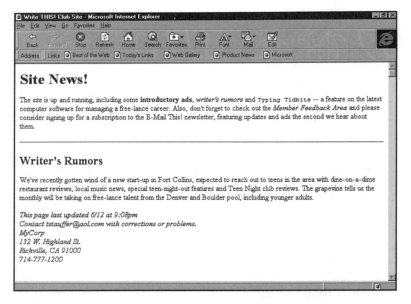

Figure 8.6   Here's some of the info you might want to include in a typical Web page <ADDRESS> container.

In this lesson, you learned how to add headings, lines, and new paragraph styles to your HTML document. In the next lesson, you'll learn how to add images.

Adding Images

9

In this lesson, you'll learn how to add images to your Web pages.

Adding Images

Images are pictures. They can be drawings, photographs, or computer paintings. They can even be pictures of text. In computing, images are files of a specific kind. They're binary files (made up of ones and zeroes) as opposed to text or ASCII files.

This means that a text editor like Windows Notepad or Mac's SimpleText won't be able to read them properly, and you'll need a graphics viewing program instead. The best-known graphics types include GIF, JPEG, TIFF, PCX, EPS, and BMP. There are several others as well.

Nearly all graphics on the Web are either in GIF or JPEG format. If you need help understanding these formats, check out Part II, Lesson 1, "Creating Web Graphics."

Graphics Help Your Web Pages

Here are a few of the enhancements your graphics will provide:

- They break text into digestible "chunks," making the page easier to read.
- They separate content so that the reader knows when a new subject has been started (or when a transition has been made).
- They provide content that is not available via text, such as a picture of your pet or your latest watercolor masterpiece.
- They add color, humor, and excitement to the medium.
- They demonstrate the author's creativity.

It's a simple matter to add images to your Web pages—all it takes is the `<IMG>` tag. Realize, however, that you're not adding the images to your HTML document. You place a pointer in your HTML document, which tells a Web browser (or similar program) how to find and load the image. The image file and HTML document need to exist separately.

The *<IMG>* Tag

When you want to insert a graphic file on a Web page, you actually do so with an URL. The URL is the specific location on the Internet where the graphic file is located. It can be on the same Web host computer that your HTML document is on, or it can be on a host somewhere else on the Internet.

To add an *inline* image to your page, use the `<IMG>` tag. This empty tag acts as a placeholder in your text where the browser will put the graphic.

Inline   Graphics files that appear exactly where you place them, along with text, on a Web document. (The other kind, *floating* images, are discussed later in this lesson.) The basic difference is that inline images aren't aligned against a margin—they are anchored in the text of the page. Floating images can be made to stick to the left or right margin.

The `<IMG>` tag is an empty tag with the following syntax:

```
<IMG SRC=image_URL>
```

IMG is the HTML image tag; it appears with all inline images. SRC means *source* and refers to the location of the image (it's on some hard drive somewhere in the world). The actual URL for the image file replaces the words image_URL.

The image_URL can be a full URL with full machine name (such as **http:// members.aol.com/tstauffer/me.gif**). Alternatively, it can refer to the graphics file's *relative* URL; in this case, you refer to the file's location relative to the directory where the Web page is.

Relative URL   One that doesn't include an entire Internet address, like: **http://www.mycon.com/people/dave.gif**. Instead, a relative URL generally includes only a path statement, like: **/people/dave.gif**. The Internet address is assumed to be the same as that of the HTML document that includes the relative URL reference. Relative URLs for images are one important reason to use the `<BASE>` tag, which is discussed in Part I, Lesson 10.

The following is sample HTML code for adding an inline graphic to the page:

```
<P><IMG SRC="rich.gif">Rich Marcheson is a private pilot and travel-
➥writer based in Southwestern Colorado. His specialties include
➥driving trips of the SouthWest, cities of the West (Salt Lake City,
➥San Francisco, Seattle, Tucson, Phoenix) and visiting national
➥parks. His work has recently appeared in <I>Utah Vacations</I>,
➥<I>In Air Magazine</I> and <I>Low Flying</I>.
</P>
```

Notice the `<IMG SRC>` command is using a relative URL—actually, it could have just as easily been a complete URL like:

```
<IMG SRC="http://www.mycom.com/writers/rich.gif">
```

Both are similarly useful, but you only need to use a complete URL if the image you're loading resides elsewhere on the Internet. If it is in a subdirectory, then something like:

```
<IMG SRC="/graphics/image1.gif">
```

will work just fine. See Figure 9.1 for an example of how this looks.

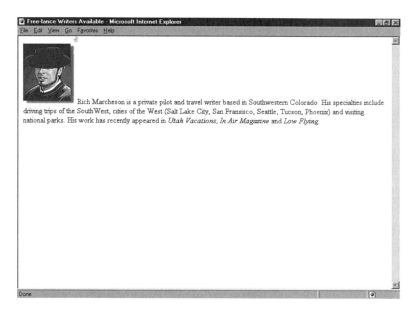

Figure 9.1 Notice that the graphic appears within the text—that's inline.

CAUTION

Use Only http You should avoid linking to files using a direct file URL to your hard drive. Remember, your computer's hard drive isn't on the Internet—your Web server's hard drive is. So, if you create an image link like `<IMG SRC="file:///clweb_site/image.gif">`, your users will not be able to see the image. Normally, Web authors don't make this mistake; instead, some older versions of Web editor programs do. So, if you use a special editing program, watch its `<IMG>` URLs.

Aligning Text and Images

On their own, Web browsers don't do much to help text and graphics share space on a Web page. Web browsers treat inline images like a character in the line of text and don't wrap text alongside the graphic.

Fortunately, you can do something about this. `<IMG>` comes with an attribute called ALIGN. ALIGN determines how text and images interact with one another on a Web page. Specifically, ALIGN controls how text that's placed on the same line as an image will line itself up along the vertical sides of the image.

The ALIGN attribute is written as:

```
<IMG ALIGN=value SRC=image_URL>
```

The possible values for ALIGN are shown in Table 9.1.

Table 9.1 Standard ALIGN Values

Value	Effect on Text
TOP	Aligns the bottom of the text to top of the image
MIDDLE	Aligns the bottom of the text to the middle of the image
BOTTOM	Aligns the bottom of the text to the bottom of the image

The BOTTOM value is the default for `<IMG>` and does not need to be specified if it's what you want to use. When using any of the standard values, Web browsers leave white space around the text on the line, and the text wraps down to the next line beneath the bottom of the image. Figure 9.2 shows how a Web browser handles each of these attribute values.

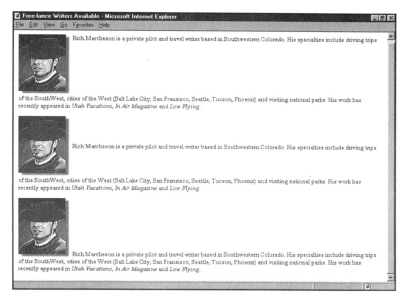

Figure 9.2 Only the text on the current line follows the selected `ALIGN` option. Text on the next line in the browser drops underneath the inline image.

Floating Images

The HTML 3.2 proposal provides more `ALIGN` values for a new type of image called a floating image. No longer tied to one line of text (with all of that awkward white space), these graphics float against one of the margins, and text wraps along the entire height of the image.

The two `ALIGN` values are `LEFT` and `RIGHT`, and they specify which margin the image will float against:

```
<P><IMG SRC="rich.gif" ALIGN=RIGHT>Rich Marcheson is a private pilot
➥and travel-writer based in SouthWestern Colorado. His specialties
➥include driving trips of the SouthWest, cities of the West (Salt
➥Lake City, San Francisco, Seattle, Tucson, Phoenix) and visiting
➥national parks. His work has recently appeared in <I>Utah
➥Vacations</I>, <I>In Air Magazine</I> and <I>Low Flying</I>.
</P>
```

Figure 9.3 shows how using these values changes the appearance of images.

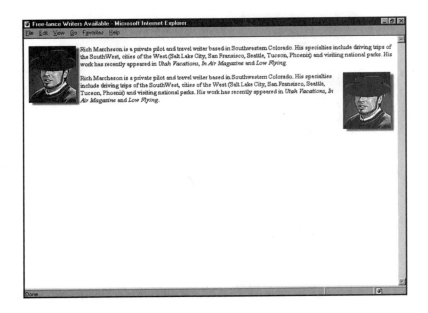

Figure 9.3 The LEFT and RIGHT values determine to which margin the graphic aligns.

To control the amount of spacing between text and floating images and between the edge of the window and the images, use the attributes VSPACE and HSPACE. VSPACE defines the space above and below a floating image, and HSPACE controls the space to the right and left of a floating image.

```
<P><IMG SRC="rich.gif" ALIGN=RIGHT VSPACE=5 HSPACE=5>Rich Marcheson
➥is a private pilot and travel-writer based in SouthWestern Colorado.
```

VSPACE, HSPACE VSPACE means vertical space, and HSPACE means horizontal space.

So, `<IMG ALIGN=LEFT HSPACE=10>` simply means, "Align this image and put 10 pixels of space to the left and right of it."

Alternative Text

Not everyone on the Internet has access to Netscape, Mosaic, Internet Explorer, or any other graphical browser. Of the millions of people on the Web, a sizable percentage still use browsers like UNIX's Lynx, which is extremely capable but doesn't display graphics. Other users keep the graphics feature of their browser turned off.

So how can you accommodate these users, even when you use graphics in your Web pages? HTML provides a simple solution: the ALT attribute (ALT means alternative). ALT defines a text string that replaces the image in browsers without graphics support. This text is often displayed in a box (to separate it from the surrounding body text). Here's an example:

```
<IMG SRC="rich.gif" ALT="Photo of Rich Marcheson">
```

Width and Height

There are two other attributes for <IMG> worth mentioning. The pair, WIDTH and HEIGHT, are designed to make your Web site faster reading.

WIDTH and HEIGHT help solve one of the Web's continually nagging problems. When people click a link to your Web pages, their browsers generally wait until all the inline images are loaded before going back and filling in the text around them. The WIDTH and HEIGHT attributes alleviate this wait.

By telling the browser the pixel dimensions of the images in your Web page, it can mock up the layout and lay in the text *before* starting to retrieve the images. If you are the reader and want to click a text link before the image finishes loading, you're free to do it. Here's an example:

```
<P><IMG SRC="rich.gif" ALIGN=RIGHT WIDTH=50 HEIGHT=70>Rich Marcheson
➥is a private pilot and travel-writer based in SouthWestern Colorado.
```

CAUTION

File Size Doesn't Change Although WIDTH and HEIGHT can be used to resize the appearance of an image, they do nothing to the actual file size of the graphic, which means the user has to wait the same amount of time for the image to download. See Part II, Lesson 1, "Creating Web Graphics," for hints on making your images download more quickly.

In this lesson, you learned how to add images to your Web pages. In the next chapter, you'll learn the basics for creating hyperlinks.

Understanding Links and URLs

In this chapter, you learn the basics of creating a hypertext link.

How Links Work

On the Web, hyperlinks are the basis of all movement and manipulation. Clicking a link on a Web page generally moves you to the related resource. Sometimes that's a new Web page; sometimes it's another Internet service, like an e-mail message or a UseNet discussion group. Whatever the case, a hyperlink requires certain elements to work correctly, and the hyperlink needs to be created by the Web author.

You use a special HTML tag, the <A> anchor tag, to create a hyperlink. The anchor requires the HREF attribute, which is used to tell the Web browser what new URL is being referenced by the hyperlink. So, in order to create a hyperlink, you'll first need to determine the URL for the target page or resource.

The Uniform Resource Locator

Every hyperlink contains a Uniform Resource Locator, or URL. The URL is the address of the Web page that appears in the Location or URL box near the top of your Web browser when you're surfing the Web. It's also the address that shows up (with most browsers) at the bottom of the screen when you move the cursor over a hyperlink.

The URL consists of two major items: the protocol and the destination (although they have all kinds of other names).

The protocol tells you what kind of Internet resource you're dealing with. The most common protocol on the Web is **http://**, which retrieves HTML documents from the Web. Others include **gopher://**, **ftp://**, and **telnet://**.

The destination can be a file name, a directory name, or a computer name. An URL such as **http://members.aol.com/tstauffer/index.html** tells you exactly where the HTML document is located and what its file name is. If the URL is **ftp://ftp.netscape.com/**, the URL is telling the browser to log in to the FTP site on the machine named **netscape.com** using the file transfer protocol.

Relative versus Absolute

There's also another distinction you can make when it comes to URLs for your hyperlinks. If a particular Web page URL is basically the same as the current page—except, perhaps, for the file name—then it's possible to use a relative URL to reference that page. Consider the following two pages:

```
http://www.yourweb.net/richt/index.html
http://www.yourweb.net/richt/resume.html
```

Both of these URLs are absolute URLs—they could both be used to reference their individual pages from anywhere on the Internet. Now, if you created a hyperlink on the first page (**index.html**) to the second page (**resume.html**), you could use a relative URL, since the rest of the information is the same.

It's a little like working with files in Windows or the Mac OS. If you save a file in a particular directory, and then decide to open a new file, you generally don't have to go flipping through your entire hard drive to find that directory again. Many programs (such as Microsoft Word) will open right to the last-used directory.

A Web browser does the same thing. When it encounters an URL that's little more than a path or file name, like **resume.html**, the browser will assume that the author meant "Use the current URL and directory, but open a new file."

So, you could use the following relative URL to refer to the second page *from* the first page:

```
resume.html
```

This is shown in Figure 10.1. If **index.html** and **resume.html** are in the same directory (and on the same Web server computer), then everything will work fine.

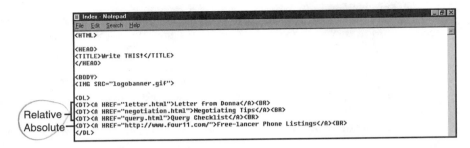

Figure 10.1   Hyperlinks to files that you create for your Web site can use relative URLs. Links to other resources should use absolute URLs.

Web Page Links

Most hypertext links by themselves are added to HTML documents using the anchor tag. This anchor, `<A HREF></A>`, surrounds the text that describes what the link points to. The URL itself must be in quotes, and it uses the HREF (hyperlink reference) attribute.

A link in HTML takes the following format:

```
<A HREF="URL">put your link text here</A>
```

So, if you want to link the text "Tips for Better Writing" with the HTML document called **tips.html** that resides in the hanger on the www.myserver.com machine, the HTML code would look like this:

```
<A HREF="http://www.myserver.com/hanger/tips.html">Tips for Better
➥Writing</A>
```

Don't Hide Links   Make sure that your link or anchor includes descriptive text. Otherwise, you'll have what is known as a *hidden* link, which simply means a link that can't be seen. This most likely won't be of much use to you.

CAUTION

Those long URLs work great for pages that are on someone else's Web server—but you don't have to type all that in if the file you're linking to is stored in the same Web directory as the document you're creating. For instance, if the file **moreinfo.html** is in the same directory and on the same machine as the page containing the following HTML code, the URL shown will work fine:

```
<A HREF="moreinfo.html">Get More Information</A>
```

Another interesting aspect of relative links is that they don't change just because you move the files. It's like furniture in your living room. Move from one address to another, and chances are that the armchair and couch could still be found if you told a friend, "Look in the living room." If you used an absolute reference ("Go to 123 Main and look in the living room"), you'd have to change part of that reference if you move the furniture.

In the same way, you'd have to change an absolute URL, like **http://www.mynet.com/ricky/page2.html**, if you moved to a new server computer. Just `page2.html`, however, would still work fine in the new location.

 TIP **Describe Links** Try to make your link text descriptive. Links that say things such as "Click here" or "Follow this link" don't give the user enough information about what he is getting into.

Linking on the Same Page

If you want to include a link that takes the user to a different part of the page that he is already on, use a # and an anchor name. Your HTML will look something like this:

```
<A HREF="#phone">Phone Number Listing</A>
```

Clicking this HTML would cause the page to scroll in the browser until the part of the page that has the target name "phone" is showing on the screen. This means that some part of your document has to include the target; the following HTML shows how this is done:

```
<A NAME="phone"><H2>Phone Numbers</H2></A>
➥You can contact any of our staff at the following numbers:
```

Here's a breakdown of what's happening in this example:

1. The original hyperlink, `<A HREF="#phone">Phone Number Listing</A>`, creates a hyperlink that looks for an internal target instead of an external file (that's what the # symbol tells the browser).

2. But, it can only find its target if you add one within the document—so, you use the `<A NAME="phone">...</A>` style tag to place that target somewhere in your document.

3. When a user clicks the link, the document moves immediately to the targeted text.

Such targets can be used for linking to specific places on other pages as well. If you have a link to a page that is very extensive, but your users will only be interested in a specific part of that page, you can use a target anchor so they will automatically go to that part of the page, as in Figure 10.2.

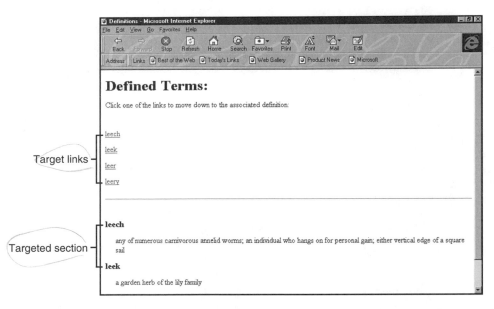

Figure 10.2 Anchor names and target links are a common way to move around on a large page of definitions or similar items.

The *<BASE>* Tag

You've already seen that relative URLs take some of the effort out of creating hyperlinks. But what if you want to make your URLs relative to some other address? You can do that with the <BASE> tag.

Take this example:

1. You've created a directory structure that begins at the URL:

```
http://www.mynet.com/
```

2. Now, within that directory you've created some subdirectories, like images, about, and products.

3. You create a page called widget.html within a new_products subdirectory of the products directory. The URL to that file would be:

```
http://www.mynet.com/products/new_products/widget.html
```

4. Now the fun begins. If you had an image that you wanted to include on the page widget.html, and that image was saved in the image directory, you'd use the UNIX convention of two dots (".."") to refer to a parent directory. So, the relative URL to the images would be:

```
../../images/widget.gif
```

5. Unfortunately, that's not much more fun than typing an absolute URL. That's why you'd use the <BASE> tag. Base is added to the <HEAD> of your document, like this:

```
<HEAD>
<BASE HREF="http://www.mynet.com/">
</HEAD>
```

6. A relative URL isn't necessarily relative to the current document—it's relative to the base HREF. To get to that image, all you'd have to enter would be:

```
images/widget.gif
```

7. Note, though, that this also changes relative URLs for the current directory. For instance, in order to load another page in the new_products directory, you'd need an URL like:

```
products/new_products/widget2.html
```

Essentially, adding a <BASE> tag means that the base URL is added together with any relative URLs to create a complete reference. In the example, the base URL http://www.mynet.com/ is added to the relative URL images/widget.gif in order to create the absolute URL:

```
http://wwww.mynet.com/images/widget.gif
```

You can make <BASE> pretty much anything you want. Then, every relative URL will be added to that <BASE>. (Absolute URLs you enter on the page are unaffected.)

Graphical Links

If you'd like users to click a graphic image (like an icon or picture) in order to move on to a new page or part of the current page, you can create a link that uses an image in the place of descriptive text. For instance, if you have an image named "icon.gif" you can use it as a link like so:

```
<A HREF="about_me.html"><IMG SRC="icon.gif
➥ ALT="Read About Todd"></A>
```

This places a highlighted border (most color browsers use blue by default) like the one shown in Figure 10.3. This lets your user know that the image can be followed like any other hyperlink.

 TIP   **Alternative Text**   Use ALT text in your clickable image, and users of non-graphic browsers will see a text hyperlink, just as they normally would. Otherwise, they won't see anything.

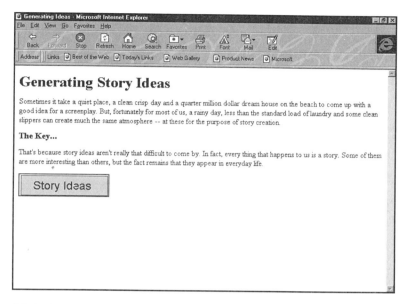

Figure 10.3   Here's a "clickable image" hyperlink.

In this lesson, you learned the basics of hyperlinks and URLs. In the next lesson, you'll learn how to create hyperlinks to other Internet services and graphical hyperlinks.

Adding HTML Links

11

In this lesson, you learn how to create hyperlinks to other Internet services and how to change pages automatically.

Internet Hyperlinks

URLs are so flexible that you can use them to create links to practically anything on the Net. You can create links to e-mail, FTP, Gopher, UseNet news, Telnet, and the search engine WAIS. This makes it possible for Web pages to put related information together. In other words, your readers no longer have to fire up individual Internet programs to get to the information you want them to see.

Partially for this reason, the Web browser has become the single most important Internet tool. From your browser, you can do just about everything else you can do on the Net. This allows Internet users the simplicity of accessing information using just one piece of software.

Regardless of the type of service accessed, each hyperlink begins with an anchor <A HREF>. From there, the only things that change are the protocols for the hyperlinks and the type of URL address used.

One-Click E-Mail

Putting an e-mail link in an HTML document is pretty easy. All you need is a valid e-mail address, which is made up of four parts: the username, the @ symbol, the machine name, and the domain name.

Here's an example of a valid e-mail address:

tstauffer@aol.com

My username is **tstauffer** and the domain name is **aol.com**. In this example, there is no machine name. However, consider an e-mail address like this:

todds@lechery.isc.edu

In this case, lechery is a machine name.

After you have a valid e-mail address, you just put mailto: in front of it. An example of an e-mail link is as follows:

```
<A HREF="mailto:tstauffer@aol.com">Send me mail!</A>
```

Figure 11.1 shows an example of a mailto: link. Many authors like to "sign" their home page by putting an e-mail link at the bottom.

E-mail link ——

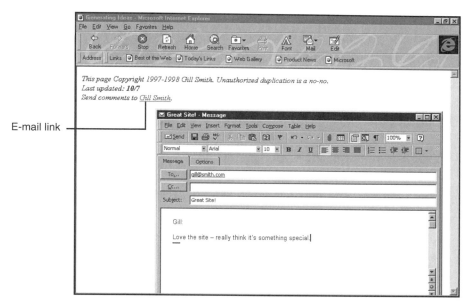

Figure 11.1 When a user clicks an e-mail link on your home page, he'll be able to write messages with his browser.

Creating a Link to an FTP Site

FTP (File Transfer Protocol) is mostly used to copy files between computers. Users of FTP have to log on to remote computers, often as guests, and get whatever files they want.

The only thing you need to put in a link to an FTP site is an Internet address to an FTP server computer. So, if a valid FTP site is ftp.microsoft.com, the link would look like the following:

```
<A HREF="ftp://ftp.microsoft.com/">Microsoft's FTP Site</A>
```

TIP   **FTP Downloads**   If you're building a Web site for a company that has a lot of files to make available, it's a good idea to put the files on an FTP server, and then just include a link to that server on your Web page. This prevents your Web page from becoming cluttered with download links.

If you're inviting your Web visitors to download a particular file from your site, you should specify the file path for them. This keeps users from trying to find their way through unknown directories.

For example, let's say you have a program (**program.exe**) in your home directory (**/users/myself/**) that you want people to access. A link to it might look something like the following:

```
<A HREF="ftp://ftp.mycom.com/users/myself/program.exe">
➡My program</A>
```

This tells the Web browser to connect with FTP, go directly to the correct directory, and immediately begin downloading the file.

Gopher Servers

Before the Web came into existence, one of the most popular ways of storing and accessing information was through Gopher sites. Gopher is basically a collection of text-based menus that store information in a hierarchical format, as shown in Figure 11.2.

Gopher is very similar to the Web except that it doesn't have any built-in multimedia capabilities, such as graphics or sound. You can incorporate a link to a Gopher site on your Web page by simply adding an anchor around the computer's address, and putting **gopher://** in front of it. So a Gopher link would look like the following:

```
<A HREF="gopher://marvel.loc.gov">The Library of Congress</A>
```

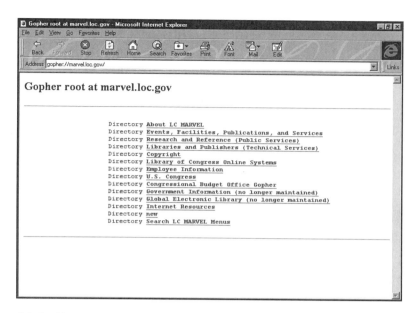

Figure 11.2 You can point your users directly to a gopher server with a simple hyperlink.

Link to Newsgroups

You may want to point people to a newsgroup because your home page relates specifically to what goes on in that group. Or, if you think that the users might have more questions than you can answer, you can include a link to a related newsgroup in the hope of decreasing the amount of e-mail you receive.

Whatever the case, putting in a link to a UseNet newsgroup is different from most other hypertext tags. To put in a link to a newsgroup, simply enter **news:** followed by the newsgroup name in the anchor. A typical newsgroup link would look like the following:

```
<A HREF="news:alt.tv.mad-about-you">Check out the Mad About You
➥newsgroup!</A>
```

Remote Login: Telnet

Sometimes you'll want the user to be able to directly access other computers, which is what the Telnet link is for. The Telnet link actually establishes a connection with another computer and asks the user for a logon name and password.

The syntax for a Telnet link is pretty straightforward: You just type **telnet://** followed by the remote computer's address. A typical Telnet link would look something like the following:

```
<A HREF="telnet://mycomputer.com/">Log on to my computer!</A>
```

TIP **Special Login** You can tell users what logon name to use for guest accounts. All you have to do is specify the logon name they should use followed by the @ sign before the machine name. So, if you want a person to access your computer with the logon name of "guest," the HTML code would be:

```
<A HREF="telnet://guest@mycomputer.com/">Log on to my system</A>
```

When the browser sees this, it notifies the user of the correct logon name.

Changing Pages Automatically

Using a process called *client-pull*, the <META> tag and its attributes allow you to automatically load another HTML page after a predetermined amount of time. You can also use these tags to reload or "refresh" the same HTML document over and over.

TERM **Client-Pull** Using the <META> tag, a Web browser (often called the "client" in official Internet speak) is instructed to automatically load (or "pull") a new page from the Web server without the user clicking anything or the Web server computer running any special programs.

The client-pull concept is based on the <META> tag, which is used in the head of your document. For client-pull, the <META> tag takes the attributes HTTP-EQUIV and CONTENT. Client-pull follows the format:

```
<HEAD>
<META HTTP-EQUIV="REFRESH" CONTENT="seconds; URL="new URL">
</HEAD>
```

The HTTP-EQUIV attribute always takes the value "REFRESH" in client-pull; it only loads a new document if the CONTENT attribute includes an URL. Otherwise, it refreshes (reloads) the current document.

The CONTENT attribute accepts a number for the amount of time you want the browser to wait before the next page is loaded (or the current page is refreshed), then a colon and the statement URL=, followed by a valid URL for the page that should be loaded automatically.

Here's an example that just refreshes the current page after waiting ten seconds:

```
<HEAD>
<META HTTP-EQUIV="REFRESH" CONTENT="10">
</HEAD>
```

In this example, we'll use client-pull to load a new page after waiting 15 seconds:

```
<HEAD>
<META HTTP-EQUIV="REFRESH" CONTENT="15; URL=http://www.mynet.com/
➡index.html">
</HEAD>
```

One of the best uses for client-pull is as part of a "front door" page to your site. You can assume that a user's browser that accepts the client-pull commands is also capable of rendering Netscape- or IE-specific commands. Users with browsers that don't recognize client-pull can click another link on the page to allow them to view regular HTML 2.0 pages.

In this lesson, you learned how to create hyperlinks to Internet services and load Web pages automatically. In the next lesson, you learn how to create HTML lists.

Creating Lists

In this lesson, you learn how to create and format HTML lists.

Using Lists in HTML

List tags, like paragraphs and preformatted text, are generally HTML containers that are capable of accepting other container and empty tags within their boundaries. These list tags are responsible for affecting the spacing and layout of text, not the emphasis, so they are applied to groups of text, and allow individual formatting tags within them.

Most HTML lists follow the form:

```
<LIST TYPE>
<LI> First item in list
<LI> Second item in list
<LI> Third item
</LIST TYPE>
```

Each of the items appears on its own line, and the list item (<LI>) tag itself is generally responsible for inserting either a bullet point or the appropriate number, depending on the type of list that's been defined. It's also possible that the item tag could insert no special characters (bullets or otherwise), as is the case with definition listings.

We'll look at each type in the following sections. The basics to remember are: Use the main container tags for list type, and the individual empty tags to announce each new list item. The type of list you choose is basically a question of aesthetics.

Ordered and Unordered Lists

It might be better to think of these as *numbered* (ordered) and *bulleted* (unordered) lists, especially when we're talking about their use in HTML. The only drawback to that is the fact that the HTML codes for each suggest the ordered/unordered names. For numbered/ordered lists, the tag is <OL>, and for bulleted/unordered lists, the tag is <UL>.

For either of these lists, a line item is designated with the empty tag <LI>. In the case of ordered lists, the <LI> tag inserts a number; for unordered, it inserts a bullet point. Examples of both follow.

An ordered list:

```
<OL>
<LI> Item number one.
<LI> Item number two.
<LI> Item number three.
</OL>
```

And an unordered list:

```
<UL>
<LI> First item.
<LI> Second item.
<LI> Third Item.
</UL>
```

To see how these look in a browser, see Figure 12.1.

Both ordered and unordered lists can take different types of internal HTML tags. It's even possible to include paragraph, line break, and header tags in lists.

TIP **No Headings in Lists** It's considered bad form to use the heading tags in bulleted lists, since your goal is probably only to change the size of the text for emphasis. Header tags are designed for page organization, not emphasis. That said, most browsers will recognize heading tags in lists.

You may see the potential for creating ordered lists that conform to standard outlining conventions (for instance, Roman numerals and letters).

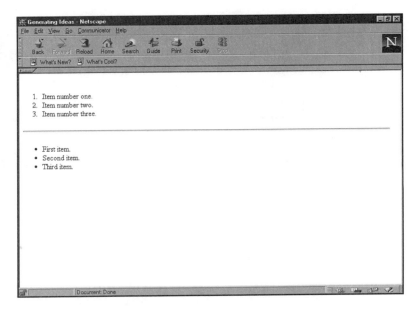

Figure 12.1 The subtle differences between ordered and unordered lists.

Numbered List Add-Ons

In order to create more effective numbered lists, you have the option of changing the numbering system and the start number for a given sequence:

- You can set the numbering style, ranging from Arabic numbers (1, 2, 3, 4) to letters (a, b, c, d; or A, B, C, D) or even Roman numerals (i, ii, iii, iv; or I, II, III, IV).
- You can set the first number in the sequence so that it's not necessary to start with 1.

Table 12.1 shows the ordered list enhancements that are possible when designing for HTML 3.2-compatible browsers.

Table 12.1 HTML 3.2 Extensions to Ordered (Numbered) Lists

Attribute	Description
TYPE=A	Sets markers to uppercase letters
TYPE=a	Sets markers to lowercase letters

continues

Table 12.1 Continued

Attribute	Description
TYPE=I	Sets markers to uppercase Roman numerals
TYPE=i	Sets markers to lowercase Roman numerals
TYPE=1	Sets markers to numbers
START	Sets beginning value of item markers in the current list

These attributes are written just like ordinary tag attributes, placed directly after the main tag itself. For example:

- <OL TYPE=A> produces a lettered list with items "numbered" A, B, C, D, and so on.

- <OL TYPE=I> yields a list that uses Roman numerals; items will be numbered I, II, III, IV, and so on.

- <OL TYPE=a START=4> displays a list with a lowercase Roman numeral in front of each list item starting with iv (the Roman numeral for 4).

Obviously, these extensions give you more options for displaying items in lists. It's a good thing, too; numbered lists are unexciting by their very nature, and they need this help to make them work like traditional outlines—the most obvious use for <OL>.

TIP **Renumber Lists** If you want to change the value of a particular list item, use the VALUE=# attribute in the <LI> tag, where # is an actual integer. The rest of the list will renumber itself from that point on.

Here's an example of a list using the special number attributes, which is shown in Figure 12.2:

```
<OL TYPE=I>
<LI> Introduction
<LI TYPE=A VALUE=1> Part One
<LI> Part Two
<LI> Part Three
</OL>
```

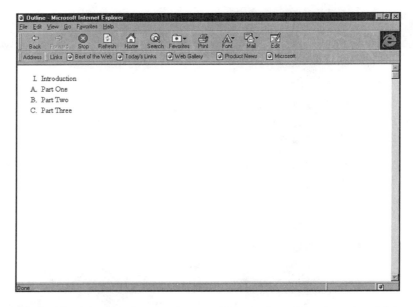

Figure 12.2 Changing starting numbers and types of numbers in ordered lists.

Bullet List Add-Ons

If you're creating pages for HTML 3.2-compatible (and beyond) browsers, you can choose the bullet styles yourself.

The new bullet styles are as follows:

- Filled circles `<UL TYPE=disc>`
- Filled squares `<UL TYPE=square>`
- Open circles (sometimes open squares) `<UL TYPE=circle>`

Directory and Menu Lists

To create a directory or menu list, we start with its respective container tag: `<DIR>` or `<MENU>`. Of these two, the directory list is probably more useful. Most browsers don't currently render the Menu command consistently…some use a bulleted list; others use no bullets.

```
<MENU>
<LI>House Salad
<LI>Fresh <B>Soup of the Week</B>
```

```
<LI>Buffalo Wings
<LI>Escargot
<LI>Liver and Onions
<LI>Turkey Sandwich, <EM>open faced</EM>
<LI>Turkey Sandwich, <EM>pre-fab</EM>
</MENU>
```

In theory, the <DIR> tag is a little more limiting. It's designed as a mechanism for listing computer file directories in HTML pages. Technically, it doesn't support interior HTML tags, although most browsers will display them. The <DIR> tag is also supposed to be limited to 24 characters (for some unknown reason) and show the file names in rows and columns, like a DIR/W command in MS-DOS, but the bulk of browsers seem to ignore both of these constraints as well.

```
<DIR>
<LI> autoexec.bat
<LI> config.sys
<LI> .signature
<LI> .password
<LI> System Folder
<LI> command.com
<LI> .kernel
</DIR>
```

Most browsers (including Netscape) will use the same font and layout for menus and directories as they will for unordered lists. In some cases, browsers will display one or the other (more often directory lists) without a bullet point, which can make them mildly useful. Some browsers can be set to a different font for directories and menus (versus ordered lists). So you may want to use these types, if only because some Web-savvy users' browsers will make an effort to display them differently.

Definition Lists

The final list tag is the definition list, which is designed to allow for two levels of list items, originally conceived to be the defined term and its definition.

The tags for this list are the container tag <DL> (definition list) and two empty tags, <DT> (definition term) and <DD> (definition). The <DT> tag is designed (ideally) to fit on a single line of your Web page, although it will wrap to the beginning of the next line if necessary. The <DD> tag will accept a full paragraph of text, continuously indenting beneath the <DT> term.

```
<DL>
<DT><B>hero</B> <I>(n.)</I>
<DD>A person admired for his or her
```

```
brave or noble deeds.
<DT><B>hertz</B> <I>(n.)</I>
<DD>A unit used in the measurement of the
frequency of electromagnetic waves
<DT><B>hex</B> <I>(n.)</I>
<DD>An evil spell or magical curse, generally
cast by a witch.
</DL>
```

Notice that standard HTML markup is permissible within the boundaries of a definition list, and that using bold and italics for the defined terms adds a certain dictionary-like quality, as shown in Figure 12.3.

 TIP   **No Extra Spaces**   Not all browsers will display definition lists in the same way, so adding spaces to <DT> items (to get them to line up with the <DD> text) is often a waste of time.

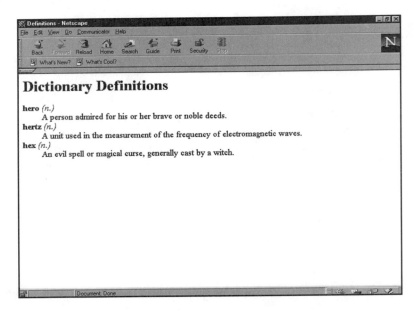

Figure 12.3   A basic definition list.

It should also be pointed out that just because definition lists allow for two different types of list items, you needn't necessarily use both. Using just the <DT> tag in your list, for instance, will result in a list not unlike an unordered list—except that nearly all browsers will display it without bullets, as shown in Figure 12.4.

```
<DL>
<DT>Milk
<DT>Honey
<DT>Eggs
<DT>Cereal
</DL>
```

And, although more difficult to find a use for, the **<DD>** item could be used on its own to indent paragraphs repeatedly. This book occasionally uses a similar device in its listings.

```
<P>I must say that I was shocked at his behavior. He was:
<DL>
<DD><I>Rude.</I> Not rude in your standard sort of affable way, or
even in
a way that would be justifiable were he immensely wealthy or criti-
cally
wounded. It was just a rudeness spilling over with contempt.
<DD><I>Unjust.</I> If there was something he could accuse you of
falsely,
he would do it. I could almost see him skulking around his apartment
after
a particularly unsuccessful party, doing his best to find things
stolen, which he
could blame on people who hadn't actually bothered to show up.
</DL>
</P>
```

The definition list offers some additional flexibility over the standard lists, then, giving us more choices in the way we lay out the list items.

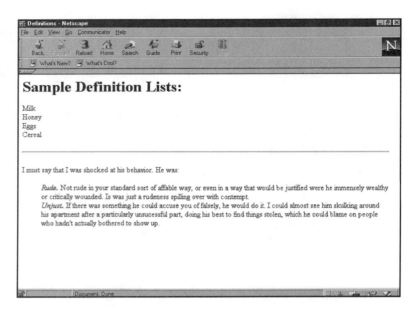

Figure 12.4 Each definition list above uses only one of the two elements.

In this lesson, you learned the different types of HTML lists. In the next lesson, you learn to create a simple table.

Formatting Basic Tables

In this lesson, you learn how to create a basic HTML table.

Creating a Table

Tables work a lot like HTML list tags, in that you must use the table container tag to hold together a group of tags that define each individual row. The main container is the <TABLE> tag, which uses enclosing tags for table rows (<TR>) and table data (<TD>). Most tables will also use an element for table headers (<TH>) that is generally used as the title text for rows and columns.

Tables take the following format:

```
<TABLE>
<CAPTION>Caption text for table</CAPTION>
<TR><TH>column1</TH><TH>column2</TH><TH>column3</TH>
<TR><TD>row1data1</TD><TD>row1data2</TD><TD>row1data3</TD>
<TR><TD>row2data1</TD><TD>row2data2</TD><TD>row2data3</TD>
...
</TABLE>
```

Notice that working with HTML tables is very similar to working with computer spreadsheets. In fact, the metaphor is the same. An HTML table consists of rows and columns. Where a row and a column meet you'll find a cell. Each individual cell is designed to be a container for data. In the case of HTML table cells, they can contain nearly any text and HTML elements, including things like hyperlinks and images.

The *<TABLE>* Tag

You begin any HTML table with the <TABLE> tag, which is actually a container tag that's designed to contain all of the elements necessary to create a table. Between the <TABLE> and </TABLE> tags, you use the <TR>,</TR> table row tags to create each row. Then, each set of <TD>, </TD> tags defines a cell, between which you place each cell's data.

1. To begin a table, enter a set of <TABLE>, </TABLE> tags in your HTML document.

2. Between the table tags, add sets of <TR>,</TR> to define the rows in your table. Add a set of these tags for each row you'd like in the table.

3. Now, in the first row definition, add a set of <TH>, </TH> table header tags for each column header you'd like to define. Type the text for each column header between each set of header tags.

4. In all of the remaining rows, add a set of <TD>, </TD> tags to define each individual cell. Between each set of data tags, enter the text for that cell.

CAUTION

Column Consistency   In order to display correctly, a table needs to have a consistent number of columns. So, in each row's definition you should create the same number of data cells. You do this by using the same number of <TD>, </TD> tag pairs.

An example of a basic table using this format might be the following:

```
<TABLE>
<CAPTION>Team Members for 3-Person Basketball</CAPTION>
<TR><TH>Blue Team</TH><TH>Red Team</TH><TH>Green Team</TH>
<TR><TD>Mike R.</TD><TD>Leslie M.</TD><TD>Rick G.</TD>
<TR><TD>Julie M.</TD><TD>Walter R.</TD><TD>Dale W.</TD>
<TR><TD>Bill H.</TD><TD>Jenny Q.</TD><TD>Fred B.</TD>
</TABLE>
```

After you work with HTML list containers, it's fairly easy to make the jump to creating tables in HTML. You can see how this table looks in Figure 13.1.

Creating Table Captions

The <CAPTION> tag is a container for reasons that may be obvious—it allows you to nest other HTML tags within the description. For instance:

```
<CAPTION><B>Table 3.1 from the book
➥ <I>Life in El Salvador</I></B></CAPTION>
```

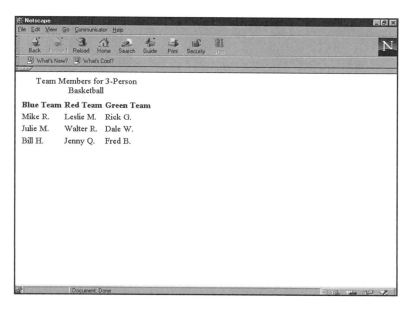

Figure 13.1 A simple table in HTML.

Just about any sort of markup tags are possible inside the <CAPTION> tags, although some—like list tags—wouldn't make much sense.

The <CAPTION> tag has one attribute, ALIGN. ALIGN=TOP and ALIGN=BOTTOM are encouraged. By default, text is also aligned to center (horizontally). TOP and BOTTOM refer to the entire table; the caption will default to the top of the table if not otherwise specified. To align the caption to BOTTOM, for instance, we enter:

```
<CAPTION ALIGN=BOTTOM>Table of Common Foods</CAPTION>
```

The <CAPTION> tag is commonly the first tag just inside the <TABLE> tag (although this placement is not required). Regardless of where you place the <CAPTION> tag, however, you must use ALIGN to force it to the bottom of the table. Otherwise, it will appear at the top, according to its default.

Here's an example of using the ALIGN attribute to the <CAPTION> tag to force the caption to the bottom, like this:

```
<BODY>
<H3>Favorite Ice Cream Flavors</H3>
<TABLE BORDER>
<CAPTION ALIGN=BOTTOM>Data from the <I>New Jersey Times</I></CAPTION>
<TR><TH>Date</TH><TH>Chocolate</TH><TH>Vanilla</TH>
```

85

```
<TR><TH>1970</TH><TD>50%</TD><TD>50%</TD>
<TR><TH>1980</TH><TD>76%</TD><TD>24%</TD>
<TR><TH>1990</TH><TD>40%</TD><TD>60%</TD>
</TABLE>
</BODY>
```

When the browser interprets this table, it should place the caption at the bottom of the table, centered horizontally, as shown in Figure 13.2.

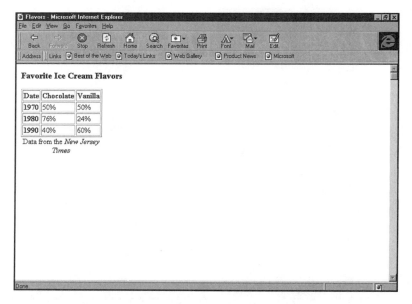

Figure 13.2 This table caption centers itself below the table.

Table Rows

Table rows (<TR>) can accept one attribute you should concern yourself with— ALIGN. The ALIGN attribute is used to determine how text will appear (horizontally) in each of the rows' data cells. For instance:

```
<TR ALIGN=CENTER><TH>Date</TH><TH>Chocolate</TH><TH>Vanilla</TH>
<TR ALIGN=CENTER><TH>1970</TH><TD>50%</TD><TD>50%</TD>
<TR ALIGN=CENTER><TH>1980</TH><TD>76%</TD><TD>24%</TD>
<TR ALIGN=CENTER><TH>1990</TH><TD>40%</TD><TD>60%</TD>
```

This example has added the ALIGN attribute (with a value of CENTER) to the rows in the previous example. Notice now that all cells center data horizontally (see Figure 13.3). This ALIGN attribute can also accept LEFT and RIGHT.

TIP **Vertical Align** Tables support another useful attribute, VALIGN, which accepts the values TOP, BOTTOM, and CENTER. Using this attribute, you can choose to align cells vertically as well as horizontally.

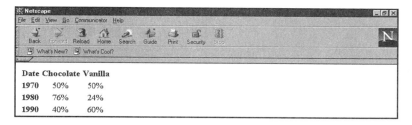

Figure 13.3 Using the ALIGN attribute with <TR>.

Table Data in Rows

You've already used the <TH> and <TD> tags to include headers and data in your tables. You may have noticed that, essentially, the only difference between the two is that <TH> emphasizes (boldfaces) the text and <TD> does not.

Technically, <TH> is a tag that the browser interprets as a header and thus displays text in a way that's distinct from the <TD> tag. In practice, this generally means it's turned bold.

Aside from accepting nearly any type of HTML markup tags within them, both tags can accept two attributes that help you align data within the cell. These are ALIGN and VALIGN. If you add these attributes, a <TH> or <TD> tag is formatted as follows:

```
<TH ALIGN="direction" VALIGN="direction">
```

ALIGN is used to align the data within the cell horizontally, accepting values of LEFT, RIGHT, and CENTER. Note that ALIGN is redundant when used with the ALIGN attribute of <TR>, unless it is used to override the <TR ALIGN=> setting.

 TIP **Override Alignment** The ALIGN or VALIGN attribute can be used in a particular cell definition to override the alignment set by that cell's row tags.

VALIGN is used to align the data vertically within cells. Possible values are TOP, BOTTOM, and CENTER. Sometimes this won't appear much different in a Web browser, especially if all of your cells contain approximately the same amount of data. In the case of two cells that are significantly different in content, though, the VALIGN attribute can make a significant difference in the appearance of the table. Figure 13.3 is an example of the VALIGN=BOTTOM attribute.

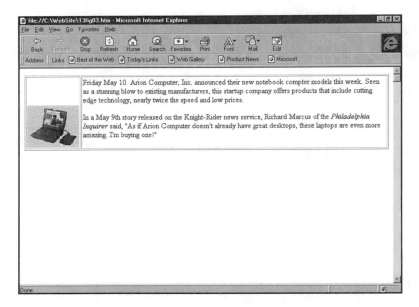

Figure 13.3 The cell on the left is set to VALIGN=BOTTOM.

In this lesson, you learned how to create a basic HTML table. In the next lesson, you'll learn how to work with advanced tables.

Working with Advanced Tables

In this lesson, you'll learn to create advanced tables using special table tags and spacing controls.

Advanced Table Attributes

Now that you have created a basic table, you can move on to a more advanced understanding of the table tags. Tables are a revolutionary step in the world of HTML. In fact, the control Web authors have over a page when they use tables has changed the way many professional Web pages are designed.

The <TABLE> tag is a complex creature that can accept many different attributes. Some of these attributes are more useful than others, so here's a look at the most useful ones:

- **ALIGN**   The ALIGN attribute is used to determine where the table appears relative to the browser window. The values are ALIGN=LEFT and ALIGN=RIGHT. As an added bonus, text will wrap around the table (if it's narrow enough) when the ALIGN=LEFT or ALIGN=RIGHT attributes are used.

- **WIDTH**   The WIDTH attribute sets the relative or absolute width of your table in the browser window. The values can be either percentages, as in WIDTH=50%, or absolute values.

  With absolute values, you must also include a suffix that defines the units used, as in **px** for pixels or **in** for inches (for example, WIDTH=3.5in). Absolute values for table widths are not recommended, since tables should react to user input (like a user changing their browser window size).

- **COLS**   The COLS attribute specifies the number of columns in your table, allowing the browser to draw the table as it downloads.

- **BORDER**   The BORDER attribute defines the width of the border surrounding the table. The default value is one pixel.

- **CELLSPACING**   The CELLSPACING attribute tells the browser how much space to include between the walls of the table and between individual cells. (The value is a number in pixels.)
- **CELLPADDING**   The CELLPADDING attribute tells the browser how much space to give data elements away from the walls of the cell. (The value is a number in pixels.)

You don't have to use all of these attributes for your table—in fact, the simple table example in the last lesson didn't use any of them. However, they do come in handy. The following sections describe each attribute.

WIDTH and *ALIGN*

By default, an HTML table takes up only as much space as needed to display the data in its cells. The table quickly grows to fill the browser window as it tries to fit all of the text in cells on one line before wrapping the text inside the cells.

You can use the WIDTH attribute to change this behavior. WIDTH accepts either fixed pixel widths or percentages of the page (so the table can grow or shrink when the user changes the size of her Web browser window). To create a table that takes up only half of the screen's width, you can add the WIDTH attribute

```
<TABLE WIDTH=50%>
```

and fix the width of the table at 50 percent of the browser window, regardless of the browser window's size. WIDTH=100% forces the table to be the exact same width as the browser window.

The ALIGN attribute is useful for any table that isn't fixed at 100 percent of the browser window, since it allows a table to be aligned to the left, right, or center of the browser window. An example is:

```
<TABLE BORDER=1 WIDTH=50% ALIGN=CENTER>
```

A table created with these attributes looks something like the table in Figure 14.1.

COLS and *BORDER*

The COLS attribute is a simple one—using it in your TABLE tag tells the browser how many columns to expect. This allows the browser to draw the table more quickly and try to render any missing cells as blank spaces in the appropriate columns.

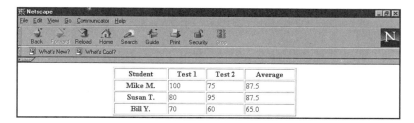

Figure 14.1 This table is set to align itself to the center and take up 50 percent of the browser window.

Since there are no column tags, the lack of a COLS attribute forces the browser to figure out the number of columns on its own. Normally this isn't difficult, but adding the attribute can help things along.

The BORDER attribute is optional. By default, every table is rendered with a border value of 1. Using the BORDER attribute, you can change this so that a table appears with a considerably thicker border or with no border at all. An example might be:

```
<TABLE BORDER=8>
```

A BORDER=8 attribute results in a table like the one in Figure 14.2. Notice that the border attribute affects the table's exterior borders. Here are the HTML codes for the table pictured in Figure 14.2:

```
<TABLE BORDER=8 ALIGN=CENTER WIDTH=50%>
<TR>
<TH>Student</TH><TH>Test 1</TH><TH>Test 2</TH><TH>Average</TH>
</TR>
<TR>
<TH>Mike M.</TH><TD>100</TD><TD>75</TD><TD>87.5</TD>
</TR>
<TR>
<TH>Susan T.</TH><TD>80</TD><TD>95</TD><TD>87.5</TD>
</TR>
<TR>
<TH>Bill Y.</TH><TD>70</TD><TD>60</TD><TD>65.0</TD>
</TR>
</TABLE>
```

CELLPADDING and *CELLSPACING*

For even more control over how your table looks, you can set the CELLSPACING and CELLPADDING attributes in the table tag.

CELLSPACING specifies how much space is between cells; the default is two.

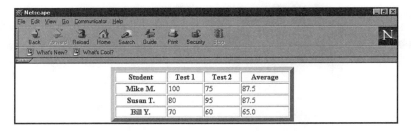

Figure 14.2   The border attribute can be used to change the appearance of your table.

CELLPADDING specifies how much space is between a cell wall and the contents of the cell. The default is one—you probably won't want to set it to zero, or your text will run into the cell and table borders. Following is an example of a <TABLE> tag that includes these attributes:

```
<TABLE CELLSPACING=4 CELLPADDING=5>
```

Figure 14.3 shows these attributes in action.

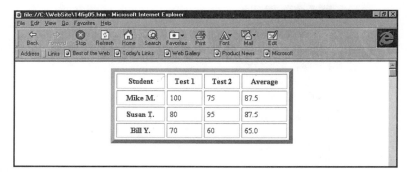

Figure 14.3   Using COLSPAN and ROWSPAN in a table.

Fusing Cells Together

Sometimes you need two or more cells with common borders (whether they're in the same row or the same column) to act as a single cell. You might fuse two cells together because they include the same information.

Whatever the reason, there are attributes for the <TH> and <TD> tags that allow you to force one cell to span more than one row or column.

COLSPAN and ROWSPAN are used to force a cell to span more than one column or row, respectively. An example is:

```
<TABLE BORDER>
<TR>
<TH>Student</TH><TH>Test 1</TH><TH>Test 2</TH><TH>Average</TH>
</TR>
<TR><TH>Mike M.</TH><TD>100</TD><TD>75</TD><TD ROWSPAN="3">N/A</TD>
</TR>
<TR>
<TH>Susan T.</TH><TD>80</TD><TD>95</TD>
</TR>
<TR>
<TH>Bill Y.</TH><TD COLSPAN=2>Dropped Course</TD>
</TR>
</TABLE>
```

Viewed in a browser, the table looks like the one in Figure 14.4.

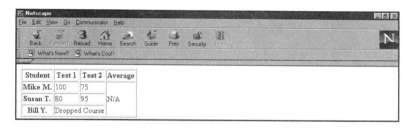

Figure 14.4 Using COLSPAN and ROWSPAN with attributes in a table.

Background Colors

Coloring cells in your table is a good idea. You can color-code rows or individual cells to make them stand out as they would on the ledger paper and financial printouts that business has used for years.

The BGCOLOR attribute accepts a color name and works with the <TABLE>, <TR>, and <TD> tags, shown in this listing:

```
<TABLE BORDER=1 CELLSPACING=2 CELLPADDING=2>
<TR><TH>JOB</TH><TH>MONDAY<TH>TUESDAY<TH>WEDNESDAY
<TR BGCOLOR=yellow><TH>Clean<TD>Mike<TD>Bill<TD>Sue<
<TR><TH>Cook<TD>Sue<TD>Mike<TD>Bill
<TR BGCOLOR=yellow><TH>Wash<TD>Bill<TD>Sue<TD>Mike
</TABLE>
```

TIP **Hex Colors** The BGCOLOR attribute also accepts three, 2-digit hex numbers that represent the RGB (red, green, blue) values for a particular color. For instance, BGCOLOR=#FFFFFF creates a white background.

As you can see in Figure 14.5, you might change the background color of tables for more than aesthetic reasons. As accountants and engineers have known for years, it's easier to communicate information in tables when you're able to shade different rows to make it clear what data is related to what other data and headers.

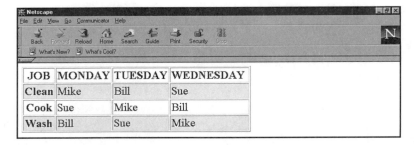

Figure 14.5 Use color in tables to make data easier to read.

In this lesson, you learned to create advanced tables using special table tags and spacing controls. In the next lesson, you learn how to use HTML tables for page layout.

Table-Based Page Layout

In this lesson, you learn how to use HTML tables for page layout.

Positioning with Tables

Since the HTML tables standard appeared on the scene, the sophistication and professionalism of Web pages has changed dramatically. The control over cells that modern browsers like Netscape and Internet Explorer (IE) offer makes it easier to put pictures, text, lists, and links wherever you want them on the page.

You do this by aligning cells, creating spanning cells (or fusing cells together), and adding the appropriate cell padding and spacing. You can also set the table border to zero so it seems as though the page has thoughtfully arranged itself.

Figure 15.1 shows an example of a simple layout. This example works well for a catalog or other product specifications, with images on one side and descriptions on the other.

One thing that hasn't really been touched on so far is the possibility of including images in tables. It's definitely possible and just about as easy as anything else you can do with tables.

The listing that follows creates a product specifications table for two of our company's computer systems. Liberal use of the ALIGN and VALIGN attributes makes this an effective table.

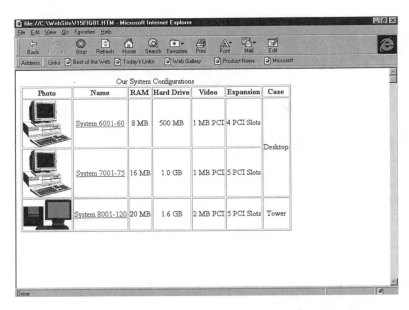

Figure 15.1   A simple layout table, good for product specifications.

```
<TABLE BORDER CELLSPACING=2 CELLPADDING=2>
<CAPTION>Our System Configurations</CAPTION>
<TR ALIGN=CENTER>
<TH>Photo</TH><TH>Name</TH><TH>RAM</TH>
➥<TH>Hard Drive</TH><TH>Video</TH><TH>Expansion</TH>
➥<TH>Case</TH>
</TR>
<TR ALIGN=CENTER>
<TD><IMG SRC="sml_6001.GIF"></TD>
➥<TD><A HREF="6001.html">System 6001-60</A></TD>
➥<TD>8 MB</TD><TD>500 MB</TD><TD>1 MB PCI</TD>➥
➥<TD>4 PCI Slots</TD><TD ROWSPAN=2>Desktop</TD>
</TR>
<TR ALIGN=CENTER>
<TD><IMG SRC="sml_7001.GIF"></TD><TD>
➥<A HREF="7001.html">System 7001-75</A></TD>
➥<TD>16 MB</TD><TD>1.0 GB</TD><TD>1 MB PCI</TD>➥
➥<TD>5 PCI Slots</TD>
</TR>
<TR ALIGN=CENTER><TD><IMG SRC="sml_8001.GIF"></TD>
➥<TD><A HREF="8001.html">System 8001-120</A></TD>
➥<TD>20 MB</TD><TD>1.6 GB</TD><TD>2 MB PCI</TD>
➥<TD>5 PCI Slots</TD><TD>Tower</TD>
</TR>
</TABLE>
</BODY>
```

Graphics enliven what would otherwise be drier, text-based tables. Notice that other HTML commands, like hyperlinks, also work well in tables.

Creating Columns with Tables

Figure 15.2 is an example of a table-based site. This is a very simple table—really only two cells in a single row. But what you're creating is an entire two-column page. One column is used for hyperlink controls, while the other is used for the main text of the page.

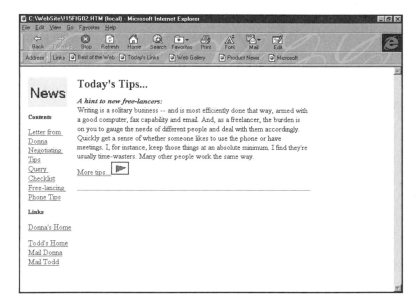

Figure 15.2 Using HTML tables to place columns of text next to each other.

In this example, the border of the table is left at BORDER=1 to show the table. In other cases, you'd want to change the BORDER to 0.

Here are the basics for creating this table layout:

1. Begin by defining the TABLE with the desired BORDER, CELLPADDING, and CELLSPACING. You can also set the WIDTH of the table either to 100 percent or to about 600 pixels.

CAUTION

Not Too Wide If you set your table to a fixed width of more than 600 pixels, you might force users with smaller monitors to scroll excessively to read your page.

2. Create the first row of your table by inserting a `<TR>` tag.

3. Now create your first cell. Between the `<TD>` tags, enter everything you want in the leftmost column. You can fix the width of this column by adding the `WIDTH` attribute to your `<TD>` tag.

4. In the next cell you create, add everything you want on the right side of the page. This can include almost any sort of HTML markup you decide on.

5. Enter the closing `</TR>` table row tags and `</TABLE>` tags.

Here's the sample code for the page shown in Figure 15.2:

```
<TABLE BORDER=1 CELLSPACING=2 CELLPADDING=5 WIDTH=600>
<TR>
<TD VALIGN=top WIDTH=100>
<IMG SRC="news.gif" WIDTH="81" HEIGHT="64"><BR>

<!-- Menu bar listing -->
<H5>Contents</H5>
<DL >
<DT><A HREF="letter.html">Letter from Donna</A>
<DT><A HREF="negotiation.html">Negotiating Tips</A>
<DT><A HREF="query.html">Query Checklist</A>
<DT><A HREF="phone.html">Free-lancing Phone Tips</A>
</DL>
<H5>Links</H5>
<DL>
<DT><A HREF="http://mynet.com/donna/index.html">
➥Donna's Home</A>
<DT><A HREF="http://members.aol.com/tstauffer/index.html">
➥Todd's Home</A>
<DT><A HREF="mailto:donna@mynet.com">Mail Donna</A>
<DT><A HREF="mailto:todds@mynet.com">Mail Todd</A>
</DL>
</TD>
<!-- END MENU BAR -->

<!--BEGIN RIGHT-SIDE CONTENT-->
<TD valign=top CELLPADDING=10>
<H2>Today's Tips...</h2>
<P>
<B><I>A hint to new free-lancers:</I></B><BR>
Writing is a solitary business -- and is most
➥efficiently done that way, armed with a good computer,
➥fax capability and email. And, as a freelancer, the
➥burden is on you to gauge the needs of different people and
```

```
➡deal with them accordingly. Quickly get a sense of whether
➡someone likes to use the phone or have meetings. I, for
➡instance, keep those things at an absolute minimum. I find
➡they're usually time-wasters. Many other people work the same
➡way. <BR>

<A HREF="tips.html">More tips...<IMG SRC="right_arrow.gif" WIDTH="33"
HEIGHT="23"></A>
</P>
<HR>
</TD>
</TR>
</TABLE>
```

This type of layout is a fairly popular one, since it allows you to place hyperlinks on one side of the page (for navigation), with text, images, and links on the other side of the page.

Nesting Tables

Another popular layout is the three-column newsletter style. This allows you to create a Web page resembling the front page of a newspaper, with headlines and columns of text (and graphics). The basics of the newsletter style are the same, although you can get a more complex effect by *nesting* the tables.

 TERM

Nesting This word comes to HTML from programming, where it describes one instance of programming logic used inside another. In the context of HTML tables, it simply means placing one table definition within another.

For a newsletter-style layout, the definition might be something like:

```
<TABLE BORDER=0 CELLPADDING=2 CELLSPACING=2 COLS=3>
```

And the first couple of rows:

```
<TR>
<TD COLSPAN=3 ALIGN=CENTER><H2>The Electronic Gazette</H2></TD>
</TR>
<TR>
<TD ALIGN=LEFT COLSPAN=2><H3>New Notebooks</H3>
<P>Friday May 10. Arion Computer, Inc. announced their new notebook
➡computer models this week. Seen as a stunning blow to existing
➡manufacturers, the startup company offers products that include
➡cutting edge technology, nearly twice the speed and low prices.</P>
<P>In a May 9th story released to the Knight-Ridder wire service,
➡Richard Marcus of the Philadelphia Inquirer said, "As if Arion
```

```
➥Computer doesn't already have great desktops, these laptops are even
➥more amazing. I'm buying one!"</P>
</TD>
```

If you've been counting columns, you know that there is still one to go. In this example, the next cell (which spans a single column) requires two rows—one row features an image, while the other row has text about the image. To do this, you can begin a new table that's completely enclosed in the cell definition:

```
<TD>
<TABLE ALIGN=CENTER VALIGN=CENTER>
<TR>
<TD><IMG SRC="perfbook.gif" ALT="Perfbook computer"></TD>
</TR>
<TR>
<TD><B>The PerfBook 400 Computer</B></TD>
</TABLE>
</TD>
```

This completes the second row of the table. You need just a row-closing tag and a closing-table tag to finish the first table:

```
</TR>
</TABLE>
```

Figure 15.3 shows the newsletter-style table layout.

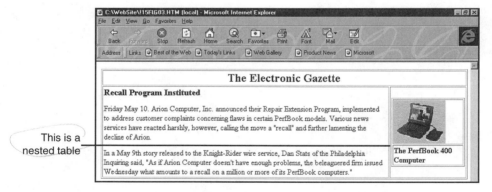

Figure 15.3   Using nested tables gives you more control over page layout (the table border is set to 1 to show the table in the figure).

In this lesson, you learned how to create table-based page layouts for your Web pages.

Web Graphics and Animation

Creating Web Graphics

In this lesson, you learn how to create graphics that look good and load quickly on the Web.

Rules for Graphics

Although adding Web graphics to your pages is a fairly painless process, creating those images can be a bit tougher. The trick with Web graphics is to keep them interesting, entertaining, and useful, yet small and unobtrusive. It takes a bit of getting used to, but the best Web designers understand that balance is the most important element for successful graphics. Here are a few basic rules:

- Graphics should have a clear purpose on your page. Graphics for the sake of having pictures around should be kept to a minimum. Most Web surfers are looking for information or services, not cool images.

- Image files should be small and load quickly. By the same token, your Web page should load quickly, too—which means it can't be overwhelmed with images.

- Take advantage of technology to improve your images. The Web palette of 216 colors, for instance, is useful for cutting down on load times. (Look for these 216-color options in your graphics creation/manipulation programs.) Certain types of graphics can be saved as *interlaced*, which causes them to appear to load more quickly.

Interlacing   By using a process called *interlacing*, certain graphics programs can save GIF and JPEG images so that they can be displayed as they load in a Web browser. This makes it easy to identify images before they've been completely downloaded. Look for this option in the **File**, **Save As** menu of your image editing programs. Also, some programs will call this option *progressive* since it allows images to be loaded as the download progresses.

Choose Clear Images

Clear images communicate their function almost instantly. But that's not to say that creating clear images is necessarily easy to do. In fact, *icons in general are* often a clever way to get a point across graphically, while keeping your graphics small and to a minimum.

If your graphics are attractive, but don't quite stand on their own, adding a little text isn't cheating. Text can be added two ways: graphically, within your image manipulation software, or via HTML. Figure 1.1 displays a World Wide Web page that combines images with graphical text to ensure clarity.

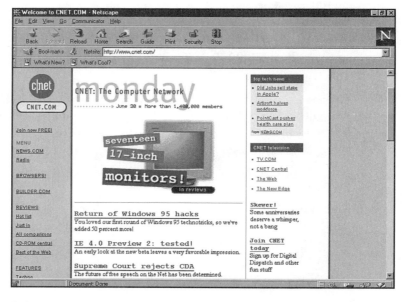

Figure 1.1   A well-designed Web site uses only a few icon images—not tons of pretty pictures—to give the impression of a highly graphical site.

Clarity is the key to the success of your design—confusing pages will more often be ignored. As you create Web pages and the images that will be used on-screen, focus on whether your ideas and intentions are clear. If you have any doubts about your icons, add descriptive text to the image for clarity.

TIP **Picture Text** Some of the best Web icons are really just "pictures of text" using interesting fonts in image-editing programs to create labeled icons.

Graphics Sizes

There are two measurements of size on the Web: the amount of the screen that an image requires, and the storage space the image's file fills. Here's how to make your images smaller for faster loading Web pages:

Leave images at about 72 dots per inch. If you're scanning images into your computer for use on the Web, they generally only need to be at a resolution of about 72–75 dots per inch (dpi). That's the dpi on typical computer monitors, so graphics look good at that resolution. More dots (like the 360 dpi of inkjet printers) is overkill for a computer monitor, and it makes the image file larger.

Use small *thumbnail* images on your page. If you want the user to be able to see larger images, you can link the thumbnail to another Web document, which contains the full-sized graphic.

Thumbnails Tiny graphical representations that link to a full screen reproduction of the initial image. Thumbnails are usually .5–1 inch square and run about 5–10 kilobytes each in storage size.

Don't use WIDTH and HEIGHT to create small images. For thumbnails, the smaller image needs to have been made smaller in an actual image manipulation program, not just with the <IMG WIDTH= HEIGHT=> attributes. That's the only way you'll create a smaller image file that will transmit more quickly over the Internet.

To minimize the size of your graphics, consider using JPEG formatting. JPEG coding compresses images to one-third or one-fifth of the total size of GIF styles. JPEG is generally recommended for photos and other high-detail images; GIF is recommended for graphical text, icons, and computer-drawn images.

Reduce the number of colors in your images. Every image you create has a palette of colors that may be added for animation and aesthetic appeal. GIF files support palettes of up to 256 colors, while JPEG files have access to over 16 million different shades.

TIP **Fewer Colors** Graphics manipulation programs often have commands that allow you to choose 16, 64, 256, or other color palettes. Some even allow you to choose a palette that only includes the colors you've actually used. Look for choices like these to make your image files smaller.

Transparent Images

Certain image-editing programs give you the ability to create transparent GIFs—essentially making one color in the image (usually the background) transparent or invisible. When a browser loads the file, the transparent portions of the image are replaced by whatever appears behind the graphic. Only the GIF graphics format (specifically GIF89a) can be saved with a transparent background.

Transparency creates graphics that float on top of the background and are not

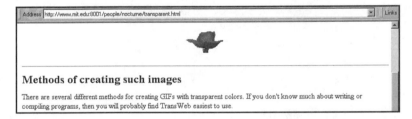

defined by a standard square picture frame, as shown in Figure 1.2.

Figure 1.2 Making the image's background transparent gives the image an interesting look on the Web page.

To create a transparent GIF:

1. Load your image in an image-editing program that supports transparency. LView Pro (**http://www.lview.com/**), UNIX's xv, and Transparency for Mac are a few options.

2. Use the program's tools to choose the transparent color. Note that every instance of that color is turned transparent. If you use the same color in

your image and for the image's background, you may end up with unsatis-factory results.

3. Use the program's **File**, **Save As** command to save the image as a **GIF89a** file.

Navigation Buttons

Little clickable icons are an exceptional way to help users move around on your site. But don't just use buttons for "next" and "previous." It's important to let users jump straight to your home page and any other important pages. You might consider looking around the Web for public domain icons (those available free from the artist) and creating clickable icons for your site.

Aligning graphics with <BR> would be as simple as:

```
<IMG SRC="news.gif"><BR>
<IMG SRC="thrills.gif"><BR>
<IMG SRC="arts.gif"><BR>
<IMG SRC="cafe.gif"><BR>
<IMG SRC="movies.gif"><BR>
```

There are an abundance of navigation-style icons and buttons available for public use on the World Wide Web. Try Yahoo!'s **http://www.yahoo.com/ Computers_and_Internet/Internet/World_Wide_Web/ Page_Design_and_Layout/** to start.

In this lesson, you learned how to keep graphics small and smart for displaying on your Web pages. In the next lesson, you'll learn how to create server-side image maps.

Creating Server-Side Image Maps

In this lesson, you learn how to create a server-side image map and add it to your page.

What Is an Image Map?

Image maps begin as normal graphics (usually in GIF or JPEG format), designed with the Web in mind. Then another program is used to map *hot zones* (clickable areas) on top of the graphics.

When put in place on a Web page, an image map allows users to access different HTML pages by clicking different parts of the graphic. Because each hot zone has an associated URL, and because each hot zone corresponds to part of the graphic, maneuvering about a Web site becomes more interesting, graphical, and interactive.

An image map can be either *client-side* or *server-side*. This lesson discusses server-side image maps. Server-side maps are the older of the two technologies and are becoming much less popular than client-side maps. Unless you've been instructed to do so by a lead Webmaster or your system administrator, you'll probably be best served by skipping to Lesson 3. This lesson is here only for those people whose corporate or organizational Web sites have standardized on the older server-side technology.

Client-Side versus Server-Side The difference between the two types of image maps is all in the way they're processed. A *client-side* image map is processed by the user's Web browser—the browser figures out where the user clicked and what the associated URL is. With a *server-side* map, the server is responsible for figuring out what page matches up with the user's click.

Creating an image map involves three steps: creating the graphic, mapping the graphic for hot zones, and placing the correct information (along with the correct programs) on the Web server itself.

 TIP   **Map Server Required**   To offer your users the option of using image maps, you must have a special map server program running on your Web server. For UNIX-based servers, this program will most often be NCSA Imagemap; other platforms have their own map server programs.

The Map Server Program

When a user clicks an image map on a Web page, the browser determines the coordinates of the graphic (in pixels) that describe where the user clicked. The browser then passes these numbers to the map server program, along with the name of the file that contains the URLs that correspond to these coordinates.

The map server program (usually NCSA Imagemap on UNIX servers) simply accepts the coordinates and looks them up in the database file that defines the hot zones for that image map. When NCSA Imagemap finds those coordinates and their associate URL, it sends a "connect to URL" command (just as a hypertext link does) that causes your browser to load the appropriate HTML document.

The Map Definition File

To determine which parts of the image map are linked to which URLs, the map server program must have a map definition file at its disposal. This file is generally a text file with the extension MAP, stored somewhere in the CGI-BIN directory for your Web site. Exactly where this file is stored depends on the combination of your Web server and map server. Let it suffice to say that you'll need to consult your server's documentation or your ISP.

The map definition file looks similar to Figure 2.1.

You can define different shapes in the file; these shapes correspond to the shapes of the hot zones that overlay the graphic that you want to use for your image. Each set of coordinates creates a point on the graphic. The coordinates are expressed in pixels, with each pair of numbers representing the number of pixels to the right and down, respectively, from the top-left corner of your graphic.

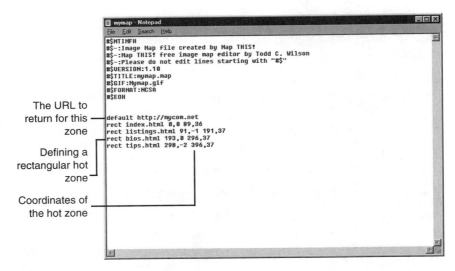

The URL to return for this zone

Defining a rectangular hot zone

Coordinates of the hot zone

Figure 2.1 A map definition file.

The Various Shapes of Hot Zones

This section briefly defines the shapes of hot zones. Hot zones can be in any of the following shapes:

- **rect** (rectangle)   This shape requires two points: the upper-left coordinates and the lower-right coordinates.
- **circle**   To create a circular region, you need coordinates for a center point and an edge point. The circle is then computed with that radius.
- **point**   A point requires only one coordinate. The map server software decides which point the mouse pointer was closest to when the shape was clicked (provided that the click didn't occur in another hot zone).
- **poly** (polygon)   You can use up to 100 sets of coordinates to determine all the vertices for the polygon region.
- **default**   Any part of the graphic that is not included in another hot zone is considered to be part of the default region, as long as no point zones are defined. If a point *is* defined, then default is redundant, since the map server will evaluate any click (outside a hot zone) and choose the nearest point.

Defining Your Image-Map Hot Zones

As a Web author, you are responsible for doing two things in the hot zone definition process. First, you need to define the hot zones to create the image map—that is, you need to decide what URL the coordinates will correspond to when the image map is clicked.

Second, you need to create the map definition file that makes the hot-zone information available to the Web server. For Windows and Macintosh users, luckily, programs that do both are available.

MapEdit for Microsoft Windows and X Window

Available for all flavors of Windows (Windows 95, Windows 3.1, and Windows NT) and for most types of UNIX, MapEdit is a powerful program that allows you to graphically define the hot zones for your image maps. You can access and download the latest version of this program from the MapEdit Web site (**http://www.boutell.com/mapedit/**).

When you have the program installed and you double-click its icon to start it, follow these steps to define your map:

1. Choose **File**, **Open/Create** from the **MapEdit** menu.

2. In the Open/Create Map dialog box, enter the name of the map definition file you want to create and the name of the graphic file you want to use for your map. You should also use the option buttons to determine whether you'll use CERN or NCSA map definitions. (Consult your map server software or ISP if you're not sure whether to use CERN or NCSA.)

3. Click the **OK** button. In the Creating New Map File dialog box, click **Yes**. After a moment, MapEdit displays your image file.

4. To create a new hot zone, choose the shape from the **Tools** menu; then click one time for each point required for the shape:

   - For a rectangle, click once to start the rectangle, then click where you'd like the opposite corner of the triangle to appear.

   - For a circle, click for the middle, then drag out the circle and click when you've got the right radius.

   - The triangle tool is actually a "polygon" tool, so click for each point in the polygon, then right-click at the last point (to connect your last point to the first point and complete the shape).

111

5. When the shape is created, the dialog box shown in Figure 2.2 appears. Enter the URL that you want to associate with your new hot zone. (You also can enter comments, if you want.) Then click **OK** to continue.

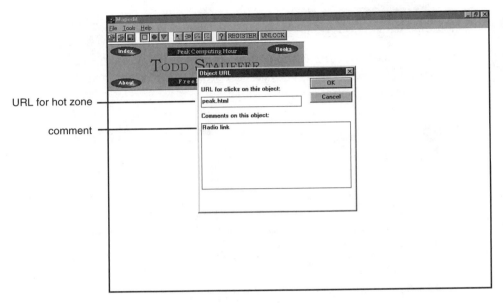

URL for hot zone

comment

Figure 2.2 Associating an URL with the hot zone.

6. Add more shapes (following steps 4 and 5 above) until you finish mapping your graphic.

7. Choose **File**, **Save**. Now you have a **.MAP** file for your image map.

TIP **Default URLs** By choosing **File**, **Edit Default URL**, you can determine whether your image map includes a default URL for clicks outside your hot zones. It's a good idea to include a default URL for every server-side image map you create. That way, if the user clicks in the wrong part of an image map, you can load a help document to explain the map to them.

WebMap for Macintosh

If you're a Macintosh user, you can use a program called WebMap, which is similar to MapEdit. You can download WebMap from **http://www.city.net/cnx/software/webmap.html**. Install the program; then double-click its icon to start it.

To create an image map in WebMap, follow these steps:

1. Choose **File**, **Open**.

2. In the Open dialog box, select the graphic that you want to use for your map and the name of the map definition file that you want to create.

3. Click the **OK** button. After a moment, WebMap displays your image file.

4. To create a new hot zone, choose the shape from the floating tool palette, and drag to create a hot zone:

   • For a rectangle, circle, or oval, click and hold the mouse in the top-left corner of your shape, drag the mouse to make the shape the desired size, then release the mouse button.

   • To create a polygon, choose the polygon shape from the tool palette, and then click once on the graphic for each point in your polygon. To complete the shape, click once on the first point you created.

5. When the shape is created, enter the URL in the space provided above the graphic file. You can use the Pointer tool (the one that looks like a mouse pointer) to select different shapes that you've created and then edit their URLs.

6. To create a default URL, use the pointer tool to click the graphic background (not a shape). `Default URL` should appear in the comment window. Then enter the default URL in the URL text box.

To create your map definition file, pull down the **File** menu and choose **Export As Text**. In the resulting dialog box, you can name your map file and save it in CERN or NCSA format. Now you're free to save the graphic and quit the program.

Adding Image Maps to Your Web Page

After you create your image map and your map definition file, you're ready to add a link for your image map to your HTML page. You can accomplish this task in a couple of ways, depending on your Web server. In essence, though, the only major difference between an image map and a clickable image is a new attribute for the `<IMG>` tag: `ISMAP`.

Image maps follow this format:

```
<A HREF="URL"><IMG SRC="graphic.ext" ISMAP></A>
```

You want the URL to access the map definition file. You'll have to ask your ISP (or figure out for yourself) where on the server the map file is stored.

Some Web servers allow you to store the map definition file anywhere on the server; the servers are smart enough to figure out that you're accessing a map definition file and take care of the rest. In that case, you could simply store the map definition file in the current directory and access it as follows:

```
<A HREF="mymap.map"><IMG SRC="mymap.gif" ISMAP></A>
```

Other servers may require you to access a particular directory on the server, such as the **/cgi-bin/** directory. In such a case, something like the following examples may be the way to access the image map:

```
<A HREF="http://www.mynet.com/cgi-bin/mymap.map"><IMG SRC="mymap.gif"
➥ISMAP></A>
```

If the server requires you to access one of these scripting directories, though, it may not want you to access the map definition file directly. Instead, the server will want you to use an alias.

Some servers store all map information in a single database file (often called `imagemap.conf`) and require you to access information within the database by using an alias. You and your Web server administrator have to determine what this alias is. In that case, your link would look more like the following:

```
<A HREF="http://www.mynet.com/bin/mymap"><IMG SRC="mymap.gif"
➥ISMAP></A>
```

In this lesson, you learned how to create and add a server-side image map to your page. In the next lesson, you'll learn to create and add a client-side image map.

Client-Side Image Maps

In this lesson, you learn how to create and add client-side image maps to your Web documents.

What Is a Client-Side Image Map?

Client-side image maps don't require a special map server program to determine where the user clicked and what URL should be accessed. Server-side maps, discussed in Lesson 2, require help from the Web server. A client-side image map, however, is interpreted by the browser itself, which simply loads the URL as if a regular hypertext link were clicked.

The advantages of using client-side image maps are considerable:

- First, they do away with the need for extra files and programs on the Web server, which should be a great relief to nonprogramming Web designers. Client-side maps are just more HTML markup—and no CGI-BIN programming.

- Related to that is the control that client-side maps offer you. As a Web author, you're not forced to deal with your Web administrator to offer image maps to your users. That's especially helpful if you get Internet access through one of the large national providers such as America Online.

- Client-side maps don't require a Web server—or the HTTP protocol—at all. In fact, they don't even have to be on the Internet. It will become more and more common to see non-Web applications for HTML in the future (like CD-ROM–based HTML archives) where a Web server isn't part of the picture. With client-side maps, you don't need a server to create an interface. Because they don't rely on the Web server, client-side maps are usually a bit quicker, too.

Create a Client-Side Image Map

To begin creating a client-side map, you need an appropriate graphic. Although client-side maps don't require a map definition file, using a map editing program (like MapEdit for Windows/UNIX or WebMap for Mac) is a sneaky way to come up with the information you *do* need for your client-side map.

Using your map editor, you can create hot zones (the clickable "shapes" that work as hyperlinks) that you'd like to use for your map. (If you need instructions for this, refer to Lesson 2.) When you've created your hot zones for a particular graphic, save your map definition file. You now have the information you need to create a client-side map.

Client-side maps require two different sections of code—the <IMG> tag and a new tag, the <MAP> container. <MAP> acts much like a map definition file does, except that it is part of the HTML document. You created the map definition file in the last section to help you with this new tag.

The Image Tag

In order to create a client-side image map, you need to add the new attribute USEMAP, as follows:

```
<IMG SRC="map_name.gif" USEMAP="#section_name">
```

Notice that USEMAP accepts a target hyperlink, just like when you create a link to another part of the same document. That's how you can store the map definition information in the same HTML document. Here's an example:

```
<IMG SRC="mymap.gif" USEMAP="#mymap">
```

That's all you need in order to display the image and tell the browser that this is a client-side image map. Now, however, you need to create the definition that the browser will use for that map.

The Map Data Tag

The <MAP> tag is a container tag that is referenced using a section-style NAME attribute. Inside the <MAP> container, you use the <AREA> tag to define each hot zone for the client-side map. Here's how it works:

```
<MAP NAME="section_name">
<AREA SHAPE="shape1" COORDS="coordinate numbers" HREF="URL">
<AREA SHAPE="shape2" COORDS="coordinate numbers" HREF="URL">
...
</MAP>
```

Notice that most of the information required for the <AREA> tag is available to you in your map definition file. So, based on the map definition file you create in a map-editing program, you can come up with a complete client-side <MAP> like the following one:

```
<MAP NAME="mymap">
<AREA SHAPE="POLY" COORDS="1,0,1,72,108,0" HREF="tips.html">
<AREA SHAPE="POLY" COORDS="154,0,109,0,88,14,154,71"
➥HREF="q&a.html">
<AREA SHAPE="RECT" COORDS="157,0,287,35" HREF="bios.html">
<AREA SHAPE="RECT" COORDS="158,38,288,71" HREF="listings.html">
<AREA SHAPE="RECT" COORDS="0,0,288,71" HREF="help.html">
</MAP>
```

That last <AREA> tag is the one you're using to define your entire graphic. According to the client-side specification, the area defined first takes precedence when two areas overlap. So, if someone clicks in one of the first four hot zones, they'll be taken to the appropriate URL. If they miss a hot zone, though, they'll be taken to help.html, where you'll tell them how to use the map!

TIP   **Default Zone**   If you elect not to create your own default hot zone, client-side maps will automatically ignore clicks that fall outside your other hot zones. This may frustrate users, but at least they won't be sent to URLs at random.

The *<AREA>* Tag

The shapes for client-side hot zones differ a bit from those for server-side maps. There are only three basic shapes. (Remember, this is when you use your map-editing program to determine coordinates.) The SHAPE attribute is used to accept these values. The numbers are given to the COORD attribute. The three basic shapes are as follows:

- **RECT**   The rectangular hot zone requires four coordinates: the top-left corner and the bottom-right corner. An example would be 1,0,55,54 which places the left at pixel 1, the top at pixel 0, the right at 55, and the bottom at 54.

- **CIRCLE**   A circular zone requires three different coordinates: center-x, center-y, and a radius. An example might be 20,20,5, which would represent a circle with its center at 20,20 and a radius of 5 pixels.

- **POLYGON**   For a polygon, each vertex requires a pair of points as its definition. (This is nearly the same as is created by most map definition programs.) A COORD value of 1,2,55,56,1,99 would create a polygon (triangle) with a vertex at 1,2, one at 55,56, and a third at 1,99.

The HREF attribute is used to give the appropriate URL for each hot zone. If no URL is desired, then the attribute NOHREF can be used to make a particular hot zone useless.

Three different examples of <AREA> tags might be:

```
<AREA SHAPE="RECT" COORDS="0,0,49,49" HREF="about_me.html">
<AREA SHAPE="CIRCLE" COORDS="75,49,10" HREF="resume.html">
<AREA SHAPE="POLYGON" COORDS="50,0,65,0,80,10,65,20,50,20" NOHREF>
```

The Clickable Image Fallback

Perhaps you want to offer a solution to browsers that can't accept client-side image maps, but don't have access to your Web server for offering a server-side map. In that case, you can make an image both a client-side map *and* a clickable graphic. Just assign the whole graphic to a link that explains that you're using a client-side map, as in the following example:

```
<A HREF="error_map.html">
<IMG SRC="mymap.gif" USEMAP="#map_data"></A>
```

In this example, if users click somewhere on the graphic, but their browser can't deal with client-side maps, they'll be taken to a page called error_map.html where you can explain the problem to them, and perhaps offer a series of clickable graphics or text links for them to use.

In this lesson, you learned how to add client-side image maps to your pages. In the next lesson, you'll learn how to add other graphical elements, such as background images.

Backgrounds and Colors

In this lesson, you learn to add background images, change font colors, and control link colors on your page.

Change the Background

Web authors have a lot of fun putting an image of some sort in the background of their page. It definitely adds personality, if that's what you're striving for. Perhaps no other single HTML command can so dramatically change the appearance of a page.

The HTML way to change the background into a graphic is to use the BACKGROUND attribute for the body tag, as in the following example, which is pictured in Figure 4.1:

```
<BODY BACKGROUND="paper.gif">
```

You've learned that graphic files should be as small as possible to speed their downloading over the Internet. And, the same is true for background graphics, most of the time.

The exception is the fact that once a background graphic is downloaded to the Web browser, it's actually displayed a little quicker if it's *physically* bigger (for example, 3×4 inches, instead of 2×3 inches). That's because the Web browser has to "tile" the image behind the Web page. The bigger the graphic, the fewer the tiles.

If you're using the same background graphic for *all* of your pages, then it's okay to send a file that's a little on the large size—both physically and in terms of kilobytes (although still not more than about 15–25 kilobytes). Once the background is in the browser's cache, it will load rather quickly.

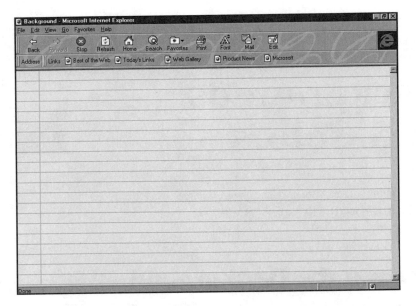

Figure 4.1   A background graphic will tile itself to fill the page. Remember to keep it light enough to show black text well, unless you also plan to change the color of the text.

If you use a different background on every page, though, the cache effect won't help as much. In that case, you'll still want to keep the file size of your background graphics fairly small.

Adding a Little Color

If you'd like to go crazy and take complete control of the look of your Web page, it's time to break out some of the color commands. As always, realize that only HTML 3.2 compliant-browsers will notice all this colorful fun—but more and more of the latest browsers do.

You can start by coloring the background. Using the BGCOLOR attribute for the <BODY> tag, you create a background color by specifying a 6-digit hexadecimal number. This attribute takes the following format:

```
<BODY BGCOLOR=#rrggbb>
...HTML Document...
</BODY>
```

The `#rrggbb` number represents the two-digit *hexadecimal* number for red, green, and blue values of the color you want added to the background of your document. An example of this is the following, which would turn the background of your page black:

```
<BODY BGCOLOR="#000000"
```

Similarly, `#ffffff` would be a white background, `#ff0000` would be red, `#00ff00` would be green, and so on.

Hexadecimal   Base-16, as opposed to base-10 (normal counting numbers), so each column in a hex number represents a digit up to 15, not nine. The rightmost column (called the "one's place" in grade school), needs single-digit numbers past nine in order to allow it to represent hex numbers.

Unfortunately, our base-10 numbering system doesn't have single digits past nine. (10, which is past nine, is a two-digit number in base-10.) So, we use letters—the first six of the alphabet. An *F* in the rightmost column represents the value 15, and an *F* in the 16's place represents 240 (15×16). So, the hex number FF is equal to 255 (240+15).

(By the way, nearly all these attributes will also accept a lot of typical color names like "yellow" or "cyan." You might try them first.)

Changing Body Text Colors

Once you've changed the background colors in your document, you may need to change the foreground (text) colors to make them readable. The default for most graphical browsers is black text, aside from hypertext links. If you change your background color so that it's also black, your user won't be able to read the text.

TIP   **Color Help**   There are a number of pages on the Web to help you pick colors for backgrounds and links. Try **http://www.bga.com/~rlp/dwp/palette/palette.html** and **http://www.phoenix.net/~jacobson/rgb.html** to start.

To change the main text color, you use the TEXT attribute to the `<BODY>` tag, which takes the following format:

```
<BODY TEXT="#rrggbb">
...HTML document.1B
</BODY>
```

In this code, #rrggbb represents another series of three two-digit hex numbers. An example appropriate for the black background would be the following, which would turn the text white:

```
<BODY TEXT="#FFFFFF">
```

It's also possible to change the colors used to represent hypertext links in HTML, using three different attributes: LINK, VLINK, and ALINK. These represent an unvisited link, a visited link, and an active link, respectively.

To change these, you'd use the following format:

```
<BODY LINK="#rrggbb" VLINK="#rrggbb" ALINK="#rrggbb">
...HTML document...
</BODY>
```

Once again, the numbers are three two-digit hex numbers that represent the red, green, and blue values of the desired color. The default values are blue for LINK, purple for VLINK, and red for ALINK. These values may also be overridden by the user if they've set different colors in their browser's preferences settings.

TIP **Active Link** What's an "active" link? If you notice, a link turns a different color right after you've clicked it—basically, just so you know you've been successful in selecting it. The ALINK value is also the color of a hypermedia link while the file is downloaded to the user's computer.

In this lesson, you learned how to change the background color, add a background image, and change font colors. In the next chapter, you'll learn to link to multimedia files.

Linking to Multimedia Files

In this lesson, you learn how to add hyperlinks to multimedia files in your Web document.

Hypermedia Links

A hypermedia link really isn't much different from any other kind of link—instead of linking to another HTML document, you link to a multimedia file. The user's browser, then, has to recognize the kind of file you've linked to, and then load a *helper application*. The helper application takes over from the browser and displays the multimedia file (see Figure 5.1).

Helper Application A small program that works with a Web browser to handle all the multimedia files that the browser doesn't feel like showing. Because many browsers aren't equipped to display digital movies, for instance, those files are passed on to a helper movie player.

Every Web browser keeps a table of hypermedia file types and the helper applications associated with each type. Whenever the browser is told to link to a file that isn't an HTML document—and it's a file that the browser doesn't otherwise know how to display—then it will load a helper application to display the file.

There are a number of multimedia files that the typical browser can handle, including:

- Graphics like .GIF, .JPEG, and .PNG (Portable Network Graphics)
- Sound files, especially .MIDI and .WAV for background sounds
- Plain text files with a .TXT extension

Files that don't fall into these categories generally require a helper application.

Figure 5.1 Here's a helper application playing the Goodtime digital movie.

Create the Hyperlink

Hypermedia links can look like any other hyperlink—they can be text, clickable graphics, or hot zones on image maps. All you have to do different is enter an URL for a multimedia file in place of an URL to an HTML document.

TIP **How Large Is That File?** Whenever you create a hypermedia link, it's a good idea to tell your user how large the file is that they're about to load. Some users may want to skip the time it would take to download a 1.5M video clip, for instance.

If hypermedia links look like other links, they're created like other links, too. Here's an example for a Windows sound file in the WAV format:

```
<A HREF="hello.wav"> Greeting from Our Chairperson (89 KB) </A>
```

Don't Link Away Unless you have the Webmaster's explicit permission, never link to a multimedia file that's on someone else's Web site. When your users access a file on their site, it may slow down their computers significantly. Also, you have no control over that file, so it may move or change, causing errors on your page.

CAUTION

Now, when your user clicks the link, the file is downloaded to her computer. After that, it's up to the browser and whatever helper applications the user has available.

Multimedia File Types

Most multimedia files are simply documents that store information outside the capabilities of HTML. That might mean digital movies, sounds, presentations, or even 3-D worlds. Table 5.1 points out a number of the major types. This list isn't exhaustive, but it should give you an idea of the types of files that can be distributed on the Web.

Table 5.1 Multimedia File Formats

File Format	Type of File	Extension
Sun Systems sound	audio	.AU
Windows sound	audio	.WAV
Audio Interchange	audio	.AIFF, .AIFC
MPEG audio	audio	.MPG, .MPEG
SoundBlaster VOiCe	audio	.VOC
RealAudio/Video	audio/video stream	.RA, .RAM
CompuServe GIF	graphics	.GIF
JPEG (compressed)	graphics	.JPG, .JPEG
TIFF	graphics	.TIF, .TIFF
Windows Bitmap	graphics	.BMP
Apple Picture	graphics	.PICT
Fractal Animations	animation	.FLI, .FLC
VRML	3-D world animation	.WRL
MPEG video	video	.MPG, .MPEG
QuickTime	video	.MOV, .MOOV, .QT
Video For Windows	video	.AVI
Macromedia Shockwave	multimedia presentation	.DCR
ASCII text	plain text	.TXT, .TEXT
Postscript	formatted text	.PS
Adobe Acrobat	formatted text	.PDF

You may have noticed that file extensions are included in the table. The reasoning behind that is simple...most Web browsers (and many Web authors) identify multimedia files by their file name extensions. So, it's very important that you name your own multimedia files with these extensions, especially when you're going to make them available to everyone on the Web (see Figure 5.2).

 TIP   **Extensions**   Even Mac users need to get in the habit of adding file extensions. Remember, it's the browser—not your server—that needs to know the file's extension.

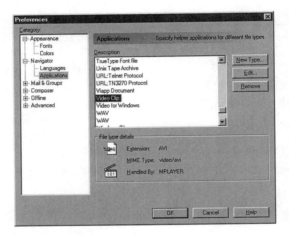

Figure 5.2   Browsers such as Netscape Navigator rely on file name extensions to decide how to deal with a particular multimedia file.

Although these are all different file types, each doesn't necessarily require a separate helper application. Many sound helpers play the majority of different sound files, for instance, and some graphics programs can handle multiple file types. For the most part, you need different helper applications for the various video, animation, and formatted text file types. But, more and more browsers are including the capability to view these files without help.

In this lesson, you learned how to add hypermedia links to your Web documents. In the next lesson, you'll learn how to add plug-in content to your Web site.

Embedding Multimedia Content

In this lesson, you learn to embed sounds and other multimedia in a Web page.

Plug-Ins

The two most popular Web browsers on the market—Netscape Navigator and Microsoft Internet Explorer—both feature support for the plug-in technology pioneered by Netscape. What's a *plug-in*? It's a small program that can do something above-and-beyond the capabilities of the browser, such as show a digital movie.

But, instead of loading a helper application, a plug-in shows the multimedia file *inside* the Web browser window, just as if it were part of the page. Basically, the plug-in programs extend the capabilities of the browser, as is shown in Figure 6.1.

Currently, the plug-in technology is a Netscape-specific standard, but other browsers, notably Internet Explorer, support Netscape plug-ins. In order to add plug-ins to your page, you need to learn a new HTML-like command. This one isn't part of the HTML 3.2 standard, so far.

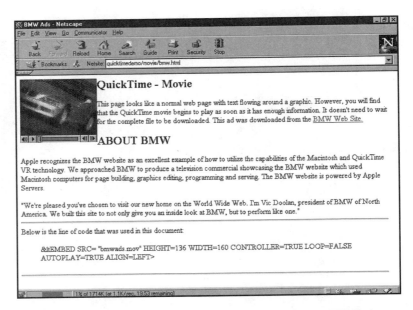

Figure 6.1 An embedded file just plays as if it were part of your HTML document. The figure shows a QuickTime video.

Embedding Multimedia Files

There's just one simple way to get a multimedia file to play in the browser window, using a plug-in: the <EMBED> tag from Netscape. It's a pretty simple tag that works much like the <IMG> tag from HTML. It does have a few extra attributes, though.

Here's how the <EMBED> container works:

```
<EMBED SRC="URL"> ... </EMBED>
```

See? It's pretty familiar looking. Even the basic attributes for <EMBED> should look pretty familiar:

- SRC="URL" tells the browser where to find the multimedia document it's going to display. Usually, the browser figures out what plug-in to use based on the file name extension—so you need to include one.
- HEIGHT="number" defines the height (in pixels) of the "window" created for the plug-in.
- WIDTH="value" defines the width (in pixels) of the "window" created for the plug-in.

- PLUGINSPAGE="URL" tells the browser where to recommend that the user look if the appropriate plug-in can't be found. For the QuickTime plug-in, you could enter the URL **http://quicktime.apple.com**, which would cause the browser to load that page if the plug-in isn't found on the user's system (and the user wants it).

Knowing this, we find that embedding a sound Macromedia Director file, for instance, could be as easy as:

```
<EMBED SRC="welcome.drc" WIDTH=144 HEIGHT=132>
```

When a Netscape-compatible browser encounters this statement, it runs the Shockwave plug-in (if the user has it installed), which is capable of playing Macromedia Director presentations in the browser window.

TIP **Plug-In Links** It's always a good idea to include a link to the company that distributes any plug-ins that you make use of on your Web page.

Each individual piece of plug-in software needs to be installed on the user's computer—most are available for download on the Web. At the same time, each Web author needs to learn, from the software company that created the plug-in, what special commands, if any, the plug-in requires in the <EMBED> tag.

The most common problem with embedded documents is saving them with the wrong file extension. It's vitally important that you make sure you use the extension that browsers expect for the various types of plug-ins. Also, remember that you need the actual plug-in software installed on your test system.

Object Tag

At the time of this writing, the <OBJECT> tag isn't part of the HTML standard, although it's proposed for the next level of HTML. The <OBJECT> tag actually replaces a number of Netscape-specific tags—<EMBED> and <APPLET>—along with some Microsoft additions such as the DYNSRC attribute to the <IMG> tag. Instead, future browsers will most likely accept the <OBJECT> tag for all of these functions.

An example of using <OBJECT> is:

```
<OBJECT DATA="cats.avi" TYPE="application/avi" WIDTH=200
➥HEIGHT=100 ALT="The Cat Movie">
<IMG SRC="cats.gif" ALT="Cats">
</OBJECT>
```

129

Here, the user's browser would display the AVI movie file if it supports that format. Otherwise, the <IMG> element will be displayed.

- The DATA attribute accepts the URL to the multimedia file.
- The TYPE attribute use MIME-type file definitions, so the user's browser can figure out whether it supports the file that's being presented. If it doesn't support that file type, it doesn't have to download the multimedia file.
- WIDTH and HEIGHT work like they do with the <IMG> tag, making loading and placement on the page work a little more quickly.
- ALT text can be added for browsers that support the <OBJECT> tag but currently have image viewing deselected in the browser's preferences settings.
- Between the opening and closing tags for <OBJECT>, nearly any HTML markup is possible. This markup is only executed by browsers that don't recognize the <OBJECT> tag.

While <OBJECT> is still gathering support, it's a useful way to incorporate a number of non-standard tags into a single HTML command.

Background Sounds

Another special case for embedding multimedia is the case of background sounds. Background sounds are simply sounds that are downloaded and played automatically when the user loads your page in his browser. The problem is, Netscape Navigator and Internet Explorer use two different standards for loading background sounds. Netscape uses embedding; Internet Explorer has its own <BGSOUND> tag.

To get them to work together, then, takes a bit of creativity. Basically, you just add both tags at the beginning of your page. Each browser will ignore the tag that isn't appropriate. Here's an example:

```
<BGSOUND SRC="Mood5.mid" VOLUME="60" LOOP=0>
<EMBED SRC="Mood5.mid" AUTOSTART=TRUE VOLUME="60" HIDDEN=TRUE>
```

This example will load and play a MIDI sound file in the background of your page. It's also possible to use a WAV format digital sounds file, but remember that MIDI files tend to be much smaller than digital sounds files. It's generally not recommended that you use a digital sounds file for your background audio, since you may be forcing your user into a very long download.

In this lesson, you learned how to embed multimedia files in your Web documents. In the next lesson, you'll learn how to find and create multimedia content.

Creating Multimedia Content

In this lesson, you learn how to create multimedia files for your Web pages.

Creating Multimedia Files

There are actually books out there that are only about augmenting your Web pages with multimedia files. Aside from obvious things—such as creating QuickTime movies or recording Windows audio sounds—you can do really amazing stuff like creating Macromedia Director projects (animation, video, sound), building presentation graphics with programs like PowerPoint, or even designing 3-D virtual reality worlds with *VRML*.

 TIP **Virtual Reality Modeling Language (VRML)** A developing standard for creating 3-D worlds for transmission over the Web. VRML is discussed in Part III, Lesson 12, "Designing for Internet Devices."

In this lesson, you'll learn how to put some of the more popular types of multimedia to use. If you develop an interest in some of the other multimedia possibilities, you'll find that most of them are rather easy to add to your Web pages.

Recording Sounds in Windows 95

A number of programs exist that enable you to create digital sounds; that is, they let you record sounds to a computer file much as you would to a cassette tape. In fact, both Windows and the Mac OS offer these capabilities as included features with the operating system.

Using Sound Recorder in Windows 95, it's simple to create WAV format sounds for transmission over the Web. Sound Recorder can be found in the Applications menu of the Start Menu, under Accessories, Multimedia, Sound Recorder. To use the program, you need a properly configured multimedia system (at least a sound card and microphone). Start up the application by selecting it in the Start menu. The application is shown in Figure 7.1.

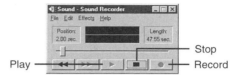

Figure 7.1 Recording sounds in WAV format with Windows 95 Sound Recorder.

Sound Recorder uses a familiar interface (with cassette recorder-style buttons) to enable you to record sounds you create through your sound card. To begin, simply click once on the **Record** button and speak into your microphone. When you're done, click the **Stop** button.

TIP **Recorder Plug-Ins** With the proper RCA-style jacks, you can plug anything into your sound card's microphone input for recording—including a cassette player, CD, or an audio feed from your VCR.

To save the new sound:

1. Choose **File**, **Save** from Sound Recorder's menu.
2. Enter an appropriate file name and choose the folder in which you'd like the sound stored (ideally, choose a folder you're using for your Web site creation).
3. Click **Save**.

From there, you can use Windows Explorer (or File Manager) to examine the file size of the save sound file…just to make sure it will be a reasonable download for your users.

TIP **Sound Quality** Sound Recorder features another command, **Edit**, **Audio Properties**, where you can adjust the quality of your recording. Generally speaking, the better the quality, the larger the file size, so try to select **Radio** or **Telephone** quality for your Web users.

Recording Mac Sounds

Mac users also have a special way to record sounds using Apple-provided tools, but it's a little more limited. Using the Sound control panel, you can create your own recordings using a microphone or any internal sound device (such as a CD-ROM drive). To do so, open the **Sound** (or **Monitors and Sound**) control panel and select **Alert Sounds** from the pop-up menu. Then, click the **Add** button. The sound controls are shown in Figure 7.2.

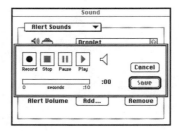

Figure 7.2   Recording sounds with the Mac OS.

After you record your sounds using the cassette-style interface, click the **Save** button to save the sounds as a Mac alert. Unfortunately, you'll notice that you haven't actually created a file (complete with its own file name) for use on your Web site.

To retrieve the sound file:

1. Go to the **System Folder** on your Mac and double-click the **System** file.
2. Scroll to the end of the folder, and you should see the various sound files available, including the one you just created.
3. While holding down the **Option** key, drag the file on the Desktop or into another folder. It's now a Mac OS sound file that you can copy or rename.

But there's one more problem—you're limiting your audience to Mac users if you post a System 7 sound file to the Web.

The answer is to convert the file with a freeware program called SoundApp.

Converting Sounds with SoundApp for Macintosh

Available as freeware for download from nearly any major Macintosh archive, SoundApp is among the most popular tools for Web authors (and users). SoundApp's own home is **http://www-cs-students.stanford.edu/ ~franke/SoundApp/index.html** on the Web.

SoundApp is basically a sound player, but it can also convert files from Mac OS sounds to more popular Web formats such as .AIFF and .WAV. Here's how to convert a sound:

1. If you've already created a Mac OS sound, use the **File**, **Convert** command in SoundApp's menu to convert the file, as shown in Figure 7.3.

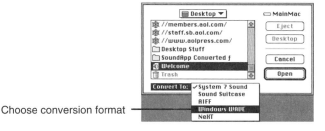

Figure 7.3 Converting files with SoundApp.

2. After you choose the file in the **Open** dialog box and select the style of conversion from the pop-up menu, click **Open**.

3. SoundApp creates a new file in the chosen file format and saves it in a new folder called SoundApp Converted. Open that folder for access to the file.

Notice that SoundApp doesn't give the new file a different name, so you need to edit the name yourself (don't forget an appropriate file extension). If you prefer, you can choose **Options**, **Preferences** from the **SoundApp** menu, and then click the **Convert** icon. In the dialog box, you can check the **DOSify Output Filenames** check box to force SoundApp to create file names with appropriate extensions.

Finding Sounds on the Web

Not all the sounds you will want to use will necessarily be those you create—you might also want to use some recognizable sounds and sound clips from movies, television, or history. Here are some great places to start in the popular Yahoo! directory:

> **http://www.yahoo.com/Entertainment/Movies_and_Films/Multimedia/Sounds/**—Yahoo!'s guide to popular archives of sounds from television and cinema.

> **http://www.yahoo.com/Computers_and_Internet/Multimedia/Sound/**—Another Yahoo! entry covers the various types of sound you can add to Web pages.

> **http://www.yahoo.com/Computers_and_Internet/Multimedia/Sound/Archives/**—Sound archives that focus on (or include) sounds other than TV and movies.

You may also find audio clips on other sites devoted to areas that interest you, such as sites from movie studios, news services, radio and TV stations, and others.

CAUTION

Copyrighted Material Always think twice about copyright issues before posting an audio file to your Web site. Many sounds that seem freely available on the Internet are actually owned by certain companies or individuals. It's up to you to secure their permission to replay the clip on your site.

Record Digital Movies

A very popular way to add multimedia pizzazz to a Web page is through the inclusion of digital movie clips. At the same time, digital movies tend to be rather large and time-consuming downloads for the average user. So, creating videos is a compromise.

It also requires a good deal of equipment. You definitely need special equipment for your Windows or Mac computer, although some models of both include video input ports. You also need special software to *digitize*, edit, and save the video as a computer file.

TIP **Digitize** As with audio, video must be *digitized*, or turned into computer recognizable ones and zeroes, before it can be saved as a computer document. The process of digitizing usually requires special computer hardware that can interpret sounds and video, and then create computer files for playback in special programs.

Digital video movies are generally in one of three different formats common to the Web: QuickTime, MPEG, or Video for Windows. Any of these is acceptable, although QuickTime and MPEG are both more easily played on computers other than Windows PCs.

Beyond creating your own movies, there are a number of areas on the Web where you can download digital clips. I recommend you start at the Yahoo! directory with **http://www.yahoo.com/Computers_and_Internet/Multimedia/ Archives/** where you'll find archived movies and other multimedia files.

In this lesson, you learned how to create some common multimedia files. In the next lesson, you'll learn specifically about QuickTime videos and special controls.

QuickTime Videos

In this lesson, you learn how to create, edit, and add QuickTime movies to your Web pages.

QuickTime Movies

QuickTime is arguably the most cross-platform of multimedia video standards, allowing you to display QuickTime movies in browsers for Macintosh, Windows 3.1, and Windows 95/NT platforms. Although QuickTime's format can support many different types of multimedia, its most popular use is digital video—most video-capture programs, for instance, can save to QuickTime formats. Also, a QuickTime plug-in program for Netscape and Internet Explorer is available for both Windows and Macintosh operating systems.

 TIP **Downloading QuickTime** You can get the QuickTime for Windows software from **http://www.quicktime.apple.com/** on the Web. QuickTime is usually included with the Mac OS, but newer versions can be downloaded from this site. The QuickTime plug-in is included with most Web browsers, but you can download upgrades from this same Web location.

Creating a digital video generally requires the use of a video camera, video-capture expansion card for your computer, and special software. It is possible, however, to piece together a slideshow-style QuickTime movie without any additional programs. All you need is the MoviePlayer application (for Macintosh) that comes with QuickTime.

Editing QuickTime Movies (Mac)

Basic editing with the MoviePlayer application for Macintosh is as easy as cut and paste. Within the same movie, for instance, it's possible to move a series of frames around within the movie file by using Copy and Paste commands.

To move frames within a QuickTime movie, complete the following steps:

1. Load the movie in MoviePlayer by choosing **File**, **Open**.
2. Hold down the **Shift** key while dragging the mouse over the section of the movie player control bar that represents the frames you want to move.
3. Choose **Edit**, **Cut**.
4. Place the movie slider at the point in the movie where you'd like the cut frames to reappear.
5. Choose **Edit**, **Paste**, as shown in Figure 8.1.

 TIP **Clear Frames** The Mac MoviePlayer application will also allow you to delete the selected frame(s) from the QuickTime movie by choosing **Edit**, **Clear**.

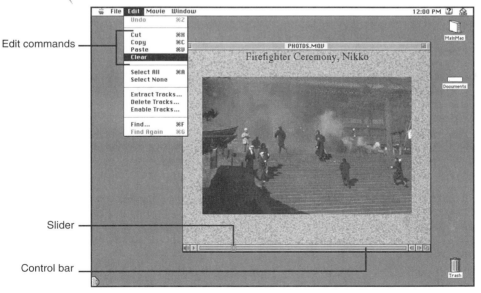

Edit commands

Slider

Control bar

Figure 8.1 The MoviePlayer application makes it possible to edit QuickTime videos.

It's also easy to merge two videos into one (assuming they are the same size) or to add a series of images to a single QuickTime video, allowing you to create a self-revolving banner or slideshow. On a Macintosh, simply copy images from an image-editing or similar program (such as Adobe PhotoShop or Graphic Converter, discussed in Part VI, Lesson 8), and then paste them into MoviePlayer.

QuickTime Plug-In Commands

If your users are going to take advantage of an embedded QuickTime movie, they're going to need some typical movie-watching controls. In MoviePlayer, Windows' Media Player, and similar applications, users are shown VCR-style controls for play, fast forward, and volume control.

When you embed a QuickTime video, you gain access to a number of optional controls that give you more say in how the video is played on the browser's page. Aside from the typical <EMBED> controls, you have access to a number of others that are specifically designed to work with the QuickTime plug-in program. Table 8.1 shows some of the possible commands for embedding a QuickTime movie as a plug-in document.

Table 8.1 Commands for a QuickTime Movie <EMBED> Command

Command	Useful Value	What It Does...
AUTOPLAY	TRUE	Causes movie to begin automatically
CONTROLLER	FALSE	Hides movie controls
LOOP	TRUE	Loops movie over and over
PLAYEVERYFRAME	TRUE	Plays every frame, even if movie is too slow
VOLUME	0 through 256	Chooses the volume level; 256 is highest
HIDDEN		If you include the HIDDEN attribute, the movie will be hidden from the user (useful for playing sounds without pictures)
HREF	URL	Allows user to click movie to move to another URL; works only if CONTROLLER=FALSE

These special attributes are added to the <EMBED> tag for QuickTime movies. An example might be:

```
<EMBED SRC="movie.mov" AUTOPLAY=TRUE CONTROLLER=FALSE HREF="http://
➥mynet.com/page2.html">
```

This command would allow the user to click the movie to move to the new Web page, but not to control the playback of the movie. Once downloaded, the QuickTime movie would begin playing all the way through without requiring any input from the users.

Digital Movie Considerations

Before adding tons of digital movies to your site, there are a couple of things you should keep in mind:

- **Digital movies are large files.** Even 30 seconds of QuickTime movie can take up hundreds of kilobytes of space, meaning your modem users will wait many minutes to download the movie. To avoid this, use only short clips and make them as small as possible when you first create them. Also, warn users ahead of time.

- **QuickTime can include other types of multimedia.** One way to make a movie smaller is to use MIDI sounds instead of digital audio in the background of your movies.

- **Try QuickTime VR.** The 3-D virtual reality type movies can be added using the same QuickTime plug-in command, and they're more suited to Web use, because they allow the user to move about and explore the virtual reality scene instead of passively watching.

In this lesson, you learned how to edit and add QuickTime movies to your Web pages. In the next lesson, you'll learn how to create and add animated GIFs.

Adding
Animated GIFs

*In this lesson, you learn how to create and add animated GIFs
to your Web documents.*

Animated GIFs

In Part II, Lesson 1, you learned that the GIF89a specification has the capability
to display gradually (*interlacing*) and offers transparent backgrounds. But that
specification also has another special capability that has become very popular on
the Web. With GIF89a, it's possible to store a number of images in a single GIF
file, and then scroll through those images automatically. That capability, along
with the right graphics program, enables you to create animated and slideshow
GIFs.

GIF animation works almost exactly like the flip-card animation that many
people learn in grade school (or create for themselves in spiral-bound note-
books). By moving quickly through similar, but slightly different, images, it's
possible to create a GIF that gives the appearance of motion. Or, you can also
create a GIF that simply has revolving graphics, like a slideshow presentation—
perhaps for an advertising billboard or something similar.

Animated GIFs are only fully displayed in Netscape 2.0 (or later) and Internet
Explorer 3.0 or later. Other browsers that don't support animated GIFs either
show the animation once, or just show the first or last image in the animation.
The latest version of Netscape Navigator also allows users to selectively turn off
animated GIFs. (Before, only the display of all images could be turned on and
off in Web browsers such as Navigator.)

To create an animated GIF, you need a program designed to handle the multiple-graphic feature of GIF89a. The shareware GIF Construction Set for Windows (Alchemy Software, **http://www.mindworkshop.com/alchemy/ gifcon.html**) is a great example of a program that walks you through the creation of animated GIFs.

 TIP **Mac Software** Mac users should check out the shareware GifBuilder (written by Yves Piquet, the program is available in most Mac archives, like MacWorld Software **http://www.macworld.com/software/**), which offers the ability to easily create animated GIFs. This program is discussed in Part VI, Lesson 9.

Creating the Animation

Creating an animated GIF with the GIF Construction Set is simple—the hard part is creating the frames or "cells" for the animation in another program. Just as in professional animation, GIF animations require a number of cells, or individual images, that, when viewed quickly one after the other, produce the illusion of movement. Generally, this means that a good animation will require quite some time spent with a graphics editing program, so that you can create all those individual images.

 TIP **Slideshows** As mentioned before, the GIF89a standard can also be used to create a slideshow of different images. In this case, you can create images that don't give the impression of movement. Instead, you'll switch abruptly between images, just as in a real-world slideshow. You'll still want to use an image editing program to make all the images the same size and give them the same number of colors, as described in Part II, Lesson 1.

If you're working in Paint Shop Pro, for instance, you create a number of different images to represent the movement for your animation, as shown in Figure 9.1.

 CAUTION **Same Size, Same Background** Unless you want a strobing effect on your animation, you should keep every frame you create the same size, with the same solid-colored background.

With the frames of your animation created, the GIF Construction Set (GCS) makes things simple with the Animation Wizard:

1. Start GCS and choose **File, Animation Wizard**. After the Wizard starts up, click **Next**.

2. Choose the **Yes, for Use with a Web Page** option button, and then click **Next**.

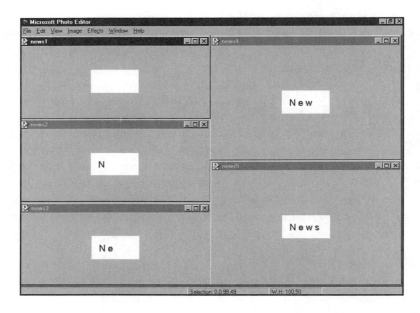

Figure 9.1   Each cell of the animation needs to be created individually to create the illusion of movement.

3. Choose the option you'd prefer for your animation's looping. Many GIF animations loop indefinitely. Click **Next**.

4. Tell the wizard what sort of images you'll be using. Note that text-oriented images you create in an image editing or drawing program are considered Drawn. Click **Next** after making your choice.

5. Choose the length of delay you'd like between each animation frame. This delay will be applied universally to each frame (you can change individual delays from within the program, discussed in the next section). Click **Next**.

6. Select the source files for each cell of your animation. Click the **Select** button, then find the first image in the Open dialog box. Once you've found it, click the **Open** button in the Open dialog box to add that image

to your list of selected images, as shown in Figure 9.2. The Open dialog box reappears automatically so you can continue selecting source images. When you're finished selecting images, click **Cancel** in the Open dialog box, and then click **Next**.

7. The final wizard screen tells you that the GIF animation is complete. You can now click **Done** to move on to the main GCS interface.

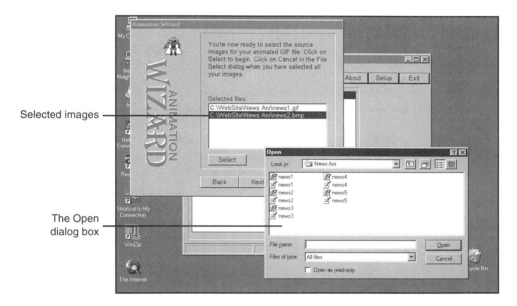

Selected images ——

The Open dialog box ——

Figure 9.2 You select each frame for your GIF animation from the Open dialog box.

Altering Your Animation

The GIF89a format stores information such as how many times to loop the animation, how long to wait between frames, and what frames occur in what order. All it takes, then, is a program capable of getting that information from you, and saving it in the correct format.

The GCS window shows you the order in which images appear in the animation, and it allows you to change certain variables (such as LOOP and CONTROL) by double-clicking the variable name in the listing:

- In GCS, LOOP allows you to determine how many times the GIF animation will repeat itself before stopping. Double-click the word **LOOP** in the GCS window to open the Edit Loop Block dialog box that will allow you to alter this behavior.

- You can also change a number of other settings that relate to each individual frame of your animation. To alter the settings, like the transparent color for a frame or the amount of delay for a particular frame, double-click **CONTROL** in the GCS window. This loads the Edit Control Block dialog box that allows you to change the transparency color, delay, and method used to remove each frame after it's been displayed.

 Removal In this context, removal (sometimes referred to as *disposal*) is a setting that determines how each cell is removed from view after it is displayed. Sometimes the image isn't removed at all; sometimes it's replaced by the subsequent image; sometimes the animation reverts to the background color before displaying the next image. Experiment with these settings to see which works best for your animation.

When you're ready to see the masterpiece you've created, click the **View** button. If your animation progresses the way that you'd hoped, you're done. Choose **File, Save** to save your new animated GIF.

 TIP **Slideshow** If you're creating a slideshow instead of an animation, use a **CONTROL** delay between each image to control how long each "slide" appears on-screen before it is replaced by the next one.

Adding the Animation

An animated GIF doesn't require any special HTML (or extended HTML) commands; instead, only the regular <IMG> tag is necessary for placing the animated GIF on your Web document. Once the file is saved (in GIF format), add it as such:

```
<IMG SRC="animated.gif" HEIGHT=50 WIDTH=50 ALT="Spinning Ball">
```

In this lesson, you learned how to create an animated GIF. In the next lesson, you'll learn how to place portable documents online.

Microsoft Office Online

In this lesson, you learn how to add portable documents and Microsoft Office documents to your Web pages.

What Are Portable Documents?

Portable Document Format is actually a file format (like GIF or MPEG) created and used by the Adobe Acrobat system. The Acrobat system is probably the most widely known (and Internet-pervasive) method for distributing portable documents. Based on Adobe's PostScript technology, certain Adobe products (such as Acrobat Distiller, Adobe PageMaker, and others) are capable of generating PDF files, which can then be viewed by Web helper applications and plug-ins. Figure 10.1 is an example of a PDF document.

Portable documents also refer to any sort of format that allows you to distribute documents intact to users, without relying on the "*machine-dependent*" nature of HTML. In other words, these are documents that can be viewed by the user, but only in one way—they generally keep the same font, layout, and display characteristics, regardless of the type of computer on which they're viewed.

Machine Dependent   Most formatted and font-filled documents can only be accurately displayed on the same type of computer. For instance, you could create (in Windows) a Microsoft Word document that included the fonts Arial and Courier New, and feel fairly sure that other Microsoft Windows users could see the file the same way you created it, since those fonts come with Windows. They don't, however, come with all Macs. When a Mac user views your document, they see a slightly different version because of the Word document's dependence on Windows standards.

continues

continued

A portable document, then, is one that's designed to include font and formatting information with the file so that users on Windows, Mac, and other computers would see very similar pages.

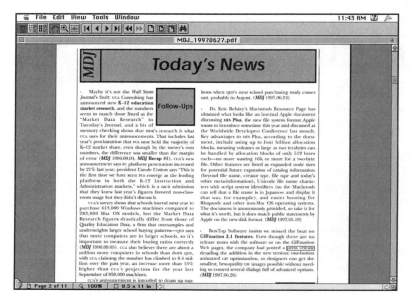

Figure 10.1   Viewing an Abobe PDF file.

You can almost think of portable documents as big graphics files. Most of these documents don't allow the user to alter them in any way, although some allow you to annotate these documents with little electronic "sticky notes." You can't change the original documents, but you can add comments that appear on top of the document.

So what qualifies as a portable document? Well, among others, Adobe Acrobat, Envoy, Common Ground, RTF files, Microsoft Word DOC files, and even ASCII text files. Each offers various advantages and tradeoffs, but all (with the exception of ASCII) also offer the ability to control the display of your text to a greater degree than you can with HTML.

Adding PDFs to Your Web Site

While Adobe distributes Acrobat Reader for free, you have to pay a decent amount of money for the products that create Acrobat files, like Adobe

Exchange. These products help you create, lay out, and save your files as .PDF format files. They can then be added to your Web site for downloading by interested users.

TIP   **Acrobat**   To find out more about Acrobat products, visit **http://www.adobe.com/**.

Adding an Acrobat file to your Web page takes nothing more than a hypermedia link with the appropriate extension. For instance:

```
Here are Abobe's <A HREF="online.pdf"> Tips for Adding Acrobat
➥Files to Web Sites</A> in Acrobat format.
```

When clicked, this link will cause the browser to download the PDF document to the user's hard drive. If the user's browser is properly configured, the document will be loaded into Adobe's Acrobat reader.

Creating Your Own PDFs

If you don't want to spend money on a program like Acrobat, you can still use other programs you have hanging around as substitute PDF files. Most of these file formats don't allow for the inclusion of graphics and don't give you much control over fonts, while the more sophisticated PDF formats do. At the same time, however, they do give you control over things like centering, text size, hard returns, font appearance (bold, italic, underlined), and similar attributes.

TIP   **Less than Perfect**   PDF formats are designed to appear *exactly* the same on different computer platforms. These makeshift PDFs (like MS Word documents) will generally have slight differences from platform to platform and version to version.

For instance, Microsoft Word documents are an easy way to distribute documents on the Web, as Word tends to be one of the most popular word processors, and most other word processors can read Word's .DOC files.

But even if a user's word processor can't read .DOC files, Microsoft offers a free Word document viewer for Windows users. The Word Viewer is designed to do just that—allow your users to view and print Word documents. Without Word or another word processor, they can't do any editing. But they can view and print your preformatted form.

TIP   **Get the Viewer**   The Word viewer can be downloaded from **http://microsoft.com/word/**. You might want to let your users know this if you offer Word documents for downloading.

Creating the Word Document

Fortunately, there's nothing special you need to do to create a Word document for viewing on the Internet. The only requirement is that you use Microsoft Word to create the documents (or a word processor that can save in Microsoft Word for Windows 2.0 and later or Word for Mac 4.0 and later formats). Save the file with a **.DOC** extension just as Windows and DOS users normally would. (Windows 95 users can use WordPad to create, view, and edit Word documents.)

Then, you can make it available as a hyperlink on your Web site, just as with any other multimedia file, as in the following example:

```
Download the file in <A HREF="file.doc> MS Word format </A>.
```

Using Rich Text Format

Another interesting way to distribute formatted documents on the Web is by using the Rich Text Format (RTF). RTF is a Microsoft file format that's designed to be more sophisticated than plain ASCII text, but less proprietary and complicated than word processing document types. Most word processors can create, view, print, and save documents in this format.

To make RTF format files available on your Web site, first save your document in your word processor as an RTF file with the .RTF extension . From there, all you have to do is include it in a hypertext link, like in the following example:

```
<A HREF="myfile.rtf">Here's a copy of my special RTF file.</A>
```

Other Microsoft Formats

Other Microsoft documents are just as easy to deliver as portable documents over the Web. Your users will need to have the appropriate application or viewer to see these, but the HTML codes aren't any different.

TIP **Helper Applications** You may want to add hyperlinks on your page that point users toward these Microsoft helper applications. They're available from **http://microsoft.com/office/** on the Web. (Click the links on this page to PowerPoint and Excel to find the viewers.)

For Excel documents, create your hyperlinks so that they include the file with an **.XLS** extension:

```
<A HREF="mysheet.xls">Here's the chart (in Microsoft Excel format)</
➡A>
```

PowerPoint presentations can be similarly disseminated. To place a PowerPoint presentation on the Web, simply include the file name with a .PPZ extension:

```
<A HREF="present.ppz">Click here to view the presentation (in
➡Microsoft PowerPoint format)</A>
```

Figure 10.2 shows a PowerPoint presentation being viewed in the PowerPoint Viewer.

Figure 10.2 Even if your users don't have PowerPoint, they can still view presentations you create with the special viewer application.

In this lesson, you learned about portable document formats and how to add them to your Web page. In the next lesson, you'll learn how to add Shockwave animations to your pages.

151

Shockwave for Macromedia Director

In this lesson, you learn how to create, save, and embed Macromedia Shockwave documents in your Web pages.

What Is Shockwave?

HTML is a very static way to present information, with graphics that don't react to the user, image maps that don't make it clear where to click, and almost no animation capabilities. To remedy that situation, you have access to technologies like animated GIFs, Dynamic HTML, and JavaScripting.

Or, you can use Shockwave. Macromedia's presentation technology, called Shockwave, is pretty much the de facto standard on the Web, even though it's not technically a standard at all. Shockwave presentations can only be created with Macromedia tools (like Director or Flash) and can only be viewed with the Macromedia Shockwave plug-in programs. But that hasn't kept Shockwave from becoming very popular.

If you've ever experienced a multimedia presentation (or played some popular adventure games like Myst), then you've probably experienced what it is that Shockwave allows you to view over the Web. Shockwave documents are animated, they're colorful, and they're interactive. Shockwave presentations even have special features that make them capable of controlling a Web page by loading new URLs in a Web browser or a frameset, as shown in Figure 11.1.

Figure 11.1 Here's an example of a Shockwave presentation being used to control a frameset.

Creating Shockwave Animations

Shockwave presentations for the Web are generally created in either Macromedia Director or Macromedia Flash. Director is the full-featured multi-media authoring application designed for all types of professional authoring such as CD-ROM interfaces, games, and kiosks. Flash, on the other hand, is a smaller, less-expensive tool designed for creating basic animations and presentations for your Web pages. If you don't already have Director, you might look into Flash.

TIP **Free Trial** A Macromedia Flash free trial version is available for download from the Shockwave site: **http://www.shockwave.com/** on the Web.

Creating Frames

With Flash, creating a quick animated presentation screen is simple. In this example, you'll create an animation suitable for the top frame of a Web interface.

153

To begin, you need to create some frames—each frame will represent a single animated movement in your presentation. Here's how you create frames for your animation:

1. Start **Flash** and choose **File, New** from the menu.

2. Now you're viewing the main interface, including the Timeline at the top of the window. Make sure you have **View, Work Area** selected so that you're seeing a blank canvas.

3. Choose **Modify, Movie** from the menu to change the size on the movie work area. In the resulting dialog box, edit the Dimensions for the movie. Click **OK** when you're done.

4. The next step is to create a series of frames within the current layer. Notice that the Timeline at the top is counting off scenes. To create new frames for the animation, drag the mouse pointer along the Timeline (within the current layer) to select the number of frames you'd like to create, as shown in Figure 11.2.

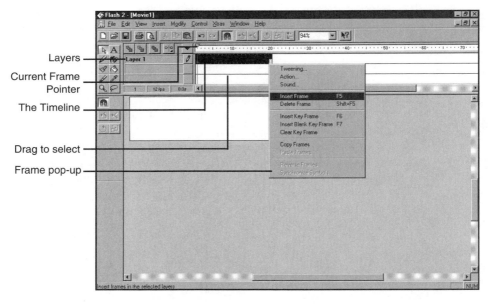

Figure 11.2   The Timeline is used to create new frames.

5. Select the **Frame Pop-Up**. In the menu, choose **Insert Frame**. This creates as many frames as you had highlighted.

Animating Objects

The next step in a simple animation involves creating the key frames. *Key frames* are those that include new images or a change in the previous images. If you're drawing every frame of your animation, then every frame needs to be a key frame. In this example, however, you can use a faster process to create a quick text movement.

 TIP **Import Also** You can just as easily use the **File**, **Import** command to add a simple image to your movie, then animate that image with the following instructions.

Here's how to animate a block of text:

1. Use the Current Frame Pointer to select the first frame.

2. In the Work Area, create some text for your animation (see Figure 11.3). Notice that the text (in this example) is placed outside of the movie area so that it doesn't appear in the movie in the first frame.

Use text tool to create text

Place text outside of movie area

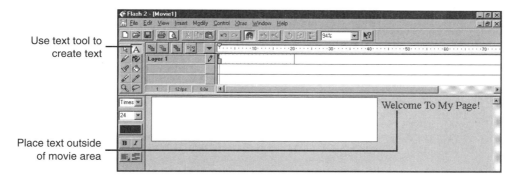

Figure 11.3 Placing text that will be animated.

3. Using the Current Frame Pointer, move to the frame that will be the end of the animation. Again select the **Frame Pop-Up** and make this frame a key frame with the **Insert Key Frame** command.

4. Select the text and drag it to its final destination in the movie area. This is the spot where you want your animated text to come to a rest.

5. In the Timeline, return the Current Frame Pointer to the first frame on your animation.

6. Now, click in the first frame. From the Frame Pop-Up menu, choose **Tweening**. The Tweening dialog box appears, as shown in Figure 11.4.

Tweening Menu ——
Options ——

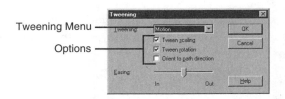

Figure 11.4 Tweening is Macromedia Flash's simple way to animate images and text.

7. Choose **Motion** from the **Tweening** menu. (The default settings for motion are fine.) Choose **OK**.

8. If all goes well, you have animated text. Use the Current Frame Pointer to place the Timeline back at Frame 1, then choose **Control**, **Play** from the menu. You should see your animation in action.

Finish and Save

This process can be used over and over to create more animated elements in your movie. Once you have an entire movie ready for the Web, you can save it as a Shockwave Flash document for placement on the Web.

To create a Shockwave file:

1. Choose **File**, **Export Movie** from the menu.
2. In the Export Movie dialog box, make sure **Shockwave Flash** is selected in the **File Type** menu.
3. Enter a name in the Export Movie text box.
4. Click the **Save** button in the dialog box.

Adding Shockwave to Web Pages

Like many other multimedia file formats, Shockwave presentations are best added to your pages as embedded multimedia by using the <EMBED> tag, discussed in Part II, Lesson 6. Here's an example of the HTML code for embedding a Shockwave Flash document for browsers that recognize the Netscape <EMBED> command:

```
<EMBED src="mymovie.swf" width=400 height=50
➡pluginspage="http://www.macromedia.com/shockwave/
➡download/index.cgi?P1_Prod_Version=ShockwaveFlash">
</EMBED>
```

Shockwave Flash also supports its own ActiveX control (discussed in Part 3, Lesson 15). To embed the document for use in an ActiveX control, use:

```
<OBJECT classid="clsid:D27CDB6E-AE6D-11cf-96B8-444553540000"
➡codebase="http://active.macromedia.com/flash2/cabs/
➡swflash.cab#version=2,0,0,0" width=400 height=50>
  <PARAM name="Movie" value="mymovie.swf">
```

The classid value should be entered exactly as pictured, as should the codebase value, which tells the browser where to automatically download the Flash ActiveX control if necessary.

In this lesson, you learned how to create a Shockwave document and add it to your Web page. In the next lesson, you'll learn the basics of Virtual Reality Modeling Language, or VRML.

Beginning VRML Worlds

In this lesson, you learn the concepts behind the Virtual Reality Modeling Language and how to add 3-D worlds to your Web site.

Understanding VRML

Virtual Reality Modeling Language, or VRML, isn't HTML at all, but the two are close cousins. Born out of a desire for a more "human" interface to the Web, VRML is a text-based description language for creating 3-D interfaces to the World Wide Web. Like HTML, VRML allows you to use just a text editor to create *worlds* that the special VRML browsers can navigate.

 TERM   **Worlds**   VRML documents are generally called "worlds," perhaps because the word "document" seems rather two-dimensional. A single ASCII listing can be used to create a world, however.

Generally, VRML worlds are simply another hypermedia link used to call a file with the file extension `.wrl` for "world." The following hypermedia link is an example of a link to a VRML world:

```
<A HREF="http://www.mynet.com/worlds/living.wrl">Enter My living
➥room.</A>
```

The VRML world would then be loaded into a helper application designed to give the user access to the VRML world, including controls for manipulating the VRML graphics in 3-D, as shown in Figure 12.1. Double-clicking different objects will generally send a command back to the browser, which can then move on to another URL.

TIP **Cosmo** Silicon Graphics, one of the founding companies in the VRML standard, offers VRML browsers and plug-ins for many different computing platforms. You can download them at **http://cosmo.sgi.com/** on the Web.

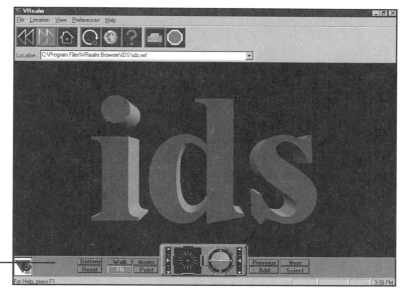

Controls to move around in the VRML world

Figure 12.1 A VRML world gives you some of the sensations of moving around in a video game.

In general, VRML browsers are configured as helper applications that recognize the model/vrml (for VRML 2.0) MIME-type and are loaded whenever a link to a .wrl file is clicked. The VRML browser can then pass links back to the Web browser, so that new worlds (or Web pages) can be loaded when items in the VRML world are selected.

Plug-ins are also available for browsers that allow the user to view VRML worlds as inline images, but this, too, is a young industry. Currently, the only standard way to include an embedded VRML world is with the <EMBED> tag, like:

```
<EMBED SRC="myworld.wrl">
```

TIP **URL Activation** Some VRML plug-ins can be activated simply by loading the **.wrl** file in versions of Netscape 3.0 and later, just as you would an HTML document.

The VRML Document

In your text editor, you'll need to start out with a new text file. Type the following as the first line of your document:

```
#VRML V2.0 utf8
```

This tells VRML browsers what format you're using. The utf8 signifies that international characters can be displayed in VRML using a special encoding standard.

CAUTION

Case-Sensitive   Most of the VRML browsers I've encountered are case-sensitive about this first line. Enter it exactly as shown.

You can also use the # sign to begin comments in your VRML document. For instance, the following is a comment that will be ignored by the VRML browser, but useful to you and others as documentation of your VRML commands:

```
# This is the left front leg of the chair
```

Coordinates and Distances

The other thing you need to do with VRML is switch over to a 3-D way of thinking. Many VRML objects and commands have coordinates, which include X, Y, and Z components, usually in that order. On your screen, X is left and right, Y is up and down, and Z is from the back of your head to the back of the monitor.

These directions are also in positive and negative numbers from a point directly in the middle of the screen or, at least, from the active part of the VRML's display (see Figure 12.2). Left is negative from center, down is negative, and into the monitor is negative.

Distances in VRML are measured in meters, while angles are given in radians. While VRML objects aren't actually rendered in meters (you'd have trouble fitting them on a computer monitor), this is a relative measurement. It allows something the size of .01 meters, for instance, to be a pencil, while something the size of 1 meter might be a table top.

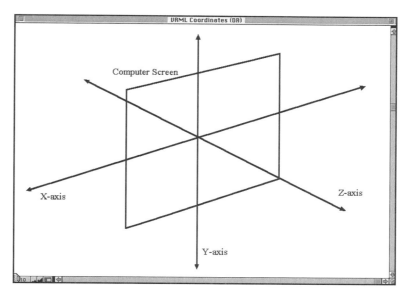

Figure 12.2 How coordinates work in VRML.

Radians are the angle (such as 45 degrees) divided by 180, times π (approx. 3.14). Most browsers will accept best-guess radians, so multiplying by 3.14 for π is acceptable.

 TIP **Radians** To get the radians of an angle in degrees, divide the degrees by 180, and then multiply by π. For instance, a 360-degree angle divided by 180 is 2; 2 times π gives you the answer—about 6.28 radians.

A VRML Template

You might start out by creating a very simple template for your VRML worlds. Starting with a new text document, enter Listing 12.1.

Listing 12.1 Creating Your VRML Template—*template.wrl*

```
#VRML V2.0 utf8
#
#Comments about this
#world go here.
#
```

Don't forget to save it as your template, perhaps calling it **template.wrl**. Now, when you go to create a new VRML world, you can use the **Save As** command in your text editor to create a new VRML document.

Nodes

The basic building block of a VRML world is called a *node*. Nodes can do a number of different things, including creating shapes, moving shapes, describing colors and textures, and creating hyperlinks. Nodes are commonly used together to achieve different effects.

Curly brackets are used (as in JavaScript and many programming languages) to represent the beginning and end of a node. An example of a shape node, for instance, would be:

```
Shape {
    appearance Appearance {
        material Material { }
    }
    geometry Cylinder {
        height 2.0
        radius 1.5
    }
}
```

A node like this might create a sphere, cone, cylinder, or other shape. The shape will be white (without color description) and centered on the screen. To change that, you'd start by changing the nodes within the Shape node, such as appearance and geometry. Within these sub-nodes, you change characteristics of the shape using the following:

- **Fields** such as height and radius are the sublevel of nodes actually responsible for defining certain behaviors.
- **Values** such as 2.0 for the height (in the example) define each distinct characteristic of a node.

Added to the information you've entered previously to create a VRML template, the preceding Shape node is actually a complete VRML world. Viewed in a browser, that world looks like Figure 12.3.

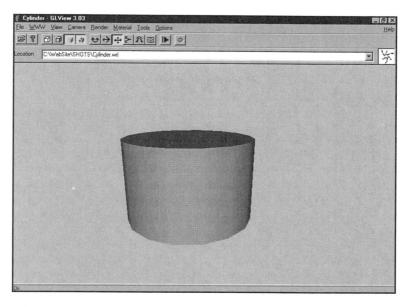

Figure 12.3   Here's the cylinder in a VRML browser. By default, it's drawn in the center of the VRML world.

In this lesson, you learned the basics of creating a VRML document. In the next lesson, you'll learn how to add shapes and text to your VRML world.

Adding VRML Objects

13

In this lesson, you learn how to add shapes and text to your VRML world.

VRML Geometry

The most basic of VRML nodes are the geometry primitives, which are simply the basic geometric shapes you can use to create 3-D worlds. These include spheres, cylinders, cones, and boxes. You'll quickly look at how to create each of these, then learn how to move them around in your virtual world.

Geometry primitives appear within the Shape node and follow this basic format:

```
geometry primitive_name {
    properties
    }
```

Spacing is unimportant, but curly brackets are required around the shape's properties.

The Sphere

Probably the easiest shape to create in VRML is a sphere. All you really need to know is what you want the radius to be in meters (that is, *virtual* meters). This is done with curly brackets. The primitive name is Sphere and the property name is radius, so an example would be:

```
geometry Sphere {radius 3}
```

Cylinders and Cones

Some other one-line primitives are cylinders and cones. Both take the property `height`, but a cylinder and a cone handle their radii differently. These shapes can also take the property `parts`, which is used to determine which parts of the shape will be rendered. The general format for `Cylinder` is the following:

```
geometry Cylinder {
   height size
   radius size
   }
```

An example for a cylinder could be the following:

```
geometry Cylinder { height 4 radius .5 }
```

This example creates a cylinder about four meters high and one meter in diameter; perfect for the columns outside of a virtual house. At the same time, a cylinder like the following might be correctly sized and rendered for an eight-ounce drinking glass:

```
geometry Cylinder {
   height .15
   radius .04
   }
```

Notice that spacing in these examples isn't important to the VRML browser, but when you have more than one or two properties, it's probably best to space them out for the sake of clarity.

The cone primitive requires a radius for its base, and a height. Since the radius of a cone changes consistently from bottom to top, you use the property `bottomRadius`:

```
geometry Cone { height 15 bottomRadius 10 }
```

This one might make a good approximation of a pine tree outside a virtual mountain cabin.

On the other hand, you might use the following:

```
geometry Cone {
   height .10
   bottomRadius .02
   }
```

This could easily represent an ice cream cone (albeit upside down for now).

The Box

The box primitive can have unequal sides, making it more or less a 3-D rectangular shape. It's also probably the most useful shape, if for no other reason than the fact that you'll generally want to use it as the floor in your virtual world.

Actually, a box is useful for representing many different things, from appliances and furniture to buildings and ceilings. Because you can stretch the box in 3-D, you have limitless possibilities.

The basic format for a box is the following:

```
geometry Box {
    size x y z
}
```

When initially rendered, x is the x-axis, y is the y-axis, and z is the z-axis.

```
geometry Box {
    size 1 1 1
    }
```

This one actually is a cube, one meter on each side. It might be good to represent a nice-sized shipping box.

An example that meets the challenge of being a virtual room's "floor" would be the following:

```
geometry Box {
    size 20 .01 25
      }
```

This is just about the right size for a reasonably dimensioned den or family room—maybe even a master suite. You can see it extending out into the distance in Figure 13.1.

Text

The final primitive, Text, accepts a string value of ASCII text and writes it to the screen. You can choose values for the spacing, justification (alignment), and width of the string, if you want to confine it to a particular size. The basic format is like the following example:

```
geometry Text {
    string ["Welcome to My World"]
    FontStyle {
      family  "SERIF"
```

```
    style   "BOLD"
    size    1.0
    spacing 1.0
  }
}
```

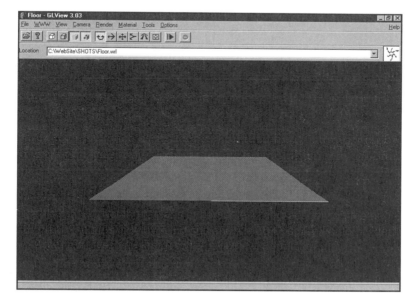

Figure 13.1 A virtual floor.

Here's a quick breakdown of the Text node:

- You enter the text you want to use after the string field, between the quotation marks. You can also close quotation marks, add a comma and re-open quotation marks to create two lines of text.
- The FontStyle node is used to enclose optional fields for controlling the appearance of the text.
- The family field accepts values SERIF, SANSSERIF, or TYPEWRITER as the font family name.
- The style field accepts values BOLD, ITALIC, or BOTH.
- The size field takes a number to indicate the font size (in virtual meters).
- The spacing field accepts a numeric value representing the character spacing.

The following is an example of Text, within a Shape node:

```
Shape {
    geometry Text {
    string ["A long,",
            "long time ago,"]
    fontStyle {
        style "BOLD"
    }
    }
}
```

Figure 13.2 shows how this text looks from within a VRML browser.

Figure 13.2   Text in your virtual world.

Moving Your Shapes Around

Here, you'll move on to using nodes that move your shapes around in the VRML world. You're using a node called Transform, which is designed to affect the location, rotation, and scale of the objects that come after it.

Here's an example:

```
Transform {
      translation -2.0 3.0 0.0
      children [
      Shape {
        geometry Cylinder {
              radius 0.3
            height 6.0
            }
        }
      ]
}
```

By default, all shapes in your VRML world are rendered at the center of the world (0 0 0), unless you transform the coordinate system for a particular shape. That's what the transform node is for. Actually, it can accept some other properties, too:

```
Transform {
      translation 2 2 0
      rotation 0 0 0
      scale 0 0 0
      children [
      ]
}
```

Translation

The `translation` field is responsible for actually moving the object in VRML space, and it uses a basic 3-D vector to do that. This vector can be seen as a 3-D description of how the object should be moved from the point of origin. Consider this part of the last example:

```
translation 2 2 0
```

Whatever shape(s) come in the *children* field of this `Transform` node will be moved two meters to the right (+2 in the x-axis), two meters up (+2 in the y-axis), and will stay at the same distance near/far (0 in the z-axis).

Children The translation field in VRML has a subfield labeled `children` that contains all of the shape nodes that are to be translated in some way.

Rotation

The rotation field allows you to choose which axis you would like to rotate the shape around, and then lets you enter an angle (in radians) for that rotation. Look at the following example:

```
rotation 0 1 0 1.57
```

The shape will rotate 90 degrees around its y-axis. This would be akin to "spinning" the shape, since the y-axis can be seen as a line from the top of the screen to the bottom of it. Here's another example:

```
Transform {rotation 1 0 0 3.14}
```

This rotates any associated shapes 180 degrees around the x-axis. This would be "flipping" the shape. The x-axis runs from left to right across the screen, so rotating a shape around the x-axis 180 degrees would turn the shape upside down.

Knowing this would allow you to flip the "ice cream cone" created earlier in the chapter, like this:

```
Transform {
        rotation 1 0 0 3.14
        children [
        Shape {
          geometry Cone {
                        height .10
            bottomRadius .02
            }
        }
      ]
}
```

Scale

The scale field allows you to choose a factor by which a shape can be sized in each access, as in the following example:

```
Transform {scaleFactor 1 4 -2}
```

This would keep any subsequent shapes the same size in the x-axis, make the shape larger by a factor of four in the y-axis, and make it smaller by a factor of two in the z-axis.

Children

The children field is used to contain any other nodes on which this transform node should act. Note the following transform example:

```
Transform {
     translation -2.0 3.0 0.0
     rotation 1 0 0 3.14
     children [
     Shape {
       geometry Cone {
                  BottomRadius 0.3
          height 2.0
          }
       }
     ]
}
```

The result is a cone that's been moved to the left, down a bit, and flipped so that the rounded bottom appears on the top, as shown in Figure 13.3.

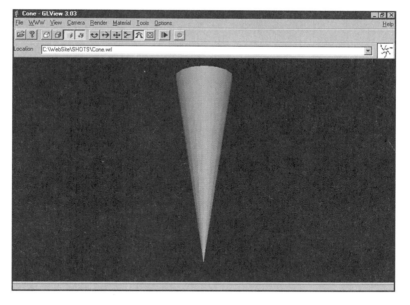

Figure 13.3 The transform node acts on its children.

In this lesson, you learned how to create and move shapes in VRML. In the next lesson, you'll learn how to change their appearance, add hyperlinks, and create a more realistic world.

Advanced 3-D Worlds

In this lesson, you learn to create hyperlinks and change the appearance of VRML worlds.

The Appearance Node

You may recall that part of the Shape node that you've used in the last two lessons is a node called Appearance. Within that node is another node, Material. It is within that node that you'll define the color of your shape.

Here's an example of a shape:

```
Shape {
       appearance Appearance {
        material Material {
          diffuseColor  0.0 0.0 0.0
          emissiveColor 1.0 0.0 0.0
          transparency  0.5
        }
      }
      geometry Box {
        size 2.0 4.0 0.3
      }
}
```

The first two properties, diffuseColor and emissiveColor, accept values for each of the red, green, and blue channels for the color desired. The values can be any decimal between zero and one.

diffuseColor is the basic color of your primitive. The emissiveColor field determines what color your shape will glow. Often you'll want these to be the same, although it's up to you as to whether or not you want your shapes to glow or have slightly duller colors.

TIP **Color Brightness** Remember with these red, green, and blue values that as you approach 1 with all values, you get closer to white. 0,0,0 is black. Everything in between is a spectrum—each color is at its "brightest" at one while the other colors remain zero.

transparency affects how solid the material appears. The default for transparency is 0, or completely solid, with a value of 1 being completely transparent.

Adding Hyperlinks in VRML

Links in VRML require another node, the Anchor node. This one accepts two basic properties, name and description as in the following example:

```
Anchor {
    url "study.wrl"
    description "Door to the Study"
        children [
                    Shape {
                        appearance Appearance {
                            material Material {
                                diffuseColor 0.6 0.4 0.0
                            }
                        }
                        geometry Box {
                            size 3.0 6.0 0.2
                        }
                    }
            ]
    }
```

The url property can accept any sort of URL, whether it's another VRML world, a regular HTML document, or a hypermedia link. The description text is similar to ALT text for the <IMG> tag. Some VRML browsers will allow the description text to pop up on-screen to help the user decide if this is a useful link for them.

As with other nodes, the node that Anchor acts on is held in the children [] node. In this case, it's a shape that looks a bit like a door. Click the door in a VRML browser, and you'll move on to the next world, as shown in Figure 14.1.

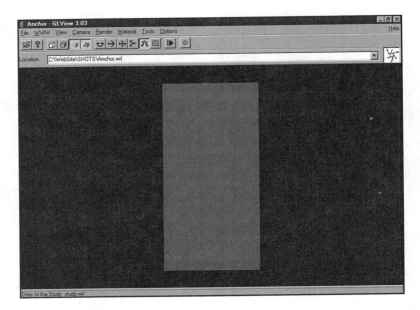

Figure 14.1   This object is an anchor—notice that the cursor changes and the link
description appears in the status bar at the bottom of the browser.

More Nodes: *IndexedFaceSet*

Creating your own shapes takes two steps, and three different nodes. The first
node, `Coordinate`, is used to lay out the coordinates for your new shape. This
doesn't actually create anything in the VRML world. Instead, the field point is
used to create invisible points in the world that represents corners of your
shape. It's basically a template for the parent node, `IndexedFaceSet`. Here's an
example:

```
Shape {
    geometry IndexedFaceSet {
        coord Coordinate {
        point [
            5  0  0,        #0
            5  -5  -5,      #1
            5  -5  5,       #2
            -5  0  0,       #3
            -5  -5  -5,     #4
            -5  -5  5,      #5
```

```
        ]
      }
    coordIndex [
          0, 1, 2, -1,      #Side A
          0, 1, 4, 3, -1,   #Side B
          3, 4, 5, -1,      #Side C
          0, 2, 5, 3, -1,   #Side D
          5, 2, 1, 4, -1,   #Side E
    ]
  }
}
```

 TIP   Prototype by Hand   When you draw your object, make it as close to 3-D as possible, and clearly label the points (starting with zero). This will help you create it in VRML.

The Coordinate node is used to create a point for each end point in the shape that you're creating.

```
coord Coordinate {
    point [
    x1-coord y1-coord z1-coord, #point 0
    x2-coord y2-coord z2-coord, #point 1
    ...,
    ]
}
```

Each coordinate for your shape requires an X, Y, and Z coordinate. This creates a point in your VRML world. Get enough points together, and you'll have a shape. But you won't be able to see anything.

The next step is to add the coordIndex node, which contains a listing of sides, as in the following format:

```
coordIndex [
    point_num, point_num, point_num, -1, #side1
    point_num, point_num, point_num, -1, #side2
    ...
    ]
}
```

Each instance of *num* represents one of the points you created with the Coordinate node. So, coordIndex is used to create each side of your shape. And, because many of the shapes you create probably won't have just three sides, you use -1 to represent the end of a shape. Depending on your mood and the number of advanced degrees in mathematics you have, the sides of your shapes could have many, many points to connect.

Putting It All Together

What you've learned so far are only the very basics of VRML, especially in the 2.0 standard. Not only can you create and position shapes, but you can also force shapes to be solid (so users can't walk through them). You can also animate shapes and add scripting commands to create incredibly advanced worlds.

 TIP **The Standard** For more on the VRML 2.0 standard, check out **http://www.vrml.org/** on the Web.

But, with what you do know, it's possible to create a fairly advanced VRML world. For instance, you could create a complete house. Listing 14.1 does just that. It's a bit long, but it doesn't use anything you haven't already seen in these lessons.

Listing 14.1 Creating a House

```
#VRML V2.0 utf8
#Creating your own house
#

Transform {                                    #move cube up above ground
        translation 0 1.7 0
            children [
            Shape {                            #define this as a
➥my_house instance
                appearance Appearance {
                    material Material {        #add color to
➥main house

                        diffuseColor 0 0 1
                        emissiveColor 0 0 .5
                    }
                }
                geometry Box {                 #create
➥house

                    size 5 8 8
```

continues

Listing 14.1 Continued

```
                            }
                        }
                    ]
                }
Shape {
    appearance Appearance {
            material Material {                              #add
➥color to roof
                    diffuseColor .5 1 .5
                    emissiveColor .5 .5 .5
                }
            }
        geometry IndexedFaceSet {                        #create roof points
            coords Coordinates {
                point [
                        5 10 0,        #0
                        5 5 -5,        #1
                        5 5 5,         #2
                        -5 10 0,       #3
                        -5 5 -5,       #4
                        -5 5 5,        #5
                ]
            }
        coordIndex [                              #draw faces of roof sides
                0, 1, 2, -1,        #Side A
                0, 1, 4, 3, -1,     #Side B
                3, 4, 5, -1,        #Side C
                0, 2, 5, 3, -1,     #Side D
                5, 2, 1, 4, -1,     #Side E
            ]
        }
    }
}
```

It takes a while to enter all of this code, but once it's in, it begins to make some sense. Figure 14.2 shows you how this looks in a VRML browser.

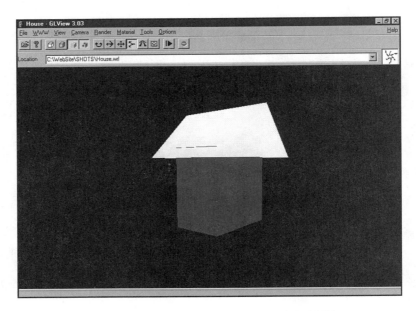

Figure 14.2   Here's a little 3-D house created completely in VRML.

In this lesson, you learned how to add color, hyperlinks, and new shapes to your VRML worlds. In the next lesson, you'll learn how to add ActiveX controls to your Web page.

Inserting
ActiveX Controls

In this lesson, you learn to use the ActiveX Control Pad to add ActiveX controls to your Web pages.

What Is ActiveX?

People have more trouble answering this question than almost any other question in the Internet world. What exactly is ActiveX, and why should you care?

ActiveX is the son (or stepson, perhaps) of Object Linking and Embedding, Microsoft's object-based technology for making applications take notice of one another. OLE allows you to embed an Excel spreadsheet in a Microsoft Word document, for instance, and then have the embedded document automatically update whenever you change the spreadsheet in Excel.

OLE also goes much further than that, as it becomes more and more a part of the Windows operating environment. The idea that you could "embed" objects in parts of the desktop isn't too far away—in fact, it's already here in certain arenas, like in Internet Explorer 4.0's Active Desktop.

So OLE and ActiveX are related. But who's the mother? Visual Basic, the popular "everyperson's" programming language for Windows, is probably the mother. Visual Basic's modus operandi is straightforward. There exist a number of *controls* that you can place in an interface window. Those controls are then scripted (in Visual Basic scripting) to allow a response to a user's input. Click a control, for instance, and a script can respond by changing windows or adding new interface elements.

Control An interface element that requires some user input. In ActiveX terms, a control is often a button, text box, or menu—just like in HTML forms. Controls can also be more advanced, though, like small game applets, stock tickers, or database interfaces for something like making an airline reservation.

Essentially, ActiveX is the child of these two technologies—OLE and Visual Basic—brought together in such a way that makes sense for the World Wide Web. ActiveX allows you to embed Visual Basic-like controls in Web pages, and respond to user input using a Visual Basic Scripting syntax (VBScript). For folks who already know Visual Basic, it's a boon. For others, it takes a bit of learning.

Adding ActiveX Controls

ActiveX controls can be difficult to grasp—and they can be even tougher to add to your documents by hand. Fortunately, there are more and more ActiveX-aware Web editors coming on the market to help you with the process. And although it's possible to add ActiveX components by hand, even Microsoft recognizes the need for a more friendly solution—which is why they've made Control Pad available for free download.

TIP **Get Control Pad** Control Pad is available for download from **http://microsoft.com/activeplatform/** and **http://microsoft.com/workshop/author/cpad/** on the Web. Many ActiveX controls and tips for using them are available from **http://www.activex.com/**, sponsored by C-Net.

Control Pad can either be used as your primary HTML editor, or just to add ActiveX controls to existing pages. Either way, adding a control is a fairly straightforward process:

1. Launch **Control Pad** and enter HTML for your page. You can also choose **File**, **Load** to load an existing HTML document into the editor.
2. Place the cursor (insertion point) where you'd like to add an ActiveX control in your document.
3. Choose **Edit**, **Insert ActiveX Control** from the menu.
4. In the resulting Insert ActiveX Control dialog box, choose the ActiveX control you'd like to add to your page. Click **OK**.

   What appears next are the visual tools for editing the ActiveX control. These tools are shown in Figure 15.1.

HTML for page in background

Change control's properties

Drag and edit control

Figure 15.1 The visual tools for editing an ActiveX control aren't the most intuitive, but it beats editing by hand.

5. After editing the control's properties, click the **Close** box on the **Edit ActiveX Control** window. The HTML codes for the controls appear in your document.

Editing ActiveX Properties

There are actually two ways to edit ActiveX control properties—the obvious one being to edit the properties while you're creating the control. The other way gets you to basically the same point—click the **Edit ActiveX Control** icon in Control Pad's window. You'll notice the icon just to the left of the HTML code that's been used to include the ActiveX object. Click it once and the visual editing tools return.

There are a couple of properties common to all ActiveX controls that you'll want to consider editing (scroll down in the Properties dialog box shown in Figure 15.1 to see some of these options):

ALIGN Follows the same basic rules of ALIGN in the HTML world.

BORDER Allows you to specify the border around the ActiveX control's embedded space.

181

CLASSID   The nearly nonsensical internal ID number that ActiveX requires to understand a control. It's entered by Control Pad, so you don't have to worry about it.

CODEBASE   This one is important, and it's a toughie. CODEBASE is an URL to the location of a downloadable version of the ActiveX control in question. When a user's browser encounters your ActiveX control, it may not have that control stored away on the hard drive. Instead, it will need to download the control. It can automatically do so, if you specify an URL directly to that control, along with the special version information.

 TIP   **The CODEBASE URL**   Microsoft's ActiveX CODEBASE URL begins with **http://activex.microsoft.com/controls/iexplorer** and finishes with the name of the file and the version. A full CODEBASE example might be: **"http://activex.microsoft.com/controls/iexplorer/btnmenu.ocx#Version=4,70,0,1161"**. Other popular codebase URLs begin from the C-Net ActiveX Web site at **http://www.c-net.com/**.

ID   Give the control a nickname for your own internal use.

To edit these properties, single-click the property in the Property window, and then change it using the text box at the top of that window. You can also change attributes like HEIGHT and WIDTH by clicking and dragging the control in Edit ActiveX Control window.

Scripting the Object

With the control in place on your page, you're now ready to actually do something with it. To do this, you need to delve into a bit of VBScript. Using Control Pad, though, makes the scripting a lot easier. Control Pad features the Script Wizard built right in—just fire it up to add scripting to your control.

1. Choose **Tools**, **Script Wizard** from the menu. In the Script Wizard dialog box, find the **Event Object** that's been added for affecting your ActiveX control, as shown in Figure 15.2.

2. Click the **plus sign** next to the Event Object to see all the possible Events.

3. Select an **Event** that you want the control to react to. In the **Insert Action** menu, choose an **Action** for responding to the Event. (You may need to click another plus sign next to the Action to see a list of possible actions.)

Select Action for each event

Select the event

Click plus sign to see possible events

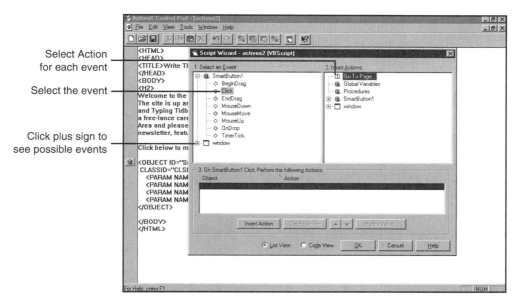

Figure 15.2 The Script Wizard keeps you pretty far from the grit of writing actual commands.

4. Toward the bottom of the dialog box, click the **Insert Action** button. This may bring up a dialog box requesting more information. Enter that information and click **OK**.

5. Click **OK** to add the scripting to your page.

To test your newly scripted page and ActiveX control, save the page to your hard drive, then load it in Internet Explorer 3.0 or later, making sure that ActiveX is turned on in the IE Options (**View**, **Options**, **Security** in some versions).

In this lesson, you learned how to add ActiveX controls to your Web pages. In the next lesson, you'll learn how to find and add Web Chat, Counters, and other elements.

Other Web Add-Ons

In this lesson, you learn how to add some other multimedia and plug-in add-ons to your pages, including counters and chat rooms.

Chat Rooms

The Web hasn't always been terribly friendly to Internet *chat*, since HTML was originally designed as a static, publishing-oriented markup language designed to show non-moving text and images, along with hyperlinks. Some folks have tried chat in HTML (combined with Web-server–based programs) that required the user to reload the document in their browser every few moments in order to see any progress in the conversation.

 TERM **Chat** On the Internet, chat refers to pretty much any technology that allows you to type comments in real time (or, live) to others around the world. Comments appear in the virtual chat room soon after you type them and hit the **Enter** key—while others in the room type responses or hold side conversations.

Until recently, however, the best way to chat on the Internet has been through the Internet Relay Chat service, which required its own Internet server computers and different client software. IRC can also be something of an exclusive club, requiring a bit of expertise before you can really take advantage of the experience.

The Web has changed quite a bit since then, and, more importantly, so have Web browsers. Now with plug-in technologies, Java, scripting, and even dynamic Web pages, chat should begin to gain more of a stronghold on the Web.

These Java add-ons tend to make chatting a little more friendly, too, like the chat areas on America Online and CompuServe.

Still, there are currently very few solutions available to the typical Web author for adding chat rooms to your pages. Most of them require access to your Web server, like:

> **ChatBox Lite (http://www.chatbox.com)**   If you have access to the back-end of a Windows NT server, you can download the freeware version of ChatBox, which supports ten users in a limited chat room.
>
> **Chat Server (http://chat.magmacom.com)**   Windows 95, Windows NT, and most flavors on UNIX can support this one, again if you have access to the server. In some browsers, it can continuously stream conversations, although others require that you hit reload every so often.
>
> **QuikChat (http://www.cs.hope.edu/~hahnfld/quikchat/)**   Any server that can run Perl scripts can use this script to create a frames-based chat room on their page. You still need access to the server, but only for a few short lines of code.

Java Chat

The addition of Java to the bag of tricks that many browsers can perform has changed some of the possibilities with Web-based chat, including the lack of a need to have access to the server-side directories of the Web server. Assuming your users have Java-capable browsers, it's possible to add a chat room to your Web site by simply adding a few lines of HTML code—if you don't mind the advertisements.

The example used here is the ParaChat service at (**http://parachat.webpage. com/**) that allows you to add a free chat room to your site, as long as you're willing to read their banner advertisements. Here's how you add the room:

1. Point your browser to the ParaChat downloading page at **http:// parachat.webpage.com/getpchat.htm** on the Web.
2. Click the **read free license** link, read the license, then click **I Accept**.
3. Fill in the form, including the URL for the chat room and the name of the room.
4. After your information has been accepted, copy the HTML code out of the browser window and paste it into a Web document. Upload the Web

document to your Web server, taking care to use the same URL that you specified in your signup form.

Once you've added the chat room, your page will look something like Figure 16.1 to users who have a Java-capable browser.

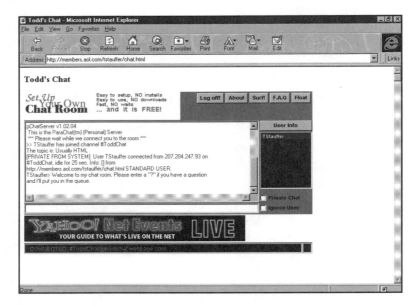

Figure 16.1   The ParaChat chat room displayed on a Web page.

Adding a Counter

If there's one thing that every single Web designer wants to know, it's the number of *hits* that their Web sites get. To determine this number, you'll want to add a counter to your page. A counter is a small program (often, but not always, requiring access to the Web server) that counts the number of times your page is loaded. This gives you a reasonably good idea of how many people are visiting your page.

Hit   In Web parlance, a hit is an instance of your Web page being loaded over the Internet. Every time someone types in your URL and loads your Web page, it's a hit.

Again, as with chat rooms, you often run into the problem of counters requiring access to the Web server. Each of them has its own instructions, setup procedure, and method for adding the counter to your individual pages. But, if you do have a bit of control over your Web server, you might consider one of these:

The Counter for Windows NT/95 (http://www.geocities.com/ SiliconValley/6742/) This exe CGI script includes the ability to configure the style of numbers used for the display or the counter.

WWWpac (http://www.psychology.uiowa.edu/WWWpac/ WWWpac.htm) This is another Windows NT/95 CGI (also available for NT Alpha) that allows you to configure the color, size, border, and other options.

WWW Homepage Access Counter (http://www.fccc.edu/users/muquit/ Count.html) A C-based counter that includes control over the style of digits used. This program can be recompiled to work with Linux, BSD, SGI, NextStep, Windows NT, VMS, Win95, and many other OSes.

Page Counter for Apache (http://www.galaxy.netwebcounter.html) This counter is designed for use with the popular Apache Web server program. The program is designed to work directly with the Web server to receive the most accurate count possible.

Kcounter (http://diakonos.hum.utah.edu/kcounter/) This AppleScript-based counter works with most popular Mac OS Web servers. Runs as a CGI, outputs basic text numbers for counter.

 TIP **Counter Included** If you deal with a customer-savvy ISP, chances are they have already added some sort of counter script or program to their Web server which you can access. Ask around.

Web-Based Counters

Your other option is to go with a service similar to the ParaChat service that offers advertiser-driven free access to chat rooms. A number of services offer a similar deal on Web page counters, which either send advertising or are offered as a free (or nearly free) public service. Check some of these out if you need a counter for your current site:

Page Count (http://www.pagecount.com/) This free access counter is added across the Net and serviced by the PageCount people, but it does send an advertisement along with the counter, as shown in Figure 16.2.

Site-Stats (http://www.net-user.com/counter/) Another free service that sends a banner ad along with the counter information.

Web Count (http://www.webcount.com/) If you get what you pay for, then Web Count may be a better service than the ad-based counters, promising accuracy and quick loading. At (currently) $3.00 a month, you get a counter in a number of styles without the ads.

Cam's Dynamic Counter Applet (http://www.local.com/counter/) For some reason, this cool little Java counter is free, while keeping track of hits on the host site. It's "dynamic" because users can watch the odometer roll over when they access your page.

Figure 16.2 The PageCount counter features a banner ad, but at least the counter is free.

Adding most of these counters is simple—usually, you'll just use an <IMG> tag that points to an URL on the host computer's site, which retrieves the page counter.

With Java applets, though, things are a bit different, requiring the <APPLET> or <OBJECT> tag. For instance, the recommended method for adding Cam's Dynamic Counter is:

```
<TABLE BORDER=4>
<TR><TD>
<APPLET ARCHIVE="http://www.local.com/counter/Counter.zip
 CODEBASE="http://www.local.com/counter/"
 COUNTER="Counter.class"
 WIDTH=75 HEIGHT=20>
 <PARAM NAME=URL VALUE="http://www.mynet.com/index.html">
</APPLET>
<TD></TR>
</TABLE>
```

While the <TABLE> tags aren't really necessary (they're designed to give the counter a nice border in this example), the rest of these tags are an example of how a simple Java applet can be added to your page. Note that the VALUE or the

<PARAM> tag needs to be changed to reflect the URL of the page that is to be counted by the counter. The rest of the URLs stay the same. (Also, note that the URLs provided are case-sensitive.)

Figure 16.3 is an example of the Java counter.

Figure 16.3   Cam's Dynamic Counter Applet in action.

TIP   **Java Help**   For more on Java, consult Part IV, Lesson 4 in this text.

In this lesson, you learned how to add chat rooms and counters to your Web pages.

Enhancing Web Pages

Frame Basics

In this lesson, you learn what frames are and how to add them to your Web pages.

Introducing Frames

Frames are basically another way to create a unique interface for your Web site. Dividing the page into different parts—each of which can be updated separately—creates a number of different interface elements.

Even a simple use of the frame specification lets you add interface graphics or a corporate logo to a site, while the rest of your page scrolls beneath it, as in Figure 1.1.

CAUTION

Version Problems   Frames are an HTML 3.2 extension to the HTML standard—that is, they haven't been around very long. Many users still have browsers that don't support frames. Only the 2.0-level (and later) versions of Internet Explorer and Netscape Navigator support them, and only the 3.0 and later AOL browser supports them. So, before using frames for your entire site, realize that not everyone will be able to view them. You might consider creating an alternate non-frames site, too.

In essence, the frames commands allow you to divide a single Web page into an interface that can load more than one HTML document at a time. Then, using special hyperlink commands, you can have a link in one frame load a new HTML document in another frame.

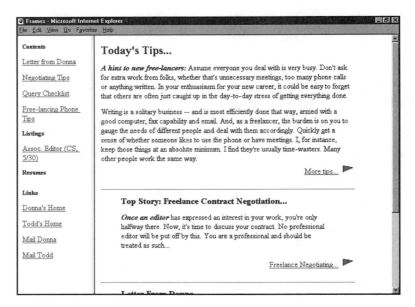

Figure 1.1   A simple frames interface.

Frames are great for the following:

- **Index links**   When you place hyperlinks in a frame column on your Web page, people can click around your Web site without being forced to constantly move back to the contents page. Because the index is always there, users simply click a new content level in the static frame.

- **Fixed interface elements**   As mentioned previously, you can force clickable graphics, logos, and other information to stay in one fixed portion of the screen while the rest of your document scrolls in another frame.

- **Image viewers or documentation interfaces**   When you want to create your own interface for browsing different documents or multimedia elements, consider using frames. This allows users to see many different HTML documents without having to reload page after page.

Creating a Frameset

Unique among the HTML-style tags so far is the <FRAMESET> tag. This container tag is required for frames-style pages. It also replaces the <BODY> tag completely on these pages.

So when you use frames, you're committed to using them completely—you can't just add frames to part of your page. On a typical page, <FRAMESET> is added like this:

```
<HTML>
<HEAD>
...HEAD elements...
</HEAD>
<FRAMESET>
...Frames and other HTML markup...
</FRAMESET>
</HTML>
```

Frameset   A short HTML document that creates a frames interface. The <FRAMESET> container replaces the <BODY> container on a page because a frameset is designed to load other HTML documents that do include <BODY> containers.

The <FRAMESET> tag accepts two attributes: ROWS and COLS. Both attributes accept numerical values (size in pixels), percentages, or a combination of both.

The value * can be used to suggest that a particular or row or column should take up the rest of the page. The number of rows or columns is suggested by the number of values you give the attribute.

These attributes take the following format:

```
<FRAMESET ROWS="numbers,percent,*" COLS="numbers,percent,*">
```

The following example creates two rows: one row that's 50 pixels long and another row that takes up the rest of the page:

```
<FRAMESET ROWS="50,*">
```

This is useful for a page that displays a fixed map or graphic at the top that you know is less than 50 pixels high. The next example creates a Web interface with two columns: one on the leftmost 25 percent of the screen and one on the other 75 percent:

```
<FRAMESET COLS="25%,75%">
```

This is a good way to set up a documentation site that offers contents in the first frame, and text and examples in the second, larger frame.

Each <FRAMESET> statement works with one attribute or the other. This means you can only create a frameset with either rows or columns. To create rows *within* columns (or vice versa), you can nest <FRAMESET> statements.

For instance, the following creates a page with two columns:

```
<FRAMESET COLS="25%,75%">
   <FRAMESET ROWS="50%,50%">
   </FRAMESET>
</FRAMESET>
```

 Nesting   A programming term that means to "place completely inside" something else. In this case, you're nesting one frameset container inside another.

In this example, the first column is divided into two rows that each take up 50 percent of that column. Although the code in the example doesn't display anything, it creates logical breaks in the page.

You'll begin to work with nested <FRAMESET> tags as you develop more advanced frame interfaces in Lesson 2, "Modifying Frames."

Adding Frames

The <FRAME> tag is used within the <FRAMESET> container to determine what actually appears in a particular frame. Each <FRAME> tag is an empty tag—like the <LI> tags you add to HTML lists. It's simply there, within the <FRAMESET> container, to determine what URL or name is associated with the particular frame it defines.

The <FRAME> tag takes the following format:

```
<FRAMESET COLS/ROWS="numbers">
<FRAME SRC="URL">
...
</FRAMESET>
```

The SRC attribute is used to tell the frame what URL should be loaded in that frame. For instance, the following code creates two frame rows: one that loads the URL MENU.HTML at the top of the Web page and one that loads the URL INDEX.HTML at the bottom of the page, as shown in Figure 1.2.

```
<FRAMESET ROWS="20%,80%">
<FRAME SRC="menu.html">
<FRAME SRC="index.html">
</FRAMESET>
```

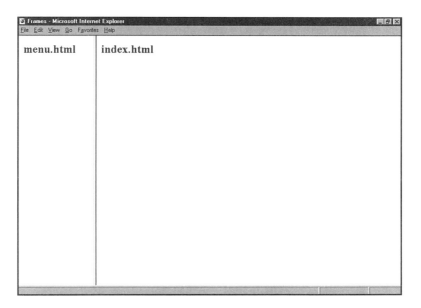

Figure 1.2 The <FRAME> tag assigns URLs to each frame window.

By using the <FRAME> tag, you create what's known as a *frame window*. Each window corresponds to a row or column definition in the <FRAMESET> tag, but nothing is drawn or displayed until an appropriate <FRAME> tag is used to define each individual window.

 TIP **Main Viewer** In most framesets, one of the frames is a *main viewer* window that you use for loading new documents. When you design a frames interface, think about which frame you'd like to use for your viewer.

Text for No Frames

The <NOFRAMES> container tag is used to contain HTML markup intended for browsers that do not support the frames specification. Text and HTML tags inside the <NOFRAMES> container are ignored by frames-capable browsers. All others should ignore the other frames tags (which they won't recognize) but display the text between the <NOFRAMES> tags.

The following is an example:

```
<FRAMESET ROWS="25%,75%>
<FRAME SRC="menu.html">
<FRAME SRC="index.html">
<NOFRAMES>
<P>This page requires a Frames capable browser to view. If you'd
➥prefer,
you can access our <a href="2_index.html">HTML 2.0 compliant pages</
➥a>
to view this information without the frames interface.</P>
</NOFRAMES>
</FRAMESET>
```

In this lesson, you learned how to create a frameset and frames. In the next lesson, you'll name the individual frames and load new pages in them.

Modifying Frames

In this lesson, you learn how to name frames and load new HTML documents within a frameset interface.

Loading Pages in Frames

So far, you've seen how to use the frames commands to split a page into two (or more) sections. For instance, you can have a logo in one frame, and a "main viewer" in the other for looking at documents. If all you're interested in is fixing a logo or advertisement at the top of your page, that's all you really need to know.

But, you can do much more than that with frames. For example, you can create an interface that works something like a remote control for a Web site. Just click a hyperlink, and a new page loads in the other frame window, as shown in Figure 2.1. The key to doing this is known as *targeting*.

Targeting   For HTML frames, targeting is how you get a hyperlink in one frame to load a new page in another frame. First, you need to name the frame that's going to accept the new page. Then, you add a target attribute to the hyperlink command, so the hyperlink knows that it needs to load its page in a new frame window.

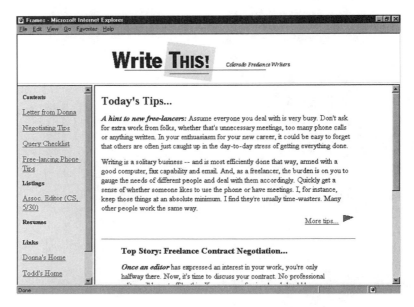

Figure 2.1 A common frameset: Click the left-side hyperlinks and a new page appears in the main viewer frame.

Giving Your Frames a *NAME*

First, you need to name your frame windows—at least, you have to name the windows you might want to change. This is accomplished with the NAME attribute to the <FRAME> tag, which takes the following format:

```
<FRAME SRC="original URL" NAME="window_name">
```

This is a little like the way that the NAME attribute works for <A NAME> links. When the frame window has a distinct name, you can access it directly from other frame windows. An example of this is the following:

```
<FRAME SRC="index.html" NAME="main_viewer">
```

CAUTION

Frame Names Although you can pretty much name your frame window anything you want, there is one restriction: You can't start the name with an underscore character (_). If you do, the name will be ignored. There's a good reason for this; the underscore is used to signal a number of "magic" target names. We get to those in the section at the end of this lesson.

Targeting A Frame

With your frame successfully named, you're ready to target that frame with a hypertext link. This is accomplished with the TARGET attribute to a typical <A> anchor tag, which follows this format:

```
<A HREF="new_URL" TARGET="window_name">link text</A>
```

The *new URL* is the new document that you want to have appear in the frame window. The *window_name* is the same name that you used to name the frame windows with the NAME attribute to the <FRAME> tag. An example:

```
<A HREF="products.html" TARGET="main_viewer">View Products</A>
```

TIP **No New URLs** Test your frameset in a browser and you'll notice that the URL doesn't change when you load a new page in a frame window. Because the URL doesn't change, you might want to put a direct URL (in regular text) at the bottom of any pages from your site that are loaded in your main viewer frame, so that users make note of the direct URL to those pages if they desire.

Frame Options

Aside from SRC and NAME, the <FRAME> tag can accept the attributes MARGINWIDTH, MARGINHEIGHT, SCROLLING, and NORESIZE. All of these additional attributes are appearance-oriented:

- MARGINWIDTH and MARGINHEIGHT are used to control the right/left margins and the top/bottom margins of the text and graphics within a frame, respectively. Each takes a numerical value in pixels, so that the following:

  ```
  <FRAME SRC="text.html" MARGINWIDTH=5 MARGINHEIGHT=5>
  ```

  creates a five-pixel border between the contents of text.html and the frame edges.

- SCROLLING can accept the values YES, NO, and AUTO, and is used to determine whether or not scroll bars will appear in the frame window. The default value is AUTO, and this is probably the best to use in most cases. Because users have all different screen resolutions and available browser window space, even short documents sometimes need to be scrolled.

- The NORESIZE attribute doesn't require a value, and is used to keep the user from resizing a frame window.

An example of SCROLLING and NORESIZE would be:

```
<FRAME SRC="text.html" SCROLLING=YES NORESIZE>
```

The example would create a frame that can be scrolled using scroll bars, but cannot be resized by the user.

The "Magic" Targets

Here's why you can't name frame windows with something that starts with an underscore. The "magic" target names all start with an underscore, which signals to the browser that they should treat this link extra special. The following are some examples:

- **TARGET="_blank"** The URL specified in this link always loads in a new blank browser window.
- **TARGET="_self"** This is used for overriding a <BASE> tag, and forcing a link to load in the same window that it's clicked in.
- **TARGET="_parent"** This causes the document to load in the current window's parent—generally, the frame window immediately preceding the current frame in the <FRAMESET> definition. If no parent exists, it acts like "_self".
- **TARGET="_top"** The document is loaded in the top frame of the window, usually giving the appearance of a non-frames page.

Basically, these magic targets are designed to let you break out of the current <FRAMESET> structure in some way. Experiment with them to see how you can move around to different windows. For instance:

```
<A HREF="newpage.html" TARGET="_top">Click for the new page
➥ in its own window</A>
```

can be used to make the linked page appear in a regular (non-frames) browser window. A link like:

```
<A HREF="ad1.html" TARGET="_blank">Click to see ad</A>
```

would load its page in a completely new window.

In this lesson, you learned how to name and target frames within a frameset interface. In the next lesson, you'll create a basic HTML form.

A Basic HTML Form

In this lesson, you learn to use the HTML form tags and add a text area to your form.

What Forms Do

The idea behind a Web form is simple—it allows you to accept information or answers from your users with varying levels of guidance. Users can be asked to:

- Type answers
- Choose answers from a list of possibilities you create
- Choose one answer from a number of options that you specify

That data is then passed on to the Web server, which hands it to a script—a small computer program—designed to act on the data and (in most cases) create an HTML page in response.

In order to deal with forms data then, you need to understand a little something about scripting, or programming, for a Web server—or know someone who does. While learning to program is beyond the scope of this book, you'll look at how these scripts work in Lesson 6 of this part, "Form Data Gathering."

Figure 3.1 shows a basic form.

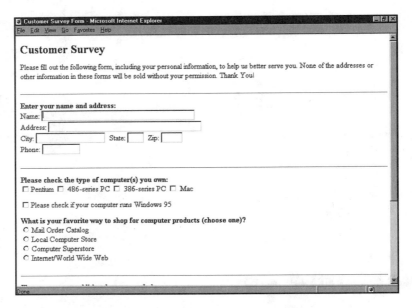

Figure 3.1   This form might be used to accept survey results.

Creating the Form

In an HTML document, forms are set between the <FORM> container tags. The form container works as follows:

```
<FORM METHOD="how_to_send" ACTION="URL of script">
...form data...
</FORM>
```

Notice that the <FORM> tag takes two attributes: METHOD and ACTION. The METHOD attribute accepts either POST or GET as its value. POST is by far the more popular, as it allows for a greater amount of data to be sent. GET is a little easier for Web programmers to deal with, and is best used with single responses, like a single text box.

So, if you plan to create a long form (with multiple entry boxes and menus), use the POST format for the METHOD:

```
<FORM METHOD="POST" ACTION="/cgi-bin/form.pl">
```

If, on the other hand, you have only one or two form elements (at most), try the GET format:

```
<FROM METHOD=GET ACTION="/cgi-bin/form1.pl">
```

The second attribute is ACTION, which simply accepts the URL for the script that will process the data from your form. Most often the script is stored in a directory called bin/ or cgi-bin/ located on your Web server.

An example of the <FORM> tag then, would be the following:

```
<FORM METHOD=SEND ACTION="http://www.yourcom.net/cgi-bin/survey.pl">
</FORM>
```

As with any HTML container tag, this example of the <FORM> tag has actually created a complete form (just like <P> and </P> is a complete paragraph). Unfortunately, your complete form doesn't *do* anything yet.

One at a Time You need to add the end tag </FORM> for your first form before creating another one in the same document. Generally, browsers will ignore any new occurrences of the <FORM> tag, since the purpose of the tag is to tell the browser how to submit data to the server, and different parts of a single form can't be submitted in different ways.

Text Fields and Attributes

One of the more common uses for forms is to accept multiple lines of text from a user, perhaps for feedback, bug reports, or other uses. To do this, use the <TEXTAREA> tag within your form. You can set this tag to control the number of rows and columns it displays, although it will generally accept as many characters as the user desires to enter. It takes the following form:

```
<TEXTAREA NAME="variable_name" ROWS=number COLS=number>
default text
</TEXTAREA>
```

<TEXTAREA> is a container tag, even though it simply puts a box for typing on the page. What's contained in the tag is the default text—so you can guide your users by letting them know what you'd like entered there. For instance:

```
<FORM>
<TEXTAREA NAME="comments" ROWS=4 COLS=40>
```

```
Enter comments about this Web site.
Good or Bad.
</TEXTAREA>                              .
</FORM>
```

The default text appears in the text box just as typed. Notice, in Figure 3.2, that text inside the `<TEXTAREA>` tag works like `<PRE>` formatted text. Any returns or spaces you add to the text are displayed in the browser window. In fact, by hitting Return or Enter after the opening `<TEXTAREA>` tag, you insert a blank line at the top of the textarea (in many browsers).

Figure 3.2   The `<TEXTAREA>` tag in action.

The NAME attribute is a *variable* name for this string of text. It gets passed on to your processing script on the Web server. ROWS and COLS can accept different numbers to change the size of the textarea box, but you should make sure that the majority of browsers can see the entire box on-screen. It's best to limit COLS to 80, and ROWS to something like 24 (the typical size for a text-based computer screen).

Variable   A programming term that means an area in computer memory used to store data. In the case of forms, the Web server script that interprets the form will ask for the value stored in this variable so that it can act on the data entered by your user.

`<TEXTAREA>` will also accept one other attribute: WRAP. WRAP can be set to OFF (which is the default if WRAP is not included), VIRTUAL, or PHYSICAL. Setting WRAP to PHYSICAL forces the browser to include actual line breaks in the text when sending it to the Web server. VIRTUAL makes the text box seem to offer line wrap, but sends a continuous stream of words to the Web server (unless the user has entered returns on his or her own).

Feedback Forms

Since `<TEXTAREA>` is commonly used to gather feedback from your Web users, this example will do just that. It's sometimes useful to have a page that allows users to quickly jot a few notes and send them off to you, saving them the hassle of creating an e-mail message.

To create a small form to do just that, enter the following in a blank Web document:

```
<BODY>
<H3>Feedback Form</H3>
<P>Please take a moment to tell us what you thought
➥ of the Web site.<BR>
Your Feedback is appreciated!</P>
<FORM METHOD="POST" ACTION="cgi-bin/feedback">
Enter your comments below:<BR>
<TEXTAREA NAME="comments" ROWS=10 COLS=70
➥ WRAP=VIRTUAL>
Dear WebMaster:
</TEXTAREA>
</FORM>
</BODY>
```

You can see how this looks in Figure 3.3. Notice in the example that some descriptive text is enclosed inside the <FORM> tag, but outside the <TEXTAREA> tag. This is completely legal—it just lets you explain what the purpose of the textarea is.

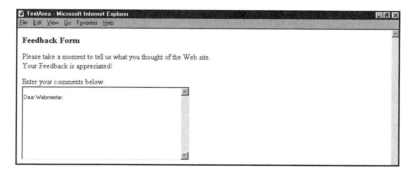

Figure 3.3 Sample textarea HTML form.

You may have realized that there's currently no way to *submit* the user's entry. You'll get to that in the next lesson.

In this lesson, you learned the basics of creating an HTML form. In the next lesson, you'll learn how to gather other types of data and submit your forms for processing.

Getting Data from Users

In this lesson, you learn to add different ways for your users to enter data on an HTML form.

Getting User Input

The <TEXTAREA> form element discussed in Lesson 3 is a fairly basic data entry tool, allowing your users to type whatever text they feel is appropriate, limited only by the number of characters they can enter. Often, however, you'll find it useful to limit the responses that your users can give. The <INPUT> tag gives you the opportunity to be a bit more picky about the type of input you're going to accept from the user.

The <INPUT> tag follows this format:

```
<INPUT TYPE="type_of_box" NAME="variable" SIZE=number
➥MAXLENGTH=number>
```

The only required attributes are TYPE and NAME. Some other *types* of the input tag will also accept the attribute VALUE. But first, let's look at the different types of <INPUT>.

TIP   Many Types As you'll see in a moment, the <INPUT> tag allows you to employ many different input types on your form, allowing you to accept data in the form of text boxes, check boxes, and option button lists, for instance.

Text Boxes

The first possible value for the TYPE attribute is TEXT, which creates a single-line text box of a length you choose. Notice that the length of the box and the maximum length entered by the user can be set separately. It's possible to have a box longer (or, more often, shorter) than the maximum number of characters you allow to be entered. Here's an example of a text box:

```
Last name: <INPUT TYPE=TEXT NAME="last_name" SIZE=40 MAXLENGTH=40>
```

When entered between <FORM> tags, this <INPUT> tag yields a box similar to the one shown in Figure 4.1. If desired, the attribute VALUE can be used to give the text box a default entry, as in the following example:

```
Type of Computer: <INPUT TYPE=TEXT NAME="computer"
➥ SIZE=50 MAXLENGTH=50 VALUE="Pentium">
```

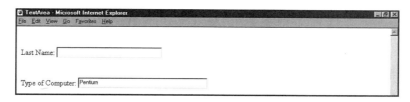

Figure 4.1   Using the TEXT option with the TYPE attribute.

Passwords

The PASSWORD option is nearly identical to the TEXT option except that it responds to typed letters by displaying bullet points or similar characters (chosen by the browser) to keep the words from being read. A sample password box could be:

```
Enter Password: <INPUT TYPE=PASSWORD NAME="password"
➥ SIZE=25 MAXLENGTH=25>
```

When characters are typed into this text box, they are shown on the screen as in Figure 4.2.

Recognize that the text is still stored as the text typed by the user—not as bullet points or similar characters.

Figure 4.2 PASSWORD hides text from people looking over your user's shoulder.

Check Boxes

The CHECKBOX value for TYPE allows you to create a check box-style interface for your form. This is best used when there are two possible values for a given choice—and no others. You can also determine whether or not a check box will already be checked (so that it must be unchecked by the user if desired), by using the attribute CHECKED. Here's an example of adding check boxes to a form:

```
Type of computer(s) you own:<BR>
<INPUT TYPE=CHECKBOX NAME="Pentium" CHECKED> Pentium
<INPUT TYPE=CHECKBOX NAME="MMX"> Pentium MMX
<INPUT TYPE=CHECKBOX NAME="Macintosh"> Macintosh
```

In this example, it's possible to check as many of the options as are presented. CHECKBOX evaluates each item separately from any others. Figure 4.3 illustrates how CHECKBOX is displayed in a browser.

Figure 4.3 Notice that Pentium is pre-checked.

Radio Buttons

Like CHECKBOX, RADIO is designed to offer your user a choice from predetermined options. The difference is RADIO is also designed to accept only one response from among its options. RADIO uses the same attributes and basic format as CHECKBOX.

RADIO requires that you use the VALUE attribute, and that the NAME attribute be the same for all of the <INPUT> tags that are intended for the same group. VALUE, on the other hand, should be different for each choice. For instance, look at the following example:

```
Choose the computer type you use most often:<BR>
<INPUT TYPE=RADIO NAME="Computer" VALUE="P" CHECKED> Pentium
<INPUT TYPE=RADIO NAME="Computer" VALUE="4"> 486-Series PC
<INPUT TYPE=RADIO NAME="Computer" VALUE="M"> Macintosh
<INPUT TYPE=RADIO NAME="Computer" VALUE="O"> Other
```

With RADIO, it's important to assign a default value, because it's possible that the user will simply skip the entry altogether. While the user can't check more than one, he or she can fail to check any of them. So, choose the most common value and set it as CHECKED, just so that the form-processing script doesn't have trouble.

Hidden Fields

This <INPUT> type technically isn't "input" at all. Rather, it's designed to pass some sort of value along to the Web server and script. It's generally used to send a keyword, validation number, or some other kind of string to the script so that the script knows it's being accessed by a valid (or just a particular) Web page. The <INPUT TYPE=HIDDEN> tag takes the attributes NAME and VALUE.

CAUTION

Not So Hidden   This isn't really terribly covert, since an intrepid user could simply use the **View Source** command in their Web browser (usually under the Edit menu) to see the value of the hidden field. It's more useful from a programmer's standpoint. For instance, on a large Web site, the hidden value might tell a multipurpose script which particular form (among many) is sending the data, so the script knows how to process the data.

The Reset Button

The <INPUT> tag has built into it the ability to clear an HTML form of entered data. RESET simply creates a push button (named with the VALUE string) that resets all of the elements in that particular FORM to their default values (erasing anything that the user has entered). An example would be the following:

```
<INPUT TYPE=RESET>
```

With a VALUE statement, you could enter the following:

```
<INPUT TYPE=RESET VALUE="Reset the Form">
```

211

The results are shown in Figure 4.4.

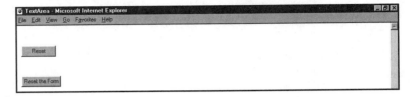

Figure 4.4   Default and named Reset buttons.

The Submit Button

The <INPUT> tag also has a type that automatically submits the data that's been entered into the HTML form. The SUBMIT type accepts only the attribute VALUE, which can be used to rename the button. Otherwise, the only purpose of the SUBMIT button is to send off all the other form information that's been entered by your user. See the following two examples:

```
<INPUT TYPE=SUBMIT>
<INPUT TYPE=SUBMIT VALUE="SEND IT IN!">
```

You can use just about anything you want for the VALUE, although it's best to remember that really small words, like OK, don't look great as buttons. To make a button larger, enter the VALUE with spaces on either end, like in the following:

```
<INPUT TYPE=SUBMIT VALUE="    GO    ">
```

Creating Pop-Up and Scrolling Menus

The last types of input that you can offer to users of your Web page revolves around the <SELECT> tag, which can be used to create different types of pop-up and scrolling menus. This is another element designed specifically for allowing users to make a choice—they can't enter their own text. The <SELECT> tag requires a NAME attribute and allows you to decide how many options to display at once with the SIZE attribute.

Also notice that <SELECT> is a container tag. Options are placed between the two <SELECT> tags, each with a particular VALUE that gets associated with <SELECT>'s NAME attribute when chosen.

The attribute SELECTED shows which value will be the default in the menu listing. An example might be:

```
Choose your favorite food:
<SELECT NAME="food">
<OPTION SELECTED VALUE="ital"> Italian
<OPTION VALUE="texm"> TexMex
<OPTION VALUE="stek"> SteakHouse
<OPTION VALUE="chin"> Chinese
</SELECT>
```

You can also use the SIZE attribute to decide to display the menu in its entirety, by simply changing the first line of the example to the following:

```
<SELECT NAME="food" SIZE=4>
```

Both examples are shown in Figure 4.5.

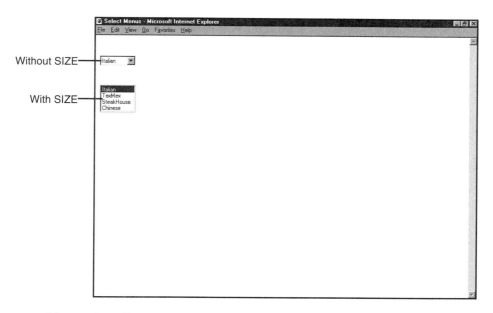

Figure 4.5   Two <SELECT> menus—a pop-up and a fixed.

In the first example, selecting the menu item with the mouse causes the menu to pop up on the page. The user can then select from the choices. In the second example, it's necessary to click the desired item.

But, what if you want to allow users to select more than one option at a time? One more attribute for the <SELECT> tag allows the user to select more than one option from the menu. Using the MULTIPLE attribute forces the menu to display in its entirety, regardless of the SIZE attribute. An example might be the following:

```
What type(s) of car does your family own (select as many as apply)?
<SELECT NAME="cars" MULTIPLE>
<OPTION VALUE="sedan"> Sedan
<OPTION VALUE="coupe"> Coupe
<OPTION VALUE="mivan"> Minivan
<OPTION VALUE="covan"> Conversion Van
<OPTION VALUE="statn"> Station wagon
<OPTION VALUE="sport"> SUV (4x4)
<OPTION VALUE="truck"> Other Truck
</SELECT>
```

In this lesson, you learned the different ways you can ask users to enter data in an HTML form. In the next lesson, you'll learn how to format pages that include HTML elements.

Form Layout

In this lesson, you learn how to format pages that include HTML form elements.

Form Design Issues

Central to the idea of form design is making the form easy for users to understand so that they follow through and fill out the form. The less incentive you give them to fill out the form, the less likely they are to try. A clean, short form is more likely to entice users than a long, confusing one.

There are some rules you should consider when building your forms so that they're easier and more effective for users:

- **Use other HTML tags to make things clear.**   You can use <BR>, <HR>, and paragraph tags to set apart different "chunks" of your form, while <B>, <I>, and even <PRE> can be used to make the form easier to read.

- **Keep your forms short.**   This isn't always possible, but when your forms are long, it's important to at least use <HR> and similar tags to break them up a bit. If forms have smaller sections, they're easier on the eye.

- **Use intuitive design.** Common sense is sometimes the key to a good form. For instance, putting the Submit button in the middle of the form will keep people from filling out the rest of it. Often it's best to use <SELECT>, radio buttons, and check boxes to keep your users from guessing at the type of info you want.

- **Warn users of unsecured transactions.**   You should tell your users if your Web server is secure—and how they can make sure that the connection is current. If you ask for credit card or similar personal information over an unsecured connection, let them know that, too.

Line Breaks, Paragraphs, and Horizontal Lines

Unlike text-oriented HTML, your best friend in form design is not really the paragraph tag—it's the line break tag. This is because you want to directly affect the layout of the forms, instead of leaving it up to the browser. Therefore, you've got to be a little more proactive. You'll end up with a lot of line break tags before your form is through.

Consider the following example:

```
<FORM>
<B>Enter your name and phone number</B>
First Name: <INPUT TYPE="TEXT" NAME="first" SIZE="30">
Last Name: <INPUT TYPE="TEXT" NAME="last" SIZE="40">
Phone: <INPUT TYPE="TEXT" NAME="phone" SIZE="12">
</FORM>
```

To get each of those text boxes on a separate line, and thus make them more pleasing to the eye, you need to add the <BR> tag.

```
<FORM>
<B>Enter your name and phone number</B><BR>
First Name: <INPUT TYPE="TEXT" NAME="first" SIZE="30"><BR>
Last Name: <INPUT TYPE="TEXT" NAME="last" SIZE="40"><BR>
Phone: <INPUT TYPE="TEXT" NAME="phone" SIZE="12"><BR>
</FORM>
```

Adding <BR> forces each subsequent text box to the next line. This is a more attractive form, and the <BR> tags make it easier for the user to understand, as shown in Figure 5.1.

TIP   **Add Instructions**   Notice the use of instructional text for these text boxes, which was put in boldface. Most of your forms will need instructions throughout, just as does any paper-based form. It's a good idea to standardize your instructions, using bold or italic tags to make them stand out from your other text.

Horizontal Lines

By placing <HR> tags in your form, you make it clear that new instructions are coming up, or that the form has reached the next logical chunk of entry. The <HR> tag simply makes it easier to look at as it guides the user through the different parts of the form. In Listing 5.1, you add <HR> tags at the logical breaks:

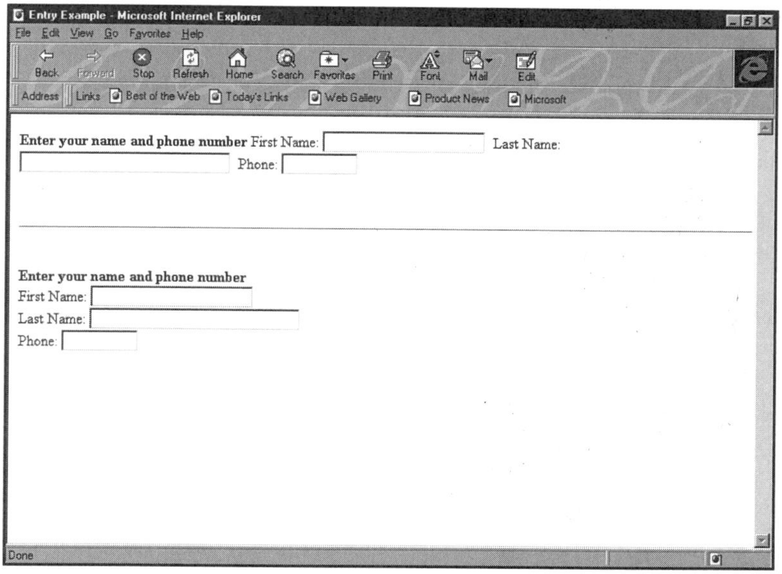

Figure 5.1 The <BR> tag makes quite a difference in form design.

Listing 5.1 Adding *<HR>* to the Form

```
<FORM>
<B>Enter your name and phone number</B><BR>
First Name: <INPUT TYPE="TEXT" NAME="first" SIZE="30"><BR>
Last Name: <INPUT TYPE="TEXT" NAME="last" SIZE="40"><BR>
Phone: <INPUT TYPE="TEXT" NAME="phone" SIZE="12"><BR>
<HR>
<B>Enter your mailing address</B><BR>
Address: <INPUT TYPE="TEXT" NAME="address" SIZE="50"><BR>
City: <INPUT TYPE="TEXT" NAME="city" SIZE="25">
State: <INPUT TYPE="TEXT" NAME="state" SIZE="2">
Zip: <INPUT TYPE="TEXT" NAME="zip" SIZE="7"><BR>
<HR>
<B>Enter your email address</B><BR>
Email: <INPUT TYPE="TEXT" NAME="email" SIZE="45"><BR>
<HR>
<B>Enter your comments below:</B><BR>
<TEXTAREA NAME="comments" ROWS="5" COLS="40">
Dear Staff,
</TEXTAREA>
</FORM>
```

217

<HR> tags make the form a little longer, as shown in Figure 5.2. But you haven't sacrificed the approachability by adding <HR> tags. Increasing the white space in a form is nearly as important as keeping it short enough so it isn't intimidating to users.

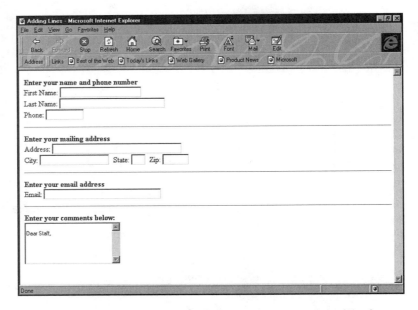

Figure 5.2   Adding <HR> tags to clearly define each new section of the form.

Paragraph Tags

Paragraph tags are basically good for keeping form data together in smaller chunks. As always, paragraph tags will add space on each side of the text that they enclose. We don't always want to add <HR> tags just because our form needs some white space.

Using paragraph tags, then, you can get the desired spacing between elements, without the horizontal line that seems to break the two apart. You can also pad the rest of the form a bit to keep it nicely spaced from the horizontal lines that you *do* use. The key is adding <P> tags as in this example, pictured in Figure 5.3:

```
<FORM>
<P>
<B>Who are you?</B><BR>
Name: <INPUT TYPE="TEXT" NAME="name" SIZE="50"><BR>
```

```
Email: <INPUT TYPE="TEXT" NAME="name" SIZE="50"><BR>
</P>
<HR>
<P>
<B>What product line do you wish to discuss?</B><BR>
Product: <SELECT NAME="product">
<OPTION SELECTED VALUE="sport"> Sporting Goods
<OPTION VALUE="home"> Home Furnishings
<OPTION VALUE="fashion"> Clothing/Fashions
<OPTION VALUE="electron"> Electronics
</SELECT><BR>
</P>
<P>
<B>Okay, fire away!</B><BR>
<TEXTAREA NAME="comment" ROWS="5" COLS="40">
Dear Staff,
</TEXTAREA>
</P>
</FORM>
```

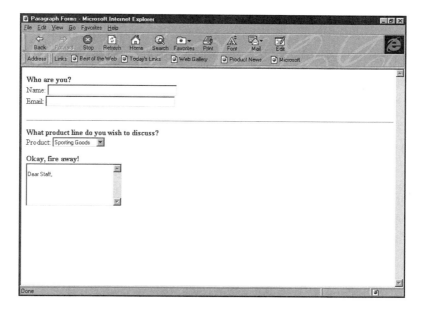

Figure 5.3 Better spacing and more conservative use of <HR> is possible when you include the paragraph tags.

Use <P> for Space Different browsers will interpret multiple <BR> tags in different ways, so it's best to use the <P> tag for sufficient spacing.

CAUTION

219

Other Tags for Form Formatting

One of the most annoying parts of setting up a form so far has been the inability to line up text box fields as they go down the page. For instance, whenever the Name: and Address: fields have been used in examples, they always look a little ragged.

The solution is the `<PRE>` tag. Because anything between the two tags uses the spacing and returns, this tag does two things. First, it allows you to line up your text boxes. Second, it eliminates the need for `<BR>` tags at the end of `<INPUT>` tags, since the browser will recognize your returns. The following is a ragged example:

```
Favorite Book: <INPUT TYPE="TEXT" NAME="book" SIZE="40"><BR>
Best Food: <INPUT TYPE="TEXT" NAME="food" SIZE="30"><BR>
Favorite Music Group: <INPUT TYPE="TEXT"
➥ NAME="music" SIZE="40"> <BR>
Personal Quote: <INPUT TYPE="TEXT" NAME="quote" SIZE="60"><BR>
```

To improve this situation, you can put this HTML between `<PRE>` tags and format them yourself:

```
<PRE>
Favorite Book:          <INPUT TYPE="TEXT" NAME="book" SIZE="40">
Best Food:              <INPUT TYPE="TEXT" NAME="food" SIZE="30">
Favorite Music Group:   <INPUT TYPE="TEXT" NAME="music" SIZE="40">
Personal Quote:         <INPUT TYPE="TEXT" NAME="quote" SIZE="60">
</PRE>
```

Remember that you need to use spaces, not tabs, to create the space between the name of the box and the text box itself. As before, you may need to play with the formatting a little to get things lined up like they are in Figure 5.4.

TIP   **Mono for `<PRE>`**   If you can, set your text editor to a monospaced font (like Courier) for editing text inside your `<PRE>` tags. Doing this will allow you to see exactly how `<PRE>` text will be displayed when viewed in a browser, since `<PRE>` forces your browser to use a monospaced font.

Using List Tags for Forms

The last little form design trick you'll look at involves using the list tags to create organization for your forms. Nearly any form element can be part of a list, and there are often good reasons to use them. Consider the following example:

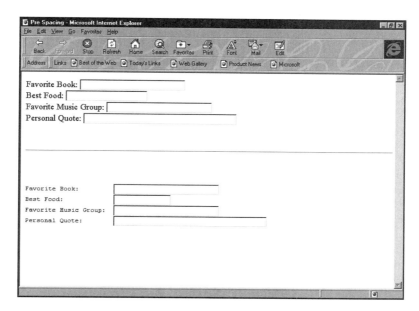

Figure 5.4 The second example is a much cleaner-looking form.

```
<DL>
<DT> Please choose the type of pet you're interested in:
<DD> <INPUT TYPE="RADIO" NAME="pet" VALUE="dog"> Dog
<DD> <INPUT TYPE="RADIO" NAME="pet" VALUE="cat"> Cat
<DD> <INPUT TYPE="RADIO" NAME="pet" VALUE="fish"> Fish
<DD> <INPUT TYPE="RADIO" NAME="pet" VALUE="bird"> Bird
</DL>
```

You've used lists in this way before—to create indented lists or outline formats that help you communicate a little better. In this case, it also makes the form *look* better, too.

A great excuse for using the <OL> tag is to create form elements that are numbered for some reason. Since the <LI> tag for an ordered list enters a number, you can simply add form elements to create a numbered form. Seen through a browser, each entry is numbered, eliminating the need for individual descriptive text.

In this lesson, you learned how to format HTML forms for easier reading. In the next lesson, you'll learn how to create CGI scripts for processing form data.

Form Data Gathering

*In this lesson, you learn how to gather data from your users
using Common Gateway Interface scripts or e-mail.*

What Is CGI?

Fill-in forms for your Web pages don't do anything by themselves. Your readers
can fill them in, but when they click the Submit button, the data won't go
anywhere.

That's where the Common Gateway Interface (CGI) comes in. By developing
CGI scripts, you can make your forms interactive. CGI scripts bring your static
Web pages to life—returning requested data, responding to user input, and
making a record of how many people access your site.

To a user, a link to a *CGI program* looks like a link to any other URL. It can be
clicked like any other link and results in new information being displayed, just
like any other link.

But, under the hood, a CGI program is much more than a normal Web page.
When a normal URL is selected, a file is read, interpreted, and displayed by the
browser. When an URL to a CGI program is selected, it causes a program to be
run on the server system, and that program can do just about anything you want
it to: scan databases, sort names, or send mail. CGI scripts allow for complex
back-end processing.

CGI changes the definition of what a Web page is. While normal pages are static
and unchanging, CGI programs enable a page to be anything you want it to be.

TERM   **CGI Programs, CGI Scripts, and CGIs**   These terms are used inter-changeably in this lesson just as they are on the Web itself.

CGI Languages

You do not write CGI scripts in HTML like you write Web pages. CGI scripts are written in other computer languages, such as UNIX shell scripts, Perl, C, AppleScript, or Visual Basic, and to write them you need knowledge of at least one of these languages.

Although a discussion of even one of them is beyond the scope of this lesson, there are strengths and weaknesses to each (and many excellent references exist, such as *CGI By Example, Special Edition Using CGI,* and *Perl 5 Quick Reference,* published by Que.

- UNIX shell scripts (or Windows NT or 95 batch files) are a good choice for small or temporary CGI programs. They are easy to write and you can see results immediately.

- Perl is a good choice for medium-complexity programs, and most plat-forms support it. It's fast, easy to program, and it's interpreted, meaning that it doesn't need to be compiled like C. Also, Perl libraries exist that automatically translate any data sent to your CGI program into a usable form. Information on Perl itself is available all over the Web, including at **http://www.yahoo.com/Computers_and_Internet/ Programming_Languages/Perl_BB**, **http://www.yahoo.com/ Computers_and_Internet/Internet/World_Wide_Web/Programming/ Perl_Scripts**, and **news:comp.lang.perl** on UseNet.

- For very complex data manipulation, it's best to use a full-fledged com-puter language, such as C. It will give you the fastest response and let you work with your information in the most flexible way. C libraries also exist for using Web data.

- Macintosh Web servers are very popular, and easy-to-create hooks exist between the Web server applications and Mac scripting languages like AppleScript and Frontier. You might start with the AppleScript/Frontier CGI tour at **http://cy-mac.welc.cam.ac.uk/cgi.html** on the Web.

A Simple CGI Script

Although CGI programs can become extremely complex, they can also be quite simple. One of the simplest is the UNIX shell script shown here:

```
#!/bin/sh
echo "Content-type: text/html"
echo ""
echo "<HTML><HEAD><TITLE>Sample</TITLE></HEAD>"
echo "<BODY>This is a <EM>simple</EM> CGI script.</BODY></HTML>"
```

The first line of this script (`#!/bin/sh`) tells UNIX what shell this program is written for; if the program were a Windows NT batch file, the line could be excluded.

The second line (`echo "Content-type: text/html"`) tells the Web server what type of information is to follow in MIME (Multipurpose Internet Mail Extension) format. *MIME* is a method of delivering complex binary data using only ASCII text characters. There are hundreds of standard MIME formats now registered, but the two most common for CGI applications are `text/html` (for HTML output) and `text/plain` (for plain ASCII output).

The third line (`echo ""`) is simply an empty space to tell the server that what follows is the data described by the "Content-type."

Finally, the fourth and fifth lines are the actual HTML data. These are sent through the server to the browser and interpreted just the same as instructions would be if they'd been read from an HTML file.

Referencing CGIs

While conventions among servers differ, most require that CGI programs be installed in a special CGI directory. This is a subdirectory of the main directory on the Web server's hard drive, and is usually called cgi-bin. If you aren't allowed to install your program in that directory (or if you're not sure), talk to your system administrator.

The system administrator will also tell you how to install the script itself, which is usually a matter of copying it from your own computer to the appropriate directory of the main Web server.

After your CGI script is in place, you can reference it from a browser like any other URL. For example, if you installed a program called **script.sh** in the cgi-bin directory, its URL would be as follows:

```
http://www.mycom.net/cgi-bin/script.sh
```

These URLs can be used like any others, including as HREFs from other Web pages or as SRC URLs for images.

Receiving Form Data

You may recall from Lesson 3 that there are two different METHODs to pass data to your CGI script. The two methods, GET and POST, cause data to be sent in different ways.

The type of METHOD used to send the data is stored in an environment variable on the Web server called REQUEST_METHOD. The GET method simply appends your form data to the URL and sends it to the server. Most servers will then store this data in another environment variable called QUERY_STRING. This string is generally limited to less than one kilobyte of data (approximately 1,000 characters), which explains why it is less popular.

Using the POST method causes the length of the data string to be stored in a variable called CONTENT_LENGTH, while the data itself is redirected to stdin (standard in). In effect, the data is made to appear to your script or program that it was typed into the server using a typical keyboard. Your script must then be designed to *parse* that input.

Parse   In English, parsing means to explain the grammatical form or function of a word. In computerese, *parsing* means something more like breaking up unreadable computer data into something that people (or, at least, programs written by people) can understand.

There are actually two steps to receiving the input: decoding and parsing. Data sent from your Web browser is encoded to avoid data loss—essentially by turning spaces into plus signs (+) and non-text characters (like !) into a percent sign (%) and a hexadecimal code.

Decode Data   There are programs designed specifically for decoding Web data. **cgi-bin.pl** is the Perl library for this. Mac Web servers might use Parse CGI for AppleScript.

Once you've worked through the decoding process, you're left with a text input that follows this format (where the ampersand simply separates each pairing of NAME and VALUE):

```
NAME1=VALUE1&NAME2=VALUE2&...
```

An example of this might be:

```
ADDRESS=1234 MAIN ST&CITY=DALLAS&STATE=TX
```

and so on. If you're not using a parsing program or library (which, ideally, would allow you to simply reassign the VALUEs in this file to variables in your script), then your script will need to accept this data, strip the ampersands, and reassign the values to appropriate variables.

Your Script's Output

Output is much easier. Because stdout (standard out) is redirected to the HTML browser, you simply need to use print (Perl and other languages), lprint (C language), or similar commands that print directly to the screen (or terminal or console). You use the print command to output HTML codes, just as if you were using your text editor.

Here's a short snippet of a Perl script to do just that:

```
print "Content-type: text\html\n\n";
print "<HTML>\n<HEAD><TITLE>Response</TITLE></HEAD>\n"
print "<BODY>\n<H2>Success</H2>\n<P>Thank you for your
➡submission<\P>\n"
print "<P>Click <A HREF="index.html">here</A> to go back <\P>
➡\n</BODY>\n</HTML>"
```

In a number of programming languages \n is the newline character, which simply feeds a Return to standard out. Otherwise, this should seem (and look) rather familiar; it's basic HTML.

Client-Side Forms

You can easily avoid all that CGI programming—just send the form data by e-mail, using a mailto URL:

```
<FORM ACTION="mailto:me@mynet.com" METHOD=POST>
```

When your user hits the Submit button, the results of the form are now forwarded to your e-mail address instead of to a CGI script. And that's great if you don't have access to your Web server's CGI directory. There is one caveat—what to do with the e-mail when it gets to your e-mail box.

The first problem is the fact that the e-mail message is still encoded in that POST format that forms use to send messages to scripts. Figure 6.1 shows an example of a typical received message—it's not a very pretty sight.

Figure 6.1 The results of a mailto: form POSTing.

The second problem is an extension of the first—you're either going to have to process all of these e-mails by hand or you need to write a program on your computer that interacts with your e-mail program in some way. Either way is probably fine for the small-business or home Web designer; at least you get the form data from users without requiring access to the server.

TIP **Parsing Utilities** There *are* utilities available for download that will help you turn form data into something more useful. Check out **http://www.yahoo.com/ Computers_and_Internet/Internet/World_Wide_Web/Programming/Forms/** for a start.

You might also notice one last problem—once the data is sent by e-mail, the page just sits there. You need to include a button or hyperlink on the page to let users move Back to a previous page. Add a clickable image, for instance, that says something like "Click after submitting" and hyperlink that button to another page.

In this lesson, you learned what a CGI is and how to incorporate CGIs into your Web sites. In the next lesson, you'll learn the basics of HTML style sheets.

Style Sheet Basics

In this lesson, you learn the basics for creating Web pages with style sheets.

What Are Style Sheets?

Style sheets are a clever way to add advanced formatting to HTML pages. You can define things like font faces, font sizes, alignment, and other characteristics—giving your page more of a desktop-published look. But style tags are also designed to be very transparent, so that older browsers can still access and display the pages.

For the real artists and designers out there, HTML is a bit too limiting. Style sheets offer a chance for some real control. And, to be honest, they're not terribly difficult to grasp, once you get into the spin of things.

The magic of style sheets is that they can become almost infinitely complicated. You can decide minute details like character spacing, color, font families, and other desktop publishing–type decisions, as shown in Figure 7.1. At the same time, however, not rendering these decisions is up to the individual user and browser, so that minimal information is lost, and the majority of users can view your information—even if they're not using the latest and greatest browser.

In this lesson, we're specifically talking about the Cascading Style Sheet (CSS) specification. Although other types of style sheet commands and syntax are possible, the major browser companies have chosen to support CSS for the time being.

New font families   Alignment

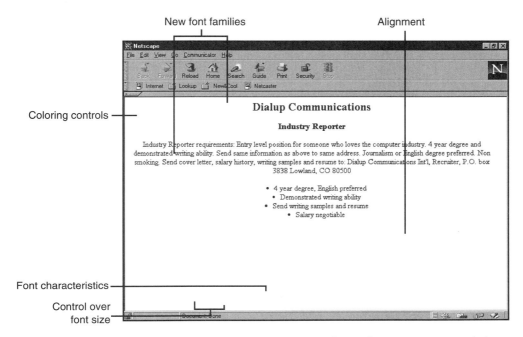

Coloring controls

Dialup Communications

Industry Reporter

Industry Reporter requirements: Entry level position for someone who loves the computer industry. 4 year degree and demonstrated writing ability. Send same information as above to same address. Journalism or English degree preferred. Non smoking. Send cover letter, salary history, writing samples and resume to: Dialup Communications Int'l, Recruiter, P.O. box 3838 Lowland, CO 80500

- 4 year degree, English preferred
- Demonstrated writing ability
- Send writing samples and resume
- Salary negotiable

Font characteristics

Control over
font size

Figure 7.1 Style sheets give amazing control over the appearance and placement of text—but only in the latest browsers.

Adding the *<STYLE>* Tag

The <STYLE> tag is the key to style sheets—it's where you'll define the behavior of your style commands. The <HEAD> section of your document is where you use the <STYLE> container to define some of the style elements you want to add to your Web page. The basic format is the following:

```
<HEAD>
<TITLE>Doc title</TITLE>
<STYLE TYPE="text/css">
HTML tag.class {special formatting}
...
<SPAN> {special formatting}
</STYLE>
</HEAD>
```

For your purposes, the TYPE attribute of the <STYLE> tag will always accept the MIME-type text/css. That stands for the Cascading Style Sheets standard for Web style, and it is basically just a standard that defines what sort of things you can do to text, images, and background on your Web page. It also determines what sort of special formatting codes you use within your <STYLE> definition—in this case, they're the codes that are recognized by most style-sheet–capable browsers.

Creating *CLASS*es

Nearly any HTML tag can be given a class, which creates a unique instance of this particular tag. If you want to create an italicized instance of the <H1> tag, for instance, you can create a new class called <H1>.italic. When that class is specified in the body portion of your document, the special formatting is used for that particular instance of the HTML tag.

Here's an example:

```
<HEAD>
<TITLE>My Styled Page</TITLE>
<STYLE TYPE="text/css">
  H1.italic { font-style: italic }
  P.red_caps { color: red; font-style: small-caps }
    .blue_Helv { font-family: Helvetica, sans-serif; color: blue }
</STYLE>
</HEAD>
```

Now, with these style definitions, you've created new classes of the familiar <H1> and <P> tags, named italic and red_caps, respectively. When you want these special instances to occur in your HTML document, use the CLASS attribute to the standard HTML tag. Therefore, the following creates the special cases for your HTML tags within the document itself:

```
<H1 CLASS="italic">This header is italicized</H1>
<P CLASS="red_caps">This text should be in red,
➥ and all small-caps.</P>
```

In the example, the class blue_Helv, which was defined with no particular element in mind, can be used with any element—the following works just fine:

```
<OL CLASS="blue_Helv">
    <LI> Item One
    <LI> Item Two
</OL>
<P CLASS="blue_Helv">The text, like the previous list, will
➥be blue Helvetica.</A>
```

TIP **Picking Names** Class names are completely of your choosing. Keep them short and descriptive and avoid spaces (use the underscore if necessary). Also avoid common HTML words and tag names, just for clarity.

A New Tag: <*SPAN*>

Notice that the original example offered another new tag, the <SPAN> tag. <SPAN> is basically a tag that enables you to create a special case for emphasizing certain text in your document. It works just like the <EM> tag, but browsers that don't recognize style sheets won't interpret the <SPAN> element in any way.

Consider this example. In the <HEAD> section, you define <SPAN>:

```
<STYLE TYPE="text/css">
  SPAN { font-style: small-caps }
</STYLE>
```

Now, in the body of your document, you can do the following:

```
<P><SPAN>Welcome to</SPAN> my home page on the Web. I'm
➥glad you could find the time to drop by and see what we've got
➥going today.</P>
```

In a style-sheet–capable browser, you see small caps used for an attractive, printed-style introduction to your paragraph. In older browsers, the text is unaffected.

Aligning Document Divisions

The style sheet standard also creates another tag, the <DIV> (division) tag, that allows you to assign attributes to a particular part of your document. <DIV> is a container tag that applies different styles to anything, including images, placed between the two tags. Ultimately, it gives the designer another level of organization for her Web page. If you think of a <DIV> as one level below the <BODY> tag, you're on the right track.

The <DIV> tag works like this:

```
<DIV CLASS="class_name" ALIGN="direction">
...HTML Markup...
</DIV>
```

Notice that the <DIV> tag can accept the same CLASS attribute that most other HTML tags can take when used with a style sheet. This allows you to create a division of your HTML pages that accepts particular style properties. In addition, the <DIV> tag can take the attribute ALIGN, which accepts LEFT, CENTER, RIGHT, or JUSTIFY.

TIP   **Don't <CENTER>**   Many browsers began accepting the <DIV> tag and ALIGN attribute early in the original HTML 3.0 draft. This is the most appropriate way to center a page or portion of the page. When possible, use this tag instead of the Netscape-specific <CENTER> tag.

Here's a look at the <DIV> tag in action:

```
<DIV ALIGN="CENTER">
<H2>Dialup Communications</H2>
<H3>Industry Reporter</H3>
<P>Industry Reporter requirements: Entry level position for
➡someone who
loves the computer industry. 4 year degree and demonstrated
➡writing
ability. Send same information as above to same address.
➡Journalism or
English degree preferred. Non smoking. Send cover letter,
➡salary history,
writing samples and resume to: Dialup Communications Int'l,
➡Recruiter,
P.O. box 3838 Lowland, CO 80500</P>
<UL>
<LI>4 year degree, English preferred
<LI>Demonstrated writing ability
<LI>Send writing samples and resume
<LI>Salary negotiable
</UL>
</DIV>
```

Because <DIV> has been supported for quite some time, you can view it in many different browsers—not just the very latest. The results are shown in Figure 7.2.

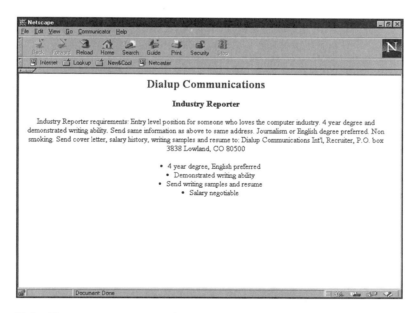

Figure 7.2 The <DIV> tag centers items in most Web browsers.

In this lesson, you learned the basic new tags of style sheets. In the next lesson, you'll learn to build new styles for your Web documents.

Adding Style Sheet Fonts and Colors

In this lesson, you learn to create style sheet elements and add them to your Web pages.

CSS Font Styles

Having seen how certain style elements can be defined for your Web page, you might be interested in learning all of the different style changes you can make to your documents. Unfortunately, this book simply isn't long enough!

The CSS style sheet definition is about 50 pages long—and it's full of possible style properties. That means things go much deeper than { color: red } in CSS. This lesson touches on some of the high points, but if you get very deep into style sheets, you'll want to consult **http://www.w3.org/pub/WWW/TR/WD-css1.html** for the latest CSS Level 1 developments and changes.

Table 8.1 offers some of the font-related CSS styles and shows how they can be used.

Table 8.1 CCS-Defined Style Properties

Property	Value	Example(s)
font-family	name of font	Helvetica, Serif, Symbol
font-size	number/percentage	12pt, +1, 120%
font-weight	number/strength	+1, light, medium, extra bold
font-style	name of style	italic, normal

Property	Value	Example(s)
font	combination of above	12pt Serif medium small caps
color	word / hex number	red, green, blue, FF00FF

Here's a quick rundown of all these style sheet properties:

The font-family property allows you to choose the name of the font that you'd like text to appear in. With any font property, you probably want to be as generic with font names (like Helvetica or Courier) as possible, because the user's browser will have to decide what that font name's closest counterpart is on the user's system. In fact, font-family allows you to specify alternative font names for different computer systems, like:

```
<STYLE TYPE="text/css">
  P.standard { font-family: Helvetica, Arial, sans-serif }
</STYLE>
```

TIP **Font Names** Font family names with spaces should be put in quotes, like: "Century Schoolbook."

The other font-related properties—font-size, font-weight and font-style—are fairly self-explanatory. Font size can be a percentage, point size, or word size, such as large or smaller. Font weight refers to the boldness of the font, with possible values like bolder, lighter, or numerical values from 100–900. Font style values determine the italic nature of the font. Possible values are italic, oblique, and normal.

The font property is basically a shorthand reference for the four that appear above it in the table. You can simply use any of the related values for font, effectively describing its entire appearance in one tag.

The possible values for color include black, red, white, green, blue, yellow, brown, gray, orange, and purple. You can also add "light" or "dark" to any of these colors. Also, remember that you're acting on a particular tag (most of the time) and that color most often refers to text color. It can be used with any text-related tag, such as <BLOCKQUOTE>, as in the following example:

```
<STYLE TYPE="text/css">
  BLOCKQUOTE.helv_red { font-family: helvetica; color: red }
</STYLE>
```

TIP   **Style Lists**   Remember that styles are not separated by commas if they are all supposed to be applied. Only lists of alternatives (like `{font-family: Helvetica, Arial, sans-serif}`) require commas.

And, you'd call it just like any other CLASS of an HTML tag:

```
<BLOCKQUOTE CLASS="helv_red">Blockquote class</BLOCKQUOTE>
```

Adding Styles to Pages

For the most part, a style sheet should be secondary to the communicative nature of your text and graphics. Ideally, this is a page that would work for both HTML 2.0 users and users with style-sheet–capable browsers. Here's a small style sheet, added to an HTML page.

Listing 8.1 is a sample of how style sheets work in a typical Web page.

Listing 8.1   Adding Font Styles

```
<HTML>
<HEAD>
<TITLE>Style Sheet Example</TITLE>
<STYLE TYPE="text/css">
 BODY.back {background: white}
 H2.ital {font-style: italic}
 H3 {text-align: center}
 P.basic {color: blue}
 SPAN {font: 14pt sans-serif; color: blue}
</STYLE>
</HEAD>
<BODY CLASS="back">
<h2 CLASS="ital">Today's Tips...</h2>
<P CLASS="basic">
<SPAN>A hint to new free-lancers:</SPAN> Assume everyone you deal
➥with is very busy. Don't ask for extra work from folks, whether
➥that's unnecessary meetings, too many phone calls or anything
➥written. In your enthuasiasm for your new career, it could be easy
➥to forget that others are often just caught up in the day-to-day
➥stress of getting everything done. </P>
<P>
Writing is a solitary business -- and is most efficiently done that
➥way, armed with a good computer, fax capability and email. And, as
➥a freelancer, the burden is on you to gauge the needs of different
```

```
➥people and deal with them accordingly. Quickly get a sense of
➥whether someone likes to use the phone or have meetings. I, for
➥instance, keep those things at an absolute minimum. I find they're
➥usually time-wasters. Many other people work the same way. </P>
<HR>
<H3 >Top Story: Freelance Contract Negotiation...</H3>
<P CLASS="basic">
<SPAN>Once an editor</SPAN> has expressed an interest in your work,
➥you're only halfway there. Now, it's time to discuss your contract.
➥No professional editor will be put off by this. You are a
➥professional and should be treated as such...
</P>
</BODY>
</HTML>
```

See Figure 8.1 to see these style changes in Internet Explorer.

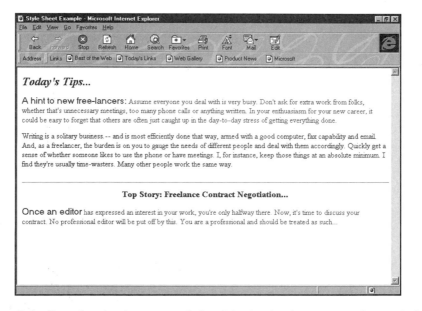

Figure 8.1 Even the simple commands for style sheets give you amazing control.

Style Overrides

You may have noticed that you have to create a class for every instance of a particular style that you want added to your page—even if you only wanted to use that style once. But that's not completely necessary.

It's possible and acceptable to create something called an *override*—a one-time implementation of a style for a particular purpose. In fact, your whole page could be overrides, if you wanted, but that might be a little tedious.

With a <STYLE> tag defined in the head of your document, you can not only use the currently defined classes for creating styles, but you can also use overrides to change the style of nearly any HTML tag. How does this work? It's similar to defining style classes, but you instead use the STYLE attribute with any legal HTML tag. The following is an example:

```
The following text is <EM STYLE="color: blue">blue and emphasized</
➡EM>.
```

You can see where the flexibility of style sheets is almost getting out of control. Although you can call these overrides for your current style sheet, the truth is that you can use these STYLE-attributed HTML tags anytime that you want to— as long as you've defined the text/css type through a <STYLE> tag in the head of your document.

TIP   **Empty Style**   If you prefer to generate your style elements on-the-fly, you can define an empty <STYLE> tag that does little more than define the TYPE as text/css. Then, use the STYLE attribute to override all the way through your document.

In this lesson, you learned how to add text styles to your Web pages. In the next lesson, you'll learn some positioning and alignment styles, and you'll learn to use one style sheet for an entire Web site.

Advanced Style Sheets

In this lesson, you learn style sheet properties for placing and aligning text, and you learn to link pages so the same style sheet can be used throughout your Web site.

Changing Text Styles

There are a number of styles in the CSS definition that allow you to decide how HTML text will be positioned and aligned on the page. These styles can be used with nearly any HTML tag, giving you control over how text and inline images appear in your document. Table 9.1 shows many of these text styles.

Table 9.1   CCS Text-Style Properties

Property	Value	Example(s)
word-spacing	number+units	1pt, 4em, 1in
letter-spacing	number+units	3pt, 0.1em, +1
text-decoration	word	underline, line through, box, blink
vertical-align	word/percentage	baseline, sup, sub, top, middle, 50%
text-align	word	left, right, center, justify
text-indent	number/percentage	1in, 5%, 3em

The properties word-spacing and letter-spacing accept *length* values, which include a number and the units of length. An example of this would be extra point-size spacing, like:

```
P.wide_text {letter-spacing: 2pt}
```

Length   In the CSS style sheet definition, length has a very specific meaning. A valid length includes a number and the measurement unit. The number can be either positive or negative; there should be no space between the number and the units. Unit measurements you can use include: px (pixels), in (inches), mm (millimeters), cm (centimeters), pt (points), em (the height of the current font), ex (the height of the current font's letter "x").

Text-decoration is used to change the appearance of text in your document, and it includes the values listed in Table 9.1. The value normal is also possible.

The properties vertical-align and text-align give Web designers much-desired control over centering and justifying text in a document. Vertical alignment is best used with elements that appear inside another element. For instance, the style definition:

```
EM.super {vertical-align: super}
```

creates a class of the <EM> tag that can be used as a superscript. So, adding that class within another paragraph creates text that is placed as a subscript compared to the surrounding text, like:

```
<P>The basic element of life is love. <EM CLASS="super">Richards, Pg.
➥11</E>.</P>
```

Background Properties

Style sheets can be used to give unprecedented control over what appears in the background of your Web page. Not only can you specify a color or an image for the background, you can also decide how the image will be repeated, whether it acts like a "watermark" and other characteristics.

Although background properties are popularly applied to the <BODY> tag (so that they affect the entire document), background properties can actually be assigned to nearly any HTML element.

Table 9.2 shows you the background properties.

Table 9.2 CCS Background Properties

Property	Value	Example(s)
background-color	name/hex number	white, #0000FF
background-image	url( )	url(image.gif), url(http://www.myoom. net/bgnd.jpg)
background-repeat	word	repeat, repeat-x, repeat y, no-repeat
background-attachment	word	scroll, fixed
background-position	direction/ percentage	top, left center, 20% 65%
background	all above	white url(image.gif) repeat-x fixed

The following describes each of the background properties:

background-color   Used to set the background color. Accepts a color name or three two-digit hexadecimal codes for red, green, and blue.

background-image   Accepts the URL to an image file.

background-repeat   This property uses one of four codes shown in Table 9.2 to determine how a background image will be repeated to cover the browser window. repeat-x sets it to repeat horizontally; repeat-y sets it to repeat only vertically.

background-attachment   Determines whether or not the background image will scroll along with the rest of the Web document.

background-position   Accepts direction names or percentages to determine the position of the top-left corner of the background image.

While all of these background properties are available in the CSS style sheet standard, you probably won't use most of them. Instead, you can use the background property as a shorthand reference to all (or any) of the other properties, like:

```
<HEAD>
<TITLE>Background Page</TITLE>
<STYLE TYPE="text/css">
  BODY.back { background: URL(http://www.bigcorp.com/back.gif)
➥white repeat-x fixed }
</STYLE>
<HEAD>
<BODY CLASS="back">
```

Alignment and Appearance

Every HTML element you use, in some way or another, ends up creating a "box" on the screen. The <P> container, for instance, creates a box of text that's usually a few lines long and a screen in length. Other tags, like the <H1> tag or the <BLOCKQUOTE> tag, are also creating boxes, even if, in some cases, the box is only one line of text tall.

The CSS style sheet definition creates a number of new properties specifically designed to help you control the appearance of those boxes. Table 9.3 shows you the box properties.

Table 9.3 CCS Box Properties

Property	Value	Example(s)
margin	length/percentage	1in, 5% 10%, 12pt 10pt 12pt 10pt
padding	length/percentage	1in, 5% 10%
border	width/style/color	medium dashed red, 2in grooved, blue
width	length/percentage	.5in, 10%
height	length/percentage	10em, 12pt
float	direction	left, right, none
clear	direction	none, left, right, both

margin and padding work in very similar ways, with the number of values included in the definition determining which sides of the page are being affected:

- A single value, like {margin: 5pt}, means that margin is applied to the top, right, bottom, and left sides of the page.
- Two values, like {padding: .5in, .4in}, means the initial value is applied to the top and bottom, while the second value applies to the right and left.
- Three values, like {padding: .5in, .4in, .3in}, means the first number applies to the top, the second to the right and left, and the third to the bottom.
- Four values, like {margin: 5em, 4em, 6em, 9em}, means the numbers apply to the top, right, bottom and left, respectively.

The difference between the two properties is that margin applies extra space outside the borders of the current element, while padding applies spaces between the edges of the element's box and the text it encloses.

The border property is a shortcut property like background. In border's case, it can accept values for the width, style, and color of the border of a particular element. The width can be thin, medium, thick, or a length; the color can be any color name or set of hexadecimal pairs; and the style values include: none, dotted, dashed, solid, double, groove, ridge, inset, outset. For example:

```
p.newborder {border: red dashed 20px}
```

The width and height elements can be used to specify the width or height of any box element, using either a length or percentage. (The value auto can also be used in individual cases to override a setting and change the width and height to normal.)

The float property can be used to allow text to flow around an element. This works the same way that ALIGN=LEFT and ALIGN=RIGHT does for images, except that the float property works for any element:

```
H3.pull_quote {float: left}
```

And, finally, the clear property can be used to determine whether or not an element will allow other elements to float to one side of it (for example, whether or not it will wrap around other elements). If clear has a value of left, then the element is moved below any floating element to its left; if the value is right, the element is moved below any images floating to the right. For instance, with the style definitions:

```
<HEAD>
<TITLE>Background Page</TITLE>
<STYLE TYPE="text/css">
  IMG.left {float: left}
  H3.no_wrap {clear: left}
</STYLE>
<HEAD>
```

The following would look like Figure 9.1 in a browser:

```
<IMG CLASS="left" SRC="images/number_one.gif">
<BLOCKQUOTE>
<H3 CLASS="no_wrap">Top Story: Freelance Contract Negotiation...</H3>
<B><I>Once an editor</I></B> has expressed an interest in
➥your work, you're only halfway there. Now, it's time to discuss
```

your contract. No professional editor will be put off by this. You
are a professional and should be treated as such...

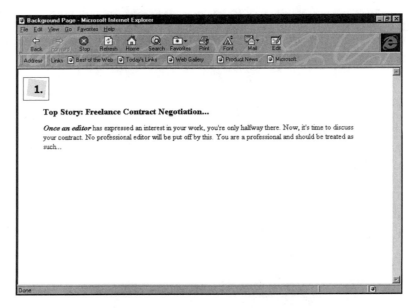

Figure 9.1 Use the clear property to avoid wrapping around a floating object.

Styles for Entire Sites

Once you've designed a comprehensive style sheet that you'd like to use with
many of your pages, you don't necessarily have to cut and paste the <STYLE>
container into the head of all your documents. Instead, you just use the special
<LINK> tag to link any new pages to the page that contains the <STYLE> container.

Using the REL attribute for the <LINK> tag, you're essentially adding the <STYLE>
elements from the linked page to the current page. Predefined style classes can
then be used in the current HTML markup.

This version of the <LINK> tag works like this:

```
<LINK TTTLE="link_doc_title" REL=stylesheet HREF="URL" TYPE="text/
➥css">
```

The TYPE can accept any style sheet type you might be interested in using—we're
sticking with CSS. The TITLE should be the same as the remote page's title (the

page with the <STYLE> stuff in it) and the HREF URL needs to be an URL to that same document. An example might be:

```
<LINK TITLE="MY STYLE" REL=stylesheet HREF="style.html" TYPE="text/
➥css">
```

You can even create a special page that holds only the style sheet, then <LINK> to that page. Then, whenever you want to change the appearance of certain elements, you can do it globally, throughout your site, regardless of the number of pages you've created.

In this lesson, you learned some advanced style sheet properties and how to link style sheets between Web pages. In the next lesson, you'll learn special Microsoft-only HTML extensions.

Microsoft HTML Extensions

In this lesson, you learn special HTML elements that Microsoft supports, even though they aren't part of the HTML standard.

HTML Extensions

The gap between official HTML and browser-specific HTML continues to widen. Netscape Navigator remains the champion of nonstandard HTML, but others, specifically Microsoft, have joined the fray. Internet Explorer, Microsoft's entry into the browser game, offers many HTML-like additions of its own—and things are only getting crazier over time.

As soon as you see some of the great pages designed for Netscape and Internet Explorer, you'll want to incorporate the new features into your own site. Before you do, though, keep a few things in mind. They're important if you're hoping to satisfy the largest possible number of readers:

- **Warn your users that you are using nonstandard tags**.   Both Microsoft and Netscape will let you add special buttons to your site that say "Download IE 4.0" or "Communicator Now!" Both companies also show you the HTML to use so that your visitors can click those icons and be transported directly to the browsers' download sites.

- **Consider creating alternate pages**.   It's not overwhelmingly difficult to create two versions of your site: an HTML 2.0-compliant site and a site with Netscape, IE, or HTML 3.2 additions. You can also create a "front door" that allows users to choose which they would prefer to view.

TIP **Dual-Purpose** You might want to make your HTML 2.0 site a low-graphics site, too, so that lower bandwidth users (those with slow modems) can choose that one over your highly graphical Netscape- or IE-only site.

- **Use HTML 3.2 whenever reasonable.** It's difficult to keep up with the HTML 3.2 standard, which is why many people just keep listening to Netscape. But, when you have the opportunity use the standard tags. (For example, use style sheets for creating strikeout text versus using the <STRIKE> tag.)
- **Make sure you don't lose information.** If you do use browser tags, make sure you're not using them in a way that means your other users are missing out on something important. Both Netscape and Microsoft are guilty of this—only IE-compatible users can see text scrolling across the screen using the <MARQUEE> tags, for instance.

Internet Explorer Add-Ons

The <BGSOUND> tag tells Internet Explorer to play an audio file when the page opens. You don't want to use a huge file, since that could take quite a while to download, but you can get people's attention with a sound or music snippet, and you can LOOP the file (play it repeatedly) as often as you want. You can use WAV, AU, or MIDI files for this purpose.

To include a background sound, you need the following HTML:

```
BGSOUND SRC="mozart.mid" LOOP=8>
```

Moving Marquee Text

Internet Explorer tries to make your pages move in several ways, one of which is the scrolling marquee. This is nothing more than a string of text that scrolls by itself across the screen, but the effect is much stronger than, say, the <BLINK> command of earlier HTML. You can draw attention to a particular sentence or phrase, or, of course, you can overdo the thing entirely and end up with a jumble of moving lines of text.

To create a scrolling marquee, enclose the text inside the <MARQUEE></MARQUEE> container. For example, the following code causes the string of text "Watch me move!" to move from the right border of the page to the left border and then start over again when it's finished.

```
<MARQUEE>Watch me move!</MARQUEE>
```

Real-Time Videos

Internet Explorer has the built-in capability to play video files in the AVI format (the standard Microsoft Windows format) using a special extension to the <IMG> tag.

The code for incorporating an AVI video file is as follows:

```
<IMG DYNSRC="videofile.avi">
```

Notice that this is similar to HTML's calling of graphics files, <IMG SRC>. DYNSRC means *dynamic source* and is used instead. (The source is dynamic—meaning an AVI movie—instead of static, like a regular GIF or JPEG image.) In practice, though, you should offer both possibilities so that readers without Internet Explorer will see something as well.

TIP   **Better Options**   Most of the time, you should use the <EMBED>, <OBJECT> or similar tags (discussed in Part II, Lesson 6) instead of the DYNSYC attribute. That way, users of non-Microsoft browsers can view your movies, too.

This would be coded as follows:

```
<IMG DYNSRC="videofile.avi" SRC="graphicfile.gif">
```

Internet Explorer will play the AVI file, while other browsers will display the GIF file.

There aren't many HTML attributes for the **DYNSRC** element, but the options you do have are important. First, you can specify when the AVI file starts playing. FILEOPEN tells it to begin as soon as the page is retrieved; MOUSEOVER tells it to start playing when the reader moves the cursor over the video image.

The other major option lets you place video controls at the bottom of the video image to let the reader take charge of what displays. The default is to have no controls; to include them, you must use the CONTROLS element:

```
<IMG DYNSRC="videofile.avi" CONTROLS>
```

Background Watermarks

Another HTML addition within Internet Explorer is the watermark background. These are similar to other background graphics, except that they don't scroll when your readers use the scroll bar.

The code for watermark backgrounds is quite simple: Add the BGPROPERTIES=FIXED element to the usual <BODY BACKGROUND> tag.

```
<BODY BACKGROUND="mypattern.gif" BGPROPERTIES=FIXED>
```

 TIP   **Other Methods**   This can also be accomplished using style sheets, which is generally a better idea than using proprietary tags, since you'll reach more users.

In this lesson, you learned Microsoft's HTML extensions. In the next lesson, you'll see the extensions that Netscape has created.

Netscape HTML Extensions

In this lesson, you learn the HTML extensions that Netscape has added to the mix.

Netscape's Additions

In Part I, Lesson 15, you saw how to use Table tags to lay out a document in such a way that the cells could be used to hold graphics, text, and various types of multimedia—making things look more like a newspaper or newsletter.

Netscape goes that scenario one better by offering the <MULTICOL> tag. Using this tag, you can easily add multiple columns to your page, as shown in Figure 11.1. Here's an example:

```
<MULTICOL COLS=3 GUTTER=15 WIDTH=600>
text and graphics for entire page
</MULTICOL>
```

<MULTICOL> is a container tag with three major attributes: COLS, GUTTER, and WIDTH:

- **COLS** is required. It tells Netscape how many columns to create.
- **GUTTER** determines how many pixels of space appear between columns. The default value is 10.
- **WIDTH** determines the overall width of your entire multi-column format, in pixels. If no WIDTH is used, the columns will stretch (or squeeze) to fill the available screen space.

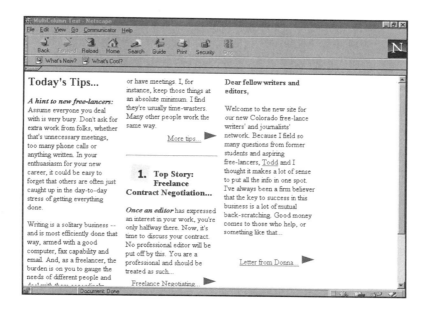

Figure 11.1 With a single container tag, it's possible to have text and graphics flow nicely along in columns.

Maximum Width If you decide to use WIDTH, you probably shouldn't go over about 600 pixels, in order for the entire layout to fit on a typical VGA (640x480) screen. If you do go over that number, you'll be forcing some of your readers to scroll the screen horizontally in order to read your text.

CAUTION

Adding Blank Space

A new Netscape tag called <SPACER> allows you to create different types of white space in your document, with more precise control. The key to <SPACER> is the attribute TYPE. It allows you to do three very different things with the tag, based on the value you give the TYPE attribute:

- **horizontal** Inserts horizontal space between words. Another attribute, SIZE, determines how much space.

- **vertical** Inserts vertical space between lines. Just like <P>, a vertical spacer automatically ends the current line of text, and then the vertical space is added before the beginning of the next line. The height of the space is determined by SIZE.

- **block** Netscape describes this one as "behaving almost exactly like an invisible image." This type of spacer focuses on WIDTH, HEIGHT, and ALIGN attributes (SIZE is ignored). The attributes work just like they would for the <IMG> tag.

Here are examples of the horizontal and vertical types:

```
This line has text here<SPACER TYPE-horizontal SIZE=50>and
text over here.<P>
This line ends now<SPACER TYPE=vertical SIZE=50>And another
line begins down here.<P>
```

The third type, block, would probably be most effective aligned to the left or right margins, with text flowing around it. An example would be:

```
<SPACER TYPE=block HEIGHT=50 WIDTH=30 ALIGN=LEFT>
```

Figure 11.2 shows the different types of <SPACER> in action.

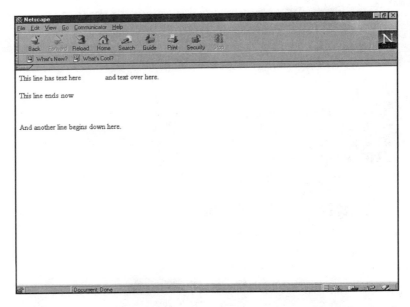

Figure 11.2 The <SPACER> tag gives you considerable control over the spacing in your Web document.

Strikeout Text

Aside from supporting the <STRIKE> tag for "strikeout" text, Netscape also supports the <S> tag, while maintaining support for the <STRIKE> tag as backward compatibility. Both are container tags, and both create strikeout text.

```
<STRIKE>This text has been struck!</STRIKE>
<S>This text has been s'ed</S>
```

Blinking Text

<BLINK> is also a container. As a tag, it's designed to make text appear in a blinking field, by forcing a cursor-style reverse field to blink on and off on top of words contained by this tag. The following is an example:

```
<BLINK>Sale Item!</BLINK>
```

Breaking Text

The <NOBR> tag prevents text from wrapping when it meets with the end of the browser screen. This is useful in situations where your user might be confused by a line wrap. (It is also supported in Internet Explorer.) This is a container tag that accepts text and markup between its tags. Its format is as follows:

```
<NOBR>test and markup</NOBR>
```

Now, this doesn't necessarily mean that users will need to scroll their browser window in order to see the text—in many cases, they just need to expand the browser window. (Or, make it considerably smaller to force the entire length of <NOBR> text to the next line.) This might be useful for addresses, programming code, a line of numbers, or similar text. The following is an example:

```
<NOBR>1234 Main Street * St. Louis, MO * 29000</NOBR>
```

The <WBR> tag is used in conjunction with the <NOBR> container to tell the browser *exactly* where you want a line break to occur, if one is necessary. It can also be used outside of the confines of the <NOBR> tag to let Netscape know where it's okay to break up a particularly long word. (Internet Explorer supports <WBR>, too.)

<WBR> doesn't usurp the responsibilities of
—it's only a suggestion. If Netscape needs to break a line of text (or a particularly long word), it will do so. If it doesn't need to break at the <WBR>, it won't. An example would be:

```
<P>When I move this Web site the new address will be
➥http://www.mycom.net<WBR>/main/tstauf/public/index.html.</P>
```

Because Netscape Navigator would interpret that address as one word, it allows you to suggest where it should be broken if the address would otherwise overlap the browser window.

TIP   No <PRE> Substitute   The <WBR> tag is only a recommendation. If the browser needs to break a line, it will do so at the <WBR> tag. For lines that are always forced to break where you want, the <PRE> tag is still your best bet (for example, if you include lines of poetry). The <BR> tag might work well, too, if you're not trying to line things up visually.

In this lesson, you learned the extensions to HTML that Netscape has created. In the next lesson, you'll learn how to design pages for other types of Web browsers.

Designing for
Internet Devices

In this lesson, you learn how to design Web pages for special devices such as WebTV.

Web Devices

While Netscape and Internet Explorer definitely make up the lion's share of the Web browsing market, more and more folks are finding a new way to get on the Web—one that doesn't involve a computer at all. As handheld computers become more powerful, they tend to be working their way onto the Internet, so that users not only get the opportunity to send e-mail, but they can also surf the Web.

Currently, one of the more popular ways of getting on the Internet without a desktop computer is WebTV, a box that hooks up to a standard TV set and a phone line in order to make Web surfing possible without a PC. The boxes include enough computing power to view the Web and translate it to a TV picture; WebTV also includes a modem and built-in software for displaying Web pages, playing sounds, and even playing some Java programs.

The problem is, since WebTV displays pages on a TV screen, a Web page only looks good on a WebTV system if it takes certain hints and tips into consideration.

WebTV Page Design

The WebTV people publish their own recommendations for how sites should be designed for display on a WebTV terminal; you can find these on the Web at **http://webtv.net/primetime/**. Their documentation is rather extensive (currently about 110 pages in Adobe portable document format), but the basics can be broken down fairly easily. In order to have a page that displays well on a WebTV system:

Put your most important text on the first screen.   TV-based Web viewers won't always be willing or able to scroll a long page of text, so design shorter screens for your site.

Reduce the number of items on your page.   TV viewers don't expect to see tons of text and links on the screen—instead they need just a few, clear choices or options.

Avoid using tags to manually break lines.   Using the <BR> tag at the end of every line of text may make a page look good on a computer, but it can make pages look very odd on WebTV.

Limit your use of form elements.   New computer users and those trying to use the WebTV interface may be overwhelmed by long HTML forms with many options, text boxes, and menus.

Don't use full red or full white.   If you need to use red or white, off-red and off-white colors work best (up to about 90% of full, bright white and red). WebTV also recommends using a charcoal background (#191919) for pages.

Avoid small text in HTML or in your images.   If you create images that include text, the text needs to be at least as large as the base font in your document. At the same time, WebTV recommends that you don't use the <FONT SIZE=> tag to make your text smaller.

Avoid large images.   Images that are too large can force WebTV users to scroll their set (the WebTV viewing area is about 540 pixels wide). Also, fine detail in images is often lost over WebTV. You can make images load faster by including HEIGHT and WIDTH information in the <IMG> tag.

 TIP   **From WebTV's Documentation**   If you don't have a WebTV Internet terminal, you can test your design for WebTV by increasing the size of your browser's display font to 18 points and narrowing the browser window to about 540 pixels (slightly narrower than a 640 × 480—standard VGA—screen).

Special WebTV Tags

Like the Netscape and Internet Explorer browsers, the WebTV software features a few of its own tags for special uses. Most of these tags are designed so that you can add WebTV-style content to your own pages, including special elements that give WebTV its unique look-and-feel.

The first tag, <SIDEBAR>, is a container tag that you can use to create a non-scrolling portion of the screen. In this sidebar (which always appears on the left side of a WebTV browser window), you can put your own codes for a table of contents, instructions, or other similar elements. Figure 12.1 shows a sample sidebar in a WebTV screen shot. The <SIDEBAR> tag follows the format:

```
<SIDEBAR>
Text and links for sidebar
</SIDEBAR>
```

WebTV Only The <SIDEBAR> tags are ignored by other browsers, which means whatever HTML and text you put in the sidebar is still displayed—just not in a sidebar. WebTV recommends that you consider creating two different pages (one for regular browsers, one for WebTV) if you plan to use the sidebar tags extensively.

CAUTION

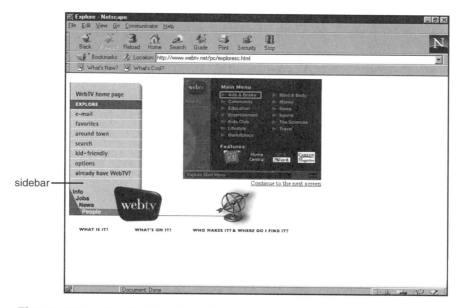

Figure 12.1 The WebTV sidebar is a convenient place to put links and controls for your WebTV viewer.

The WebTV browser also recognizes two new attributes to the <BODY> tag: CREDITS and INSTRUCTIONS. Both of these attributes accept an URL to Web pages that include the desired information. For example:

```
<BODY CREDITS="about_us.html">
```

For CREDITS. the page can contain information about the author or company behind the page; for INSTRUCTIONS, you can include the URL to a Web page with hints and tips on navigating your site.

WebTV will preload pages that use the REL="next" attribute for the <LINK> tag. Although this tag is not exclusively a WebTV tag (it's part of the HTML 3.2 specification), this is a significant use of the tag. Pages that are marked as the "next" page in a sequence will be loaded in the background by WebTV. This means the page appears much more quickly when the user decides to jump to it.

Include the <LINK> tag in the head of your document, along with the REL="next" and HREF attributes, like:

```
<HEAD>
<LINK REL="next" HREF="http://www.mynet.com/todd/page2.html">
<TITLE>Page One</TITLE>
</HEAD>
```

Like any HREF attribute, either a complete URL or a relative URL (such as **page2.html**) is acceptable.

In this lesson, you learned the special techniques and codes recommended for creating attractive WebTV-oriented Web pages.

Scripting

Overview of Scripting and Programming

In this lesson, you learn the differences between JavaScript, VBScript, and Java.

Java versus JavaScript

Java and JavaScript are not the same and they are not interchangeable, even though this is a common mistake. Java is a full-fledged programming language in the spirit of C++. Designed for the more advanced programmer, its strength is the ability to run in a *virtual machine* that can be created by a Web browser.

Virtual Machine This concept is the reason for all the hype surrounding Java. The idea is that every computer in the world can pretend to be a less sophisticated "Java-standard" computer. Usually a computer is defined by the sort of computer components it uses. For instance, Intel-brand processors usually run the Windows operating system—you can't run the current Mac OS on an Intel computer. But Java creates a standard computer completely in software. This software program (which mimics all the functions of a typical computer) is the "virtual" machine. Instead of programming specifically for Windows or the Mac OS, then, programmers simply write the program for the virtual machine. Because Web browsers can create this machine, it's possible to run a Java program from within the Web browser, making sites more interactive and entertaining.

Java, then, is similar to the programming languages used to build full-fledged applications that can be run on PCs, Macs, and UNIX machines. It's well-suited for the Internet, but not necessarily exclusive to the Web.

JavaScript Defined

JavaScript, on the other hand, is a less complex scripting language similar to AppleScript, Visual Basic Scripting (VBScript), and other scripting languages. Although JavaScript is similar in some surface ways to Java, it doesn't require you to worry as much about some of the program's underlying structure. It's a bit limited in that way, but still very useful.

TIP **JavaScript or JScript?** Microsoft calls its implementation of JavaScript *JScript*, even though they are basically the same.

Here's another way to think about it: Java applets almost always require a special little window on the Web page to run because they are complete applications. JavaScript, on the other hand, is actually part of your HTML code. It doesn't create any special windows—it just makes your Web pages a little more dynamic (see Figure 1.1).

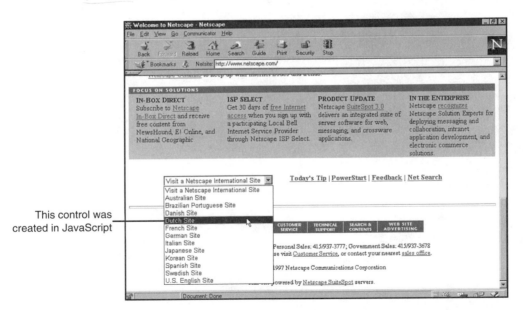

This control was created in JavaScript

Figure 1.1 There usually aren't many hints as to whether a page is using JavaScript. In this case, Netscape uses JavaScript (instead of a CGI script) to load new pages with this pop-up menu.

JavaScript isn't really an extension of HTML, although it works directly with HTML from within Web documents. It allows pages to be more dynamic and interesting, as well as giving you more control over what your users see and do. In fact, JavaScript is at the heart of what Netscape calls Dynamic HTML.

TIP **Dynamic HTML** Dynamic HTML is introduced in Part V, Lesson 1 and discussed throughout that entire Part of this book.

So, why do they have similar names? Aside from the confusion that it throws novice computer users into, there is a reason for the similar names—JavaScript uses a fairly Java-like syntax. Of course, that's not really saying much, since Java is rather like C++ and C++ is based on C. In essence, JavaScript is easy to pick up for anyone who's ever programmed in one of these strains of modern object-oriented programming languages.

What About Other Scripting Languages?

JavaScript is easily the most popular Web scripting language, which isn't terribly surprising considering it was both first to market and created by Netscape. JavaScript is even being considered for inclusion in aspects of the HTML 4.0 standard, so you can rest assured that the Web world is serious about JavaScript, and more browsers will support it in the future.

Support for JavaScript Only the 3.0 and later versions of Netscape and Microsoft browsers support JavaScript (some others, like WebTV, may support JavaScript by the time you read this). If you decide to create documents that incorporate JavaScript, be aware that only a few of the latest browsers can interpret it.

CAUTION

However, VBScript is running an important second place in the Web scripting world, and Internet Explorer is also playing a part in shaping Web browsing. VBScript has two things going for it: It's the basic scripting language recommended for ActiveX controls, and it's very much like Visual Basic, the popular Windows programming language. While both Java and JavaScript are platform-neutral, VBScript and ActiveX make a very Windows-centric play for control of the Internet.

The following lessons focus more on JavaScript than on VBScript, if only because JavaScript is the more widely accepted, is already cross-platform, and uses a slightly more approachable syntax. VBScript proponents will often already be proficient with Visual Basic, and hence won't gain as much from instruction.

Part IV will look at VBScript in some detail, however, because it's important to Microsoft's implementation of Dynamic HTML, and becoming more and more a part of the everyday Web.

What Is a Script?

Before moving on to other lessons, it's important to discuss two basic concepts in Web scripting. These define what a script is and what it does. The first concept is the *function*; the second is *event handling*.

A script within an HTML document will generally have two parts. The <HEAD> of your document will have a special script container that includes definitions for all of the functions that your script will use. A function is just that—it's a bit of code designed to do something. A function is usually designed to receive a value of some kind, do a bit of math or other processing, then return a new value.

 TIP   **Function Definitions**   Actually, functions can be defined anywhere in your document, although the head is the generally accepted norm.

Function *calls*, found within the body of your document, send and receive those values. These bits of code are simply designed to carry out the task of sending and receiving values—in general, function calls do very little processing on their own.

There wouldn't really be much point in having the functions separated from the function calls if the calls always went in a particular order. The whole point of having functions separated out is so that they can be reused or used out of order.

So, enter event handling. The reasoning behind event handling is simple—wait until the user does something, then react to it. If a particular button is clicked, then a value is sent to one of your functions. If he enters a value in an HTML form and hits the Tab key, send that value to another function…and so on. Event handling is the key use of JavaScript in Web pages, as we'll see in upcoming lessons.

While programs in the past were procedural—that is, they required humans to think like computers, doing all your data entry in a predetermined order—this new system of event handling works more like a shopping mall. If you have a particular problem you want to address, you simply head to the store that can help you out. When you're done, you head back to the middle of the mall, then work your way to some other store that interests you.

In programming, a function is like one of those stores. When a particular piece of information needs to be retrieved from the user, or if a certain calculation needs to be performed, a function is called on to solve that problem. But, functions are only invoked when the user does something that the script needs to react to. That's why it's called event handling.

In this lesson, you learned the basics of scripting and the difference between programming and scripting languages. In the next lesson, you'll learn the basics of VBScript.

VBScript Basics

In this lesson, you learn what VBScript is, how it works, and why you might want to use it.

Why Use VBScript?

VBScript is Microsoft's own answer to other scripting languages on the Web, including the popular and formidable JavaScript from Netscape. Both offer similar functionality and purpose, even going so far as to duplicate their abilities and create very similar-looking interfaces using somewhat different coding methods. It might seem on the surface that there isn't much point in using VBScript, especially since Microsoft also offers an implementation of JavaScript (called "JScript" by Microsoft) that you can use with Internet Explorer.

But, there are some good reasons to use VBScript:

You already know Visual Basic or Visual Basic Scripting. Microsoft's popular Visual Basic programming language is how many, many people get involved in programming. VBScript is a subset of Visual Basic, making it very easy for those programmers to learn. If you prefer a minimum of trouble when trying to script for the Web, you'll probably go with the familiar VBScript.

You want to work with ActiveX. Although Microsoft is beginning to develop hooks for JavaScript and other scripting languages to access ActiveX components, VBScript is overwhelmingly the choice of Microsoft—and most ActiveX proponents. The tutorials, help files, documentation, tools, and components themselves tend to assume you're using VBScript.

You plan to implement Microsoft's vision of dynamic HTML. Dynamic HTML, in its infancy, is a point of contention between Netscape and Microsoft. Microsoft's vision includes the use of slightly more proprietary tools while offering more freedom to access data. If you decide that Microsoft is the leader in Dynamic HTML, you'll probably need to learn some VBScript.

You want to stick with Microsoft's tools. Some users prefer the idea of using tools and concepts that come from one vendor, and Microsoft is overwhelmingly that vendor. If it's your opinion that more can be accomplished using only Microsoft tools and technologies, then VBScript should be your choice for Web scripting.

VBScript is generally used to either dynamically respond to user input on the page (initiating a script when a button or image is clicked, for instance) or to respond to some action taken by an ActiveX component. Since each ActiveX component creates its own event handlers and actions, it's probably easiest to use a tool like the ActiveX Control Pad to add those parts of your script. But, other VBScripts can be added directly from a text editor.

TERM

ActiveX Component Small, sophisticated programs somewhat akin to Java applets. Generally designed to perform one basic task, ActiveX components have been created for doing anything from accepting a simple text box entry to displaying an arcade-like game on the Web. One advantage with VBScript is the fact that it can be used in conjunction with ActiveX components to receive and process data from users.

Adding VBScripts to Pages

The <SCRIPT> tag is used to add scripting elements to your pages, regardless of the scripting language or browser that you plan to write for. Within those tags you'll add all of the scripting commands, including those that react to user input, those that process data, and those that respond using dialog boxes, HTML, text, or some other element. With the exception of a few HTML tags that accept scripting language within them, all VBScript commands will appear between the <SCRIPT> tags.

Nearly all VBScript-enhanced pages will have <SCRIPT> containers in at least two places: once in the head of the document and another time in the body. The head is generally where you find functions and procedures, which are the heart of your VBScript.

Here's an example of a script in the Head of a document:

```
<HTML>
<HEAD>
<TITLE>Simple Script Page</TITLE>
<SCRIPT LANGUAGE="VBScript">
<!--
Sub Button1_OnClick
      MsgBox "Thanks for clicking"
End Sub
-->
</SCRIPT>
</HEAD>
```

Notice two important details about this:

- As mentioned before, all scripting commands appear between the <SCRIPT> tags. This is so that browsers that recognized scripting know what language you're using and what commands should be considered part of the script.

- The <SCRIPT> container itself appears between HTML comment tags. That's because browsers that don't recognize scripting will ignore the <SCRIPT> tags, but may try to execute the commands within the script as HTML. That would result in a lot of confusing text and, probably, some weird HTML effects in your pages.

Within your VBScript-enabled pages themselves, it's also possible to add <SCRIPT> containers and scripting codes. This is possible in two ways. Here's an example of the first:

```
<BODY>
<SCRIPT LANGUAGE="VBScript">
document.write "<H2>Welcome to My Page</H2>"
</SCRIPT>
```

A scripting container and commands can appear anywhere in the body of your document, although it's probably best to place them at the beginning or the end. These containers are useful for scripting commands that will create HTML elements.

Another example is:

```
<BODY>
<FORM NAME="MyForm">
<INPUT TYPE="Button" Name="MyButton" Value="Click Me">
<SCRIPT FOR="MyButton" EVENT="onClick" LANGUAGE="VBSscript">
```

```
        MsgBox "You Got Me!"
    </SCRIPT>
    </FORM>
    </BODY>
```

In this case, the scripting commands appear in the document near the HTML elements that they're designed to respond to. Either way is valid.

A Sample VBScript

One of the main reasons for using VBScript is *event handling*, which means creating scripting solutions that respond to user input. With VBScript, event handling is rather simple, using the sub command in the function section of your script. (That's the section that appears in the head of your document.)

The following listing is a complete Web page, including a VBScript.

```
<HTML>
<HEAD>
<TITLE>Hello World Example
</TITLE>
<SCRIPT LANGUAGE="VBScript">
<!--
Sub MyButton_OnClick
        MsgBox "Hello World"
End Sub
-->
</SCRIPT>
</HEAD>
<BODY>
<H1>Hello World Example:H1><HR>
<FORM>
<INPUT NAME="MyButton" TYPE="BUTTON" VALUE="Click Me>
</FORM>
</BODY>
</HTML>
```

A few interesting points come out of this example:

- Handling an event is simple in VBScript, requiring no special scripting commands for the FORM element itself. Instead, you can create a sub routine in the head of your page that knows to be aware of a particular user action.
- The event handler, OnClick, is simply associated with the NAME you give the button in the <INPUT> tag. To create an event handler within a sub routine, you simply add the event handler after an underscore (_).

- Scripting languages in general introduce a new HTML form TYPE for
  <INPUT> called BUTTON. It works almost exactly like RESET or SUBMIT except
  that it does nothing on its own. It is scripting that reacts to a BUTTON, not
  HTML.

CAUTION

Not in Netscape   Remember, though, that VBScript will not work (at least
currently) in Netscape Navigator and other non-Microsoft Web browsers. You
can use event-handling concepts, but you'll want to use JavaScript to reach the
most users.

In this lesson, you learned the basics of adding a VBScript to your page. In the
next lesson, you'll see a more advanced example and learn other event-handling
techniques in VBScript.

VBScript Events and Objects

3

In this lesson, you learn how to create more advanced VBScripts, including using VBScript for event handling and using objects to load new HTML documents.

Event Handling in VBScript

As you learned in Lesson 2, VBScript is very adept at handling events generated by the user, usually as a result of something the user has entered or clicked. The range of events that VBScript can handle goes well beyond the OnClick handler, although the process for dealing with most other events is basically the same.

The most obvious example of using event handling to deal with user input revolves around the HTML forms tags. One use of VBScript is to check the input generated by users before the form is submitted—to make sure they enter what seems to be valid addresses, ZIP Codes, and phone numbers, for instance.

Before creating such a script, though, it's useful to know a few of the *events* associated with many form elements that are available to VBScript authors. Table 3.1 shows some of these.

TERM   **Event**   An action taken by the user to which your script reacts. It is also, however, a type of JavaScript procedure that is used to react to events. The event name _OnClick, for instance, responds to the event that is generated when a user clicks an HTML button.

Table 3.1   Form Events in VBScript

Event Name	What It Handles
_OnClick	Reacts to user clicking a form element.
_OnFocus	Reacts to the user placing *focus* on an element.
_OnBlur	Reacts to the user moving focus from the element.
_OnChange	Reacts to the user changing data or changing selections in an element.
_OnSelect	Reacts to the user selecting the contents of an element.

You may have noticed that some of the events listed in Table 3.1 react to a change in focus. *Focus* is simply the text or element currently selected or highlighted for editing in the browser window. If the user is in a text box that requests his first name, then he hits the Tab key to move to the next text box, the First Name text box has lost focus.

In programmer's parlance, the movement of focus is called a *blur*. In this example, the First Name text box receives a blur event when the user changes focus by hitting the Tab key. It's just like being at a party. When you first meet someone and begin talking to her, you focus on that one person. When the conversation wanes a bit, you change your focus to someone else.

Also, note that onSelect is different from the focus-oriented events because it waits for the user to actually choose or highlight something in the element, not just move the cursor to that element.

Creating Event Handlers

In VBScript, events are handled using the Sub routine in the head of your document. If you've included any scripting in your page at all, VBScript will automatically look for an event handler every time the user changes something on the page. If it finds one in a Sub routine, the event handler is executed automatically, as long as it relates to the event that took place.

An example might be creating an event handler for a form that requests an address. In this example, you'd like to check the ZIP Code box to make sure that your user has entered a five-digit (US) ZIP Code so that your company's literature might be reasonably assured of reaching this customer. Here's the full document for error checking.

```
<HTML>
<HEAD>
<TITLE>VBScript Form Element Validation</TITLE>
<SCRIPT LANGUAGE="VBScript">
<!--
Sub zipCode_OnBlur
        Dim TheForm
        Set TheForm = Document.MyForm
        If IsNumeric (TheForm.zipCode.Value) Then
                If TheForm.zipCode.Value < 99999 And
TheForm.zipCode.Value > 9999 Then
                End If
                Else
                        MsgBox "Please enter a numeric, five-digit Zip
➥code."
                End If
End Sub
-->
</SCRIPT>
</HEAD>
<BODY>
<P>Please fill in the following form:</P>
<FORM NAME="MyForm">
<PRE>
Name:      <INPUT TYPE=TEXT NAME="Name" SIZE=50>
Address:   <INPUT TYPE=TEXT NAME="Address" SIZE=60>
City:      <INPUT TYPE=TEXT NAME="City" SIZE=20> STATE <INPUT
➥TYPE=TEXT NAME="State" SIZE=2>
Zip Code: <INPUT TYPE=TEXT NAME="zipCode" SIZE=5>
Phone:     <INPUT TYPE=TEXT NAME="Phone" SIZE=10>
<INPUT TYPE=SUBMIT NAME="Submit" Value="Submit">
</PRE>
</FORM>
</BODY>
</HTML>
```

A couple of things in the script's Sub procedure need explaining:

- The keyword Dim is used to create new variables in VBScript. While not absolutely necessary, it's a good idea to get in the habit of creating variables this way. Whenever you want a new variable to occur only within a particular function, use the Dim statement, followed by the exact variable name.

- The form data is being referenced through the document object (Document.MyForm). Most parts of a document are available in this Internet Explorer-defined *object*. So, the Set command is required to make TheForm become a shortcut to that particular object, instead of receiving the value within that object.

273

Object   A collection of variables and values. In VBScript, the HTML document itself is given an object that holds a bunch of variables in it, including variables related to the forms in that document. So, it's possible to get the value of a particular form element (in the example) with a statement like `zipValue = Document.MyForm.zipCode.Value`. But what if you don't want the value? If you just want to shorten all the references used for a particular part of an object, you use the `Set` command, so that `Set TheForm = Document.MyForm` makes it possible to get at values with a little less typing, for example, `zipValue = TheForm.zipCode.Value`.

- The built-in function `IsNumeric` simply makes sure that the value held by the variable in parentheses is a number.

Here's what happens when the user loads this page:

1. The user begins entering data in the form text boxes.

2. The user switches to the Zip Code text box (using the Tab key or the mouse) and enters some text.

3. When the user leaves the text box (either by clicking somewhere else or hitting the Tab key), the script recognizes that the Zip Code box has lost focus, so it begins processing.

4. The script looks at the form object and finds the value for the Zip Code box.

5. The script then determines if the Zip Code value is a number. If it is, the script looks to see if the numerical value is between 9999 and 99999, (checking to see if it's a five-digit number).

6. If all of this is true, then the script stops executing—and the user never knows it happened.

7. If one of the criteria is not met, then the script tosses up a message box that asks the user to reenter the data in the Zip Code box.

Other VBScript Tricks

Although there isn't space to cover VBScript in much detail, VBScript does share some similarities with JavaScript, which is covered more completely in this text. In the meantime, there are a few interesting bits of code that you can quickly add to a VBScript-aware page.

TIP **Expert Tutors** Microsoft has excellent tutorials and documentation that cover everything that VBScript can do—check it out at **http:// www.microsoft.com/vbscript/** on the Web.

Here are some things to try in VBScript:

- Use the form object to place a new value in a form element. Notice in this example script that you can set a text box to a new value, which will then appear on your page. Here's the example:

```
<HTML>
<HEAD>
<TITLE>Simple Script</TITLE>
<SCRIPT LANGUAGE=VBScript>
 Sub AddButton_OnClick
     Dim TheForm
     Set TheForm = Document.MyForm
     TheForm.Result.Value = Cdbl(TheForm.Num1.Value) +
➥ TheForm.Num2.Value
End Sub
-->
</SCRIPT>
</HEAD>
<BODY>
<P>Add these two numbers:P>
<FORM NAME="MyForm">
<PRE>
First Number:     <INPUT TYPE=TEXT NAME="Num1" SIZE=2>
Second Number:     <INPUT TYPE=TEXT NAME="Num2" SIZE=2>
<INPUT TYPE=BUTTON NAME="AddButton" Value="Add Them Up">
Result:           <INPUT TYPE=TEXT NAME="Result" SIZE=5>
</PRE>
</FORM>
</BODY>
</HTML>
```

TIP **The Cdbl () Function** When you want to add two numbers together, you need to set one of them to specifically be a number, using the Cdbl () built-in function. This function changes the enclosed variable's value into a "double-float" number, which is simply confusing programmer-speak for a decimal number. If you don't specifically change at least one of the variables to a number, you'll end up adding together "strings of text," so that 1 plus 2 would be 12.

- Use built-in functions to add the time and date to your page, like the following:

```
<BODY>
<H3>Welcome to My Page</H3>
<SCRIPT LANGUAGE="VBScript">
Document.Write "It's" & Time() & "on" & Date() & "."
</SCRIPT>
</BODY>
```

- Or, open a new window with a new HTML document in it using the Window object. The command, within <SCRIPT> tags, would be: window.open ("page.html", "Window Name");

In this lesson, you learned about VBScript event handlers and objects. In the next lesson, you'll learn how to add Java applets to your pages.

Adding Java

In this lesson, you learn how to add Java applets to your pages.

The Java Language

You've probably heard at least a little something about Java if you've spent much time on the Internet. *Java*, in a nutshell, is a full-fledged computer programming language that's designed to work a lot like some other popular languages—notably a programming language called C++. (Many popular Macintosh and Windows applications are written in C++.)

 TIP   **Good Books**   Programming in Java is well beyond the scope of this book; we'll just be looking at how to add finished Java programs to our pages. For more on Java, check out *Special Edition Using Java* and *Java by Example*, both by Que.

The difference with Java (from, say, C++) is that it's also designed to run on nearly any sort of computer that might be connected to the Internet. It's popular for programmers who want to write programs for use on the Web, because once the program is downloaded, it can be run by nearly anyone who visits the Web:site.

Java Applets

For the most part, Java programs end up being very small when they're used on Web sites, for the same reason that Web authors try to keep everything else small—it takes time to download files across the Internet. These small programs are often called *applets* because, unlike full-sized computer applications, applets generally perform only one specific function, like the applet shown in Figure 4.1.

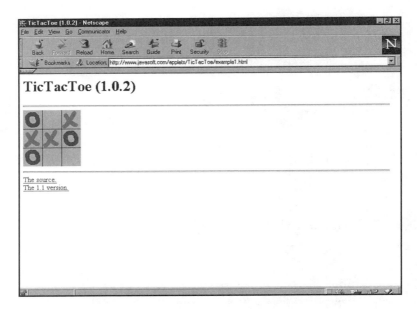

Figure 4.1 Here's an example of a single-function Java applet being displayed in Netscape Navigator.

If you're not going to write Java applets yourself (or have someone else do it for you), you might want to check out what the Web has to offer in the way of freeware and shareware Java applets for your site. A good place to start is **http://www.yahoo.com/Computers_and_Internet/Programming_Languages/Java/Applets/** from Yahoo!.

For the most part, Java applets are either small games, Web communications enhancements, or ways to display data from internal databases on Web sites. It's also typical to see Java applets that are responsible for presenting animated information screens or simple animated cartoons.

The future holds more possibilities for Java, but for now, the applets are still in the infancy stage where a lot of folks are just proving to themselves that they can create a program at all. There are, indeed, a fair number of clocks, calculators, and tic-tac-toe games that have been created.

Adding Java Applets

You add Java applets in HTML 3.2-compatible browsers with the <APPLET> container tag. The <PARAM> tag offers certain parameters to the browser concerning the applet (such as the speed at which something should display, initialize, and so on). <APPLET> accepts the attributes CODE, CODEBASE, HEIGHT, and WIDTH.

An <APPLET> tag follows the general format:

```
<APPLET CODEBASE="applet_path_URL" CODE="appletFile.class"
➥WIDTH="number" HEIGHT="number">
<PARAM NAME="attributeName" VALUE="string/number">
...
Alt HTML text for non-Java browsers
</APPLET>
```

- CODEBASE is the path (in URL form) to the directory on your server containing the Java applet. (It's basically like an URL without the final document name.)
- CODE takes the name of the applet. This file always ends in .class, to suggest that it's a compiled Java class. CODE should always be just the file name, because CODEBASE is used to find the path to the Java applet.

 TIP Relative URLs Notice that CODEBASE and CODE work together to create a complete URL. So, for a relative URL, CODEBASE isn't required if the applet is in the same directory as the Web page.

- The WIDTH and HEIGHT attributes accept the number in pixels for the Java applet on your Web page.

An example of the first line of <APPLET> would be the following:

```
<APPLET CODEBASE="http://www.myserver.com/applets/"
➥ CODE="clock.class"
HEIGHT="300" WIDTH="300">
```

<PARAM> is a bit easier to use than it may seem. It essentially creates a variable, assigns a value, and passes it to the Java applet. The applet must be written to understand the parameter's name and value. NAME is used to create the parameter's name; it should be expected by the applet. VALUE is used to assign the value to that particular parameter. It could be a number, bit of text, or even a command that causes the applet to work in a particular way.

 TIP Know Your Params Understanding the <PARAM> tag might enable you to use freeware/shareware Java applets on your own pages. By passing your own parameters to general purpose applets, you may find them useful for your particular Web site.

The following shows a simple <PARAM> tag:

```
<PARAM NAME="Speed" VALUE="5">
```

In this case, the Java applet has to recognize and know what to do with a variable named Speed that has a value of 5.

The alternative HTML markup in the <APPLET> container enables you to offer HTML text to browsers that aren't Java-enabled. A Java-aware browser ignores the markup (and displays the applet window instead), while non-Java browsers ignore everything but the markup. An example would be the following:

```
<APPLET CODE="counter.class" HEIGHT="20" WIDTH="20">
<P>You need a <I>Java-aware</I> browser to see this counter!</P>
</APPLET>
```

This displays the text, instead of the applet, when it encounters a browser that doesn't support Java.

Using the *<OBJECT>* Tag

Although still at the "recommended" stage, it's highly likely that browsers past the 4.0 level of Netscape Navigator and Internet Explorer (especially since Microsoft is championing the tag) will also include support for the more universal <OBJECT> tag, which is currently the basis for adding ActiveX components to Web pages. Soon, the <OBJECT> tag will be useful for adding nearly any sort of plug-in, component, or applet, if the governing bodies of HTML have their way.

Here's an example of the <OBJECT> tag:

```
<OBJECT
        CODETYPE="application/java-vm"
        CODEBASE="http://www.mynet.com/"
        CLASSID="java:program_name"
        HEIGHT=100
        WIDTH=100
    >
    <PARAM NAME="options" VALUE="xqz">
        Your browser does not know how to execute Java
➥applications.
    </OBJECT>
```

There are a couple of differences with this tag that are worth noting:

CODETYPE This attribute uses a MIME-style data type definition to tell the browser what sort of plug-in is coming. In this case, `application/java-vm` tells the browser it's a Java applet.

CLASSID Instead of the CODE attribute, CLASSID is used to identify the name of the Java applet. Notice that the CLASSID attribute does not require (and actually cannot use) a file name that includes the `.CLASS` extension.

All other attributes are pretty much the same for using the `<OBJECT>` and the `<EMBED>` tag.

Wait on Object Because only the very latest browsers support the `<OBJECT>` tag for Java applets, you'll probably be better off using the `<APPLET>` tag to add applets to your page for now; `<APPLET>` should be retained for backward-compatibility reasons. Wait to change over to using the `<OBJECT>` tag until a majority of people are using the 4.0 or later versions of Internet Explorer and Netscape Navigator.

CAUTION

In this lesson, you learned how to add Java applets to your Web pages. In the next lesson, you'll begin programming in JavaScript.

Scripting with JavaScript

In this lesson, you learn how to add JavaScript to your Web documents and use some of the basic commands.

Entering Scripts in Your Web Documents

You don't need any special new tools for adding JavaScript to your HTML documents; your text editor will work just fine. You will, however, want to test, test, and test again while you're writing JavaScript code, so be sure you've got the 3.0 (or later) version of Netscape or Internet Explorer (IE) handy for loading these pages.

 TIP **Browser Tests** Actually, you might want copies of both Netscape and IE for this chapter, just to make sure everything works in both. (The 3.0 versions of both reportedly have slight differences in what JavaScript makes them happy.)

Scripting for JavaScript begins in much the same way that scripting with VBScript begins—by using the <SCRIPT> tag.

Adding the *<SCRIPT>* Tags

The <SCRIPT> tag is used to add JavaScript commands to your HTML pages. This is done so that Netscape and compatible browsers can determine which text is actually scripting commands and which text should be displayed in the browser window. <SCRIPT> is a container tag that can accept the attribute LANGUAGE, which enables you to specify the scripting language used (JavaScript is generally the default). Here's how it works:

```
<SCRIPT LANGUAGE="JavaScript">
Script Code
</SCRIPT>
```

Figure 5.1 shows <SCRIPT> tags in a Web document.

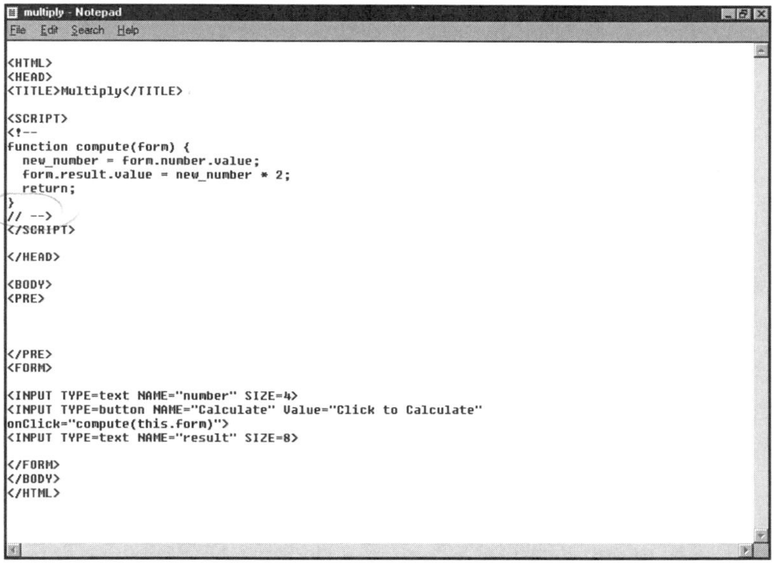


```
<HTML>
<HEAD>
<TITLE>Multiply</TITLE>

<SCRIPT>
<!--
function compute(form) {
  new_number = form.number.value;
  form.result.value = new_number * 2;
  return;
}
// -->
</SCRIPT>

</HEAD>

<BODY>
<PRE>



</PRE>
<FORM>

<INPUT TYPE=text NAME="number" SIZE=4>
<INPUT TYPE=button NAME="Calculate" Value="Click to Calculate"
onClick="compute(this.form)">
<INPUT TYPE=text NAME="result" SIZE=8>

</FORM>
</BODY>
</HTML>
```

Figure 5.1 Whenever you add JavaScript statements to your page, you need to separate them with the <SCRIPT> tag.

Hiding Scripts in Your Documents

While it's possible that old browsers that don't recognize JavaScript will just skip over the <SCRIPT> tag, it's also possible that the browser will attempt to interpret your script commands or other text as HTML markup. So, you've got to be careful about how you "hide" the script stuff.

For non-JavaScript browsers, surround the script commands with the HTML comment tag:

```
<SCRIPT>
<!--
script commands
// -->
</SCRIPT>
```

In order to keep everything happy, we've got to add all these special commands. You might have even noticed that we have to put two slashes ("//") in front of the closing HTML comment tag. This is because JavaScript will choke when it sees -->; it will try to interpret that as scripting code. (To JavaScript, that looks like two minus signs and a greater than sign.) So, you need to comment the comment.

TIP   **Comments**   Two slashes together // are the comment command in JavaScript.

In fact, it's always a good idea to create comments within your script that document what you're doing in your programming. Using the two slashes, then, you can keep up a running commentary about your script:

```
<SCRIPT>
<!--
script command    // One-line comment
...script commands...
/* Unlimited-length comments, must be
ended with */
// comment to end hiding -->
</SCRIPT>
```

Looks like you can fill a decent-sized page with nothing but comments. Notice that you've solved the HTML comment problem with a *single-line* JavaScript comment. Single-line comments start with two forward slashes and must completely fit on a single line with a return at the end. Multiline comments can be enclosed in an opening comment element (/*) and a closing comment element (*/).

To create a scripting page from scratch in Windows NotePad, start out with something like Figure 5.2.

The Hello World Example

It's something of a tradition in the learning of a new programming language to begin your studies by creating a "Hello World" program. The whole point of a hello world example is to get up and running with the programming syntax and complete a script before you've learned much of anything about the language. It gives you a sense of accomplishment and shows you how the most basic syntax (in this case, the <SCRIPT> tags) works.

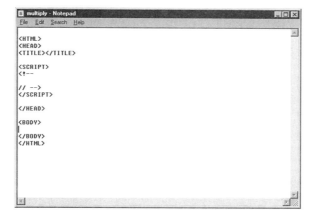

Figure 5.2 Getting all your commenting out of the way before the real scripting begins.

Although you haven't learned how to do anything with a script yet, here's one quick command for the purpose of getting your first JavaScript page to work. It's `document.write`, and it's something called a "method" in JavaScript. (A method is basically a *variable* that does something automatically.)

In this case, the method `document.write` prints text to your Web page. Listing 5.1 is a complete HTML page that includes a basic JavaScript.

 TERM **Variable** A name assigned to a particular value, like in algebra. It used to be that computer programmers created variables like X, so that X=10 would assign a value to the variable X. These days, you're more likely to see variable names such as `recent_Value` or `newResult`.

Listing 5.1 Hello World Example

```
<HTML>
<HEAD>
<TITLE>Hello World JavaScript Example</TITLE>
</HEAD>
<BODY>
<H3>The following text is script generated:</H3>
<SCRIPT LANGUAGE="JavaScript">
<!--
/* Our script only requires
one quick statement! */
document.write("Hello World!") // Prints words to Web document
```

```
// end hiding-->
</SCRIPT>
</BODY>
</HTML>
```

Save this document, and then load it in a JavaScript-capable browser. If your browser is capable of dealing with JavaScript, then your output should look something like Figure 5.3. If it's not, then you'll just see the header text.

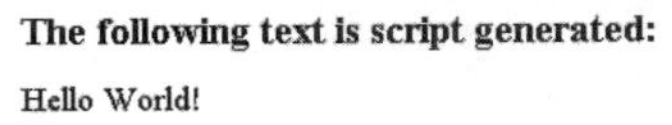

The following text is script generated:

Hello World!

Figure 5.3   The Hello World example uses a JavaScript command to print text to the browser window.

In this lesson, you learned the basics of adding JavaScript commands to a Web page. In the next lesson, you'll learn about JavaScript variables and functions.

JavaScript Functions and Variables

In this lesson, you learn how to create functions and variables in JavaScript.

JavaScript Functions

Back before there were windows and icons, programs were written to print data to screens. If you ever tried any programming back then, you might have used something like BASIC, FORTRAN, or COBOL—all of which, at least originally, were procedural languages. (Do the first step; then think; then do the next step, and so on.)

But that kind of programming meant you got one kind of program that resulted: Q&A-style programs. You'd get a menu with your choices all in text, or the program would ask you for the next number in the sequence or something. These days, you can click just about any icon you want in a program like Microsoft Word—in any order.

JavaScript, like many of the latest, most innovative computer programming languages, breaks out of the procedural mold a bit. In JavaScript, every little thing we do is separated out into a function—for performing a math equation, for instance. The functions don't have to be used in any particular order, just like you don't have to click the icons in Microsoft Word in any particular order.

What Is a Function?

A *function* is basically a "mini-program." Functions start by being "passed" a particular value; they work with that value to make something else happen and then "return" a new value to the body of your program, shown in Figure 6.1.

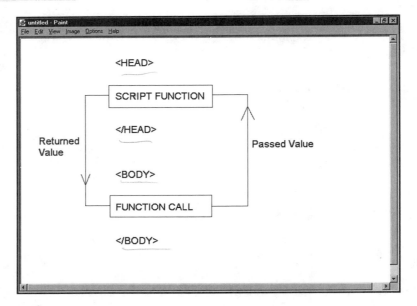

Figure 6.1   Here's (kinda) how a JavaScript program works in your document.

In JavaScript, there are two times you need to worry about functions

Declare the function.   Declaring is when you (programmatically) say, "Browser, I'm going to have this function, and this is what it's going to do." The browser, when it loads a page, will make note of the different functions that you've declared.

Call the function in the body of your script.   Generally, your script will be just a series of function calls. There isn't a whole lot of calculating done in the guts of your script. You send a value out to a function to be computed, and then receive the results back in the body.

Declaring Functions

A good rule, although it's not necessary, is to declare your functions in the head of your HTML document. The function declaration needs to appear between

<SCRIPT> tags, but you can have more than one set of <SCRIPT> tags in a document. A single set of <SCRIPT> tags doesn't necessarily define an entire script—it just sets script elements apart from other HTML tags. Function declarations look like the following:

```
<SCRIPT>
<!--
  function function_name(value_name) {
  ...function code...
  return (new_value)
}
// end hiding -->
</SCRIPT>
```

The value_name for the function is just the variable name that you assign to the passed value for the duration of the function. When the body of your JavaScript document calls this function, it will generally send along a value. When that value gets to the function, it needs a name. If the function is designed to perform simple math, for instance, you might call the passed value old_num.

When you create a variable in programming, you're really just creating a name for a slot in the computer's memory. You can then assign a certain value to that slot, and refer to it by its new name. For instance:

1. If you create a variable called num_1, you could assign the value 5 to that variable.
2. Then you could tell the script to "add num_1+10."
3. If you did it right, the script would return the answer: 15.

Also, notice that the entire calculating part of the function is between curly brackets. An example of a function declaration might be:

```
<SCRIPT>
<!--
  function get_square(old_num) {
  new_num = (old_num * old_num)
  return (new_num)
}
// end hiding -->
</SCRIPT>
```

In the example, you've created a function called get_square, which accepts a value, names it old_num, and then squares that value and assigns it to a variable named new_num. At least, that's what the function is supposed to do. It won't do

289

it yet, because this is just a declaration. It doesn't even know what actual values to work with until you *call* the function.

 TIP **Readable Scripts** By the way, all the extra spacing in these JavaScript commands and functions is for the benefit of humans, not computers. You can add spaces to make things a little easier to read. But you don't have to count the spaces on the page to make sure you get things right.

Function Calls

You *call* the function from the body of your script, which is generally in the body of the Web document. There are two things to remember about functions and function calls:

- It doesn't really matter where you declare functions (although, as mentioned, it's best to declare them between the <HEAD> tags).
- But, it is best to put the function calls of your script close to the parts of your document where they're needed (this will become more obvious as we work with JavaScript).

A function call always appears between <SCRIPT> tags, and it looks something like this:

```
function_name(value);
```

In this function call, the function_name should be the same as the function name that you use in the function declaration, but the value can be anything you want to pass to the function. You can put most anything in the parentheses—a variable name, an actual number, or a string of text—as long as the function is designed to accept such a value.

For instance, the get_square function works equally well if you use:

```
<SCRIPT>
num = 5;
num_squared = get_square (num);
</SCRIPT>
```

Here's what is happening in this function call:

1. You've assigned the value 5 to the variable num.

2. Then that variable (and hence the 5) is passed to the function get_square, which was declared in the previous section.

3. When that number gets up there to the function, it's renamed old_num in the example, and then it's squared mathematically by the commands in that function.

CAUTION

Pass Good Values Remember, though, that you should be passing a value that the function expects. If you pass a string of text to a function designed to perform math functions, you won't get anything useful.

Returning an Answer

Here's the sample function and function calls you've used in this lesson:

```
<HEAD>
<TITLE>Testing</TITLE>
<SCRIPT>
<!--
  function get_square(old_num) {
  new_num = (old_num * old_num)
  return (new_num)
}
// end hiding -->
</SCRIPT>
</HEAD>

<BODY>
HTML stuff
<SCRIPT>
<!--
num = 5;
num_squared = get_square (num);
alert ("The number squared is: " + num_squared);
// end hiding -->
</SCRIPT>
```

Down there in the body of the Web document, notice that your function call is in the same place where it has been—on the right side of an equal sign.

In JavaScript (and in most programming), that's actually an *assignment*. What you're telling the script is, "Set the variable num_squared equal to the value of the function get_squared when we send it the value num."

TIP **Assign versus Compare** In JavaScript, the equal sign is used to *assign* values to variables. So when you type **num = 5**, it isn't a question—you just put the number 5 in the variable num. This is in contrast to a comparison, which is two equal signs (==). You use the comparison when you want the script to decide whether or not two values are equal, as in, "does 5==4?"

This may take a little leap of thought, but JavaScript does two things with function calls:

1. First, the call is used to pass a value to the function.

2. Then, when the function returns a value, it *takes the place* of the original function call.

Look at the following example:

```
num_squared = get_square (5);
```

After the math of the get_square function is completed and the value is returned, the entire function call (get_square (5)) is given a value of 25. This, in turn, is assigned to the variable num_squared.

In this lesson, you learned how to add functions, variables, and function calls to your Web page. In the next lesson, you'll learn how to create statements and conditions in JavaScript.

JavaScript Statements

In this lesson, you learn the JavaScript statement and how to create conditions.

JavaScript Statements

If you have any experience with programming languages, you'll be familiar with JavaScript's small set of statements. JavaScript includes the conditional statement `if...else` and the loop statements `for`, `while`, `break`, and `continue`. You'll also get to know some of the associated JavaScript operators.

 TIP **Using Statements** Remember that, in most cases, you'll use these statements in functions. These are the commands in JavaScript you'll use to actually process data.

The key to many of these statements is called the *condition*, which is simply a bit of JavaScript code that needs to be evaluated before your script decides what to do next. So, before you look at JavaScript statements, take a look at the conditions and operators that JavaScript recognizes.

Comparison Operators

Comparisons are generally enclosed in parentheses, and they are always small snippets of code designed to evaluate as true or false. For instance, the following is a conditional statement:

```
(x == 1)
```

If x does equal 1, then this condition is valid.

This is why it's important to recognize and use the correct *operators* for conditions.

Operators JavaScript operators are similar to operators in simple mathematics. While you have plus (+) and minus (−) operators, programming also has special operators for comparing one value to another.

For instance, an assignment (assigning a value to a variable) is always `true` in JavaScript, so that the following condition:

```
(errorLevel = 1)
```

is always true, since it's an assignment. Although it may seem to make sense to use an equal sign in this instance, you actually need to use the comparison operator == for this condition. See Table 7.1 for a listing of the comparison operators.

Table 7.1 Comparison Operators in JavaScript

Operator	Meaning	Example	Is True When...
==	equals	x == y	x equals y
!=	not equal	x != y	x is not equal to y
>	greater than	x > y	x is greater than y
<	less than	x < y	x is less than y
>=	greater than or equal to	x >= y	x is greater than or equals y
<=	less than or equal to	x <= y	x is less than or equals y

So, you have a number of different ways to create conditions by using comparisons. Realize that conditions are not necessarily limited to numerical expressions. For instance, look at the following:

```
(carName != "Ford")
```

This will return the value `false` if the variable `carName` has the value of the string `Ford`.

TIP **Value Replaces Comparison** When a comparison is evaluated, the actual comparison—for example, (myLife="good")—is set to either true or false—it's given a value that could be assigned to a variable if necessary. (Actually, in computing, "true" is usually represented by the value 0 and "false" is usually -1.) It helps to think of the stuff that's enclosed in parentheses as actually being given the value of "true" or "false" when the comparison is made.

The "If...Else" Condition

So how do you put these comparisons and operators to use? JavaScript offers the if...else conditional statement as a way to create either/or situations in your script. Here's how it works:

```
if (condition) {
   script statements }
else {
   other statements }
```

The *condition* can be any JavaScript that evaluates to either true or false. The statements can be any valid JavaScript statements. For example:

```
if (x == 1) {
   document.write("X equals 1!");
   return;
   }
   else {
   x = x + 1;
   }
```

The else and related statements are not required if you simply want the if statements to be skipped and the rest of the function executed. An example might be:

```
if (errorLevel == 1) {
   return (false);
   }
```

In this case, if the condition is false (errorLevel does not equal 1), then the rest of the function will be executed. If it is true, then the function ends.

Loop Conditions

The next two condition types are used to create loops—script elements that repeat until a condition is met. These loop statements are for and while.

A for loop looks like this:

```
for (initial_counter; condition; add to counter) {
    JavaScript statements
    }
```

This is how it works:

1. You'll generally start a for loop by initializing your "counter" variable.

2. Then, you'll evaluate the counter to see if it's reached a certain level.

3. If it hasn't, then the loop will perform the enclosed statements and increment your counter.

4. If the counter has reached your predetermined value, then the for loop ends.

   For example:

```
for (x=0; x<10; x=x+1) {
    y = 2 * x;
    document.write ("Two times ",x," equals ",y,"<BR>");
    }
```

You start by initializing a counter variable (x=0), and then evaluating the counter in a conditional statement (x<10). If the condition is true, then the loop will perform the enclosed scripting. Then it will increment the counter—in this case, add 1 to it. When the counter reaches 10 in this example, the loop will end.

The while loop is similar to the for loop, except that it offers a little more freedom. while is used for a great variety of conditions. The basic look is like:

```
while (condition) {
  JavaScript statements
    }
```

As long as the condition evaluates to true, the loop will continue. An example would be the following:

```
x = 0;
while (x <= 5) {
    x = x +1;
    document.write (X now equals ",x,"<BR>")
    }
```

As long as the condition remains true, the `while` statement will continue to evaluate. In fact, the risk with `while` statements is that they can be "infinite loops" if the expression never evaluates to false. A common mistake is the following:

```
while (x=5) {
   x = x +1;
   document.write (X now equals ",x,"<BR>")
   }
```

The condition is actually an assignment, so it will always evaluate to true. In this example, the loop would continue indefinitely, and the output would always be `X now equals 6`.

Stopping and Restarting Loops

Two other keywords, `break` and `continue`, can be used in `for` and `while` loops to change the way the loop operates when certain conditions occur.

An example of `break` would be:

```
for (x=0; x < 10; x=x+1) {
   z = 35;
   y = z / x;
   if (y == 7)
      break;
   }
```

`break` will immediately stop the loop when encountered. In this example, the loop is terminated when x is equal to 5, since 35 divided by 5 equals 7. When the condition (y == 7) evaluates to true, the `break` command is executed, the loop stops and you move on to the next script element.

`continue` is basically used to skip a particular increment. For instance:

```
while (x < 10) {
   x = x +1;
   if (x == 5)
      continue;
   y = y + x;
   }
```

In this case, when the condition (x == 5) evaluates to true, the `continue` statement will cause the loop to move directly back to the `while` statement, thus skipping over the last line (y = y + x). When the condition is false, the last line will execute normally.

Adding to Variables

So far, you've seen statements like x = x + 1 in many of these examples to increment (add to) the values in your loop statements. JavaScript allows you to do this in other ways, using *unary* operators. A unary operator is an operator that requires only one operand, as in the unary increment operator:

```
x++
```

In fact, you can increment with either x++ or ++x. The difference is in when the increment occurs, for instance, if x equals 2:

```
y = x++
```

y will be assigned the value 2, then x will be incremented to 3. In the following example, though:

```
y = ++x
```

x will first be incremented to 3, then y will be assigned 3. This is especially significant in loop statements. Where x++ would work as you've seen x = x + 1 work increment in past examples, it should be noted that the following will actually increment x before performing the rest of the script elements:

```
for (x=0; x < 5; ++x) {
    y = x;
    }
```

In this case, the first assignment to y would actually have a value of 1, instead of 0.

Subtracting from Variables

Decrementing (subtracting from) variables works the same way, with both x— and —x as possibilities. Both work similarly to x = x - 1, except that —x will decrease before being assigned or used in a loop statement.

It is also possible to assign variables at the same time you increment or decrement. Generally, you would do this with an expression like the following:

```
x = x + y
```

However, this is also possible with the unary operators += and -=. For instance, the above could be written as:

```
x += y
```

Similarly, the two following two expressions yield the same result:

```
y = y - 2
y -= 2
```

In this lesson, you learned about operators, comparisons, and conditions in JavaScript. In the next lesson, you'll learn how to handle user input.

Handling User Input

In this lesson, you learn how to deal with user input in JavaScript.

Handling User Input

Although it's possible to create an entire page using nothing but JavaScript commands, most of the time that won't do you much good. JavaScript is a scripting language that's designed to react to user input, not just work by itself. It's a lot like Windows or the Mac OS in that respect. Most of what these operating systems do is wait for the opportunity to respond to things you do with the keyboard or the mouse.

In HTML, most of the elements that invite user input are in the HTML Forms specifications. It's there that you can create buttons, text boxes, and menus that invite user input. And, using these elements in conjunction with JavaScript allows you to handle user input in very interesting ways. Figure 8.1 shows one possibility.

JavaScript Events

In fact, the strength of JavaScript, more than anything else, is in *event handling*. That is, it's best at responding to something a user does on your page. This is generally done in response to some HTML tag. Here's the basic format for an event handler:

```
<TAG event_handler="JavaScript code">
```

- `<TAG>` can be just about any form or hyperlink tag. Most other tags don't have the capability to accept input from the user.
- The `event_handler` is the browser's code for some action by the user.
- The `JavaScript code` will most often be a function call.

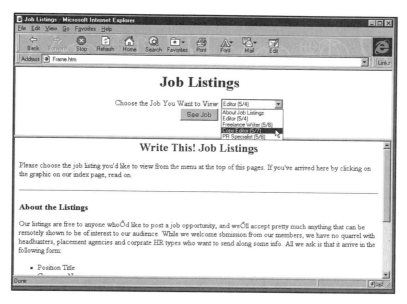

Figure 8.1 Using JavaScript, it's possible to allow users to navigate your pages by using menus.

For instance, you could use an input text box to send data to a function you've written, as with the following code:

```
<INPUT TYPE="text" NAME="number" SIZE="4">
<INPUT TYPE="button" NAME="Calculate"
➥onClick="result=compute(this.form.number.value)">
```

Here's what happens in this example:

1. An event is created when the user clicks the **Calculate** button.

2. When that happens, the value `this.form.number.value` is sent to a function called `compute`. Notice that the variable `this.form.number.value` is JavaScript's object-oriented way of storing the value of the text box named *number* in the first statement.

3. The function `compute` runs computations of the value, and returns a new value to the function call.

4. The new value is assigned to the variable `result`, which the script can now use in other processing.

Returning Values from Functions

Your average object is usually just a bunch of grouped variables. For instance, a typical browser has a JavaScript object called this, which (in the preceding example) means "variables for this page." Within this is a subcategory called form, which means "the form variables." So, the name this.form is basically where "the form variables for this page" are stored.

> **TIP**   **Keyword: This**   Actually, this is a special keyword in JavaScript used to refer to the current object. In the case of our example, the current object is, in fact, where the "variables for the page" are stored. It's too bad the JavaScript people called it "this" because that's a commonly used pronoun in the English language. Try to think of this as a completely different word in this lesson.

When you add the NAME attribute to an <INPUT> tag (for an HTML form), you're creating another variable within this object. For instance, NAME="mynumber" creates this.form.mynumber. The value of that form variable is stored at this.form.mynumber.value.

Take a look at that last example again:

```
<INPUT TYPE="text" NAME="number" SIZE="4">
<INPUT TYPE="button" NAME="Calculate"
➥onClick="result = compute(this.form.number.value)">
```

You don't necessarily have to pass the specific value to a function in order to use it. All you need to do is send the name of the object that you want the function to concentrate on. That way, it can deal with more than one value from that object.

Here's how that would work with the previous example and a new function:

1. Your user enters something in the <INPUT> text box. That value is stored in the this.form.number.value document variable.

2. Now you want to send whatever the user typed to a function. You can make the function call similar to:

```
<INPUT TYPE="button" NAME="Calculate" onClick="result =
➥compute(this.form)">
```

3. You also design the function to work with the <INPUT> value. So, your function will look something like the following:

```
function compute(form) {
  new_number = form.number.value;
  new_number = new_number * 2;
  return (new_number);
}
```

4. The function received what's known as a *pointer* to the object responsible for storing information in the form. After the function has its hands on that pointer (which the function calls `form`), it's able to access data within that function by using the object variable scheme, as in `form.number.value`.

Pointer   A pointer is a value that tells a programming function where to look for a particular object. In the case of these examples, the object in question is a collection of variables that tell JavaScript things about the current browser page, such as "What's the value stored in the variable called 'number'?"

Storing a New Value

If the function knows how to find the data storage object (and it does, since it's been given a pointer), it can also store new values in variables within that object.

So, you can change a few more things. In the original handler, you were assigning the results of the function call to a variable called `result`. This time, though, you won't assign it to a variable at all:

```
<INPUT TYPE=text NAME="number" SIZE=4>
<INPUT TYPE=button NAME="Calculate" Value="Click to Calculate"
onClick="compute(this.form)">
<INPUT TYPE=text NAME="result" SIZE=8>
```

Here's what this bit of scripting is doing:

1. In the second line, you're just telling the browser to run the `compute()` function when the Calculate button is clicked, instead of assigning the value to a variable like `result`.

2. To store the result, you use the object pointer. Here's the new function:
```
function compute(form) {
  new_number = form.number.value;
  form.result.value = new_number * 2;
  return;
}
```

3. In line three of the function declaration, notice the new variable `form.result.value`. Now, the function call sets the function in motion, and passes it the object pointer.

4. The function creates its own new variable within the object, called `result`, and gives it a new value. When the function returns, the next line of script is activated. That line is:
```
<INPUT TYPE="text" NAME="result" SIZE="8">
```

5. Notice the NAME. Because there's already a value assigned to this NAME, that value will be displayed in the text box (just as if it were default text). In your case, it happens to be the answer, as shown in Figure 8.2.

Figure. 8.2 Your text box script, complete with a result.

Types of Events

There are a number of different events that a typical browser will recognize, and for which you can write handlers. Even the simplest handler should call a function you've declared previously, then return to that point (the function call) in the Web document. Table 8.1 shows you some of the events for which there are associated handlers.

Table 8.1 Events and Event Handlers

Event	Means...	Event Handler
blur	User moves input focus from form box	onBlur
click	User clicks form element or link	onClick
change	User changes a form value	onChange
focus	User gives a form box input focus	onFocus
load	User loads the page in Navigator	onLoad
mouseover	User moves mouse over a link	onMouseOver
select	User selects form input field	onSelect
submit	User submits a form	onSubmit
unload	User exits the page	onUnload

You can probably figure out what most of these do from the table. It should also make you realize how scriptable your Web page really is.

You can create alert dialog boxes, for instance, which tell your user that a particular field is required—or that it needs to be filled with a certain number of characters. You can even say "Good-bye" to users as they leave your page, perhaps displaying a phone number or other useful information. You'll see some examples of alert boxes and other devices in the other JavaScript lessons.

In this lesson, you learned how to handle user input and pass it to JavaScript functions. In the next lesson, you'll learn how to create and work with JavaScript objects.

Working with JavaScript Objects

In this lesson, you learn how to create and use objects in JavaScript.

The JavaScript Object Model

An object, for the purposes of this lesson, is basically a collection of properties. Often, these properties are variables, but they can also be functions or JavaScript methods. Properties within objects are accessed using the following notation:

```
objectName.propertyName
```

For instance, if you created an object called myComputer, you might have properties called diskspace, monitor, and cdspeed. You could assign values to those properties like this:

```
myComputer.diskspace = "2.4 GB"
myComputer.monitor = "17-inch VGA"
myComputer.cdspeed = "6x"
```

What you've basically done is assigned values to variables that happen to all be associated with one another, since they're part of myComputer. So, you could pass this object to a function using the following function call:

```
<SCRIPT>
printSpec (myComputer);
</SCRIPT>
```

And then use the pointer to that object to access each of the individual variables:

```
<SCRIPT>
function printSpec (computer) {
    document.write ("Disk space = " + computer.diskspace + "<BR>">);
    document.write ("Monitor = " + computer.monitor + "<BR>");
    document.write ("CD Speed = " + computer.cdspeed + "<BR>");
    return;
    }
</SCRIPT>
```

Methods

Methods, then, are basically functions associated with objects. For instance, one of the methods we've used quite a bit is document.write, which is really just a function provided by JavaScript that allows you to write HTML marked-up text to the current document.

Notice that write is the function, and document is the associated object. Netscape Navigator and other JavaScript browsers define certain basic objects, like document, that are designed to make it easier for you to deal with the document or window in question. You'll learn about some of those standard objects later in this lesson.

You can even create your own methods by simply assigning a function name to an object variable, following the format:

```
object.methodname = function_name
```

Creating New Objects

JavaScript offers you the special keyword this, which acts as a placeholder. It's used to represent the current object involved in a function call. An example would be the following:

```
<FORM NAME="MyForm">
<INPUT TYPE="Text" NAME="first" onClick="check(this)">
</FORM>
```

This sends a pointer to the current object to the function check. In this case, the actual object is document.myform.first, but the keyword this can be used here, since it's clear what the current object is.

That's part of how you create your own objects. It's done in two steps. First, you need to define a function that outlines the basic object you'd like to create. This is your own personal object definition for this new type of object.

For instance, if you wanted to create a data object that could be used to describe a person, you might use the following function:

```
function person(name, height, weight, age) {
    this.name = name;
    this.height = height;
    this.weight = weight;
    this.age = age;
    }
```

Notice the use of this. In the case of the example here, this refers to the object that's being created by another keyword, new. Using new is the second step in creating our new object. The following is an example:

```
car1 = new car("Ford Mustang", 4, 280, 71) ;
```

The keyword new creates a new object. It also tells the object-creating function person that the name of this new object will be Ford Mustang. So, when the function is called, Ford Mustang will replace this and the assignment will work like this:

```
car1.name = "Ford Mustang";
car1.seats = 4;
car1.horsepower = 280;
car1.year = 71;
```

Of course, you won't see any of this happen. But, it's now possible for you to access this data just like a regular object, like in the following:

```
document.write("This car was made in19",car1.year);
```

Built-In Objects

In authoring scripts, there are a number of things you're likely to do over and over again. Instead of forcing you to write your own functions and create your own objects to achieve this, JavaScript includes some of these often-used calls in the language itself. The built-in objects tend to store useful values or offer convenient methods. The functions usually perform some fairly intensive calculating that you'll often need to use.

You'll learn about two major built-in objects available for you in JavaScript:

- The first is the String object, which helps you manipulate your strings.
- The Math object holds certain constant values for you to use in your script and methods that make it a little easier to perform some mathematical functions.

307

Strings of Text

The first object, the `string` object, is interesting if only for the fact that you don't actually have to use the notation `string.property` to use it. In fact, any string you create is a `String` object. You can create a string as simply as this:

```
mystring = "Here's a string"
```

The string variable `mystring` can now be treated as a `String` object. For instance, to get a value for the length of a `string` object, you can use the following assignment:

```
stringlen = mystring.length
```

When you create a string (and JavaScript makes it a `string` object), the value of its length is stored in the property `length`. It also associates certain methods with the object, like `toUpperCase`. You could change a string to all uppercase letters with the following line:

```
mystring = mystring.toUpperCase
```

If the string had the value `Here is a string`, this assignment would change it to `HERE IS A STRING`. Table 9.1 shows some of the other methods available with string objects.

Table 9.1 Methods for JavaScript *String* Objects

Method	*Works...*	*Example*
anchor	between <A NAME=> tags	mystring.anchor (section_name)
big	between <BIG> tags	mystring.big()
blink	between <BLINK> tags	mystring.blink()
bold	between <B> tags	mystring.bold()
charAt	by choosing single letter at index	mystring.charAt(2)
fixed	between <TT> tags	mystring.fixed()
fontcolor	between <FONT COLOR=> tags	mystring.fontcolor("red")
fontsize	between <FONT SIZE=> tags	mystring.fontsize(2)
indexOf	by finding index of certain letter	mystring.indexOf("w")
italics	between <I> tags	mystring.italics()

Method	Works...	Example
lastIndexOf	by finding occurrence before indexOf	`mystring.lastIndexOf ("w")`
link	between <A HREF=> tags	`mystring.link ("http://www.com")`
small	between <SMALL> tags	`mystring.small()`
strike	between <STRIKE> tags	`mystring.strike()`
sub	between <SUB> tags	`mystring.sub()`
substring	by choosing part of a string	`mystring.substring (0,7)`
sup	between <SUP> tags	`mystring.sup()`
toLowerCase	by changing string to lowercase	`mystring.toLowerCase()`
toUpperCase	by changing string to uppercase	`mystring.toUpperCase()`

Most of these methods should be fairly self-explanatory—they allow you to use the method to create and print text as if it were between HTML tags.

For instance, the following two script lines would have the same results:

```
document.write("<BIG>" + mystring + "</BIG>");
document.write(mystring.big);
```

Some of the other tags take some explaining—especially those that deal with indexes. Every string is "indexed" from left to right, starting with the value 0. So, in the following string, the characters are indexed according to the numbers that appear under them:

```
Howdy, boy
0123456789
```

In this case, using the method `howdystring.charAt(4)` would return the value y. You could also use the method `howdystring.indexOf("y")` which would return the value 4.

The *Math* Object

The Math object basically just holds some useful constants and methods for use in mathematical calculations. The Math object's properties are mathematical constants like E, PI, and LOG10E (logarithm, base 10, of E). You can use these by simply adding the name as math's property, as in the following example:

```
var pi_value = Math.PI;
area = Math.PI*(r*r);
```

Table 9.2 shows you the various properties for Math.

Table 9.2   Properties for the *Math* Object

Property	Value
.PI	Pi (approximately. 3.1416)
.E	e, Euler's constant (approximately 2.718)
.LN2	natural log of 2 (approximately 0.693)
.LN10	natural log of 10 (approximately 2.302)
.LOG10E	base 10 log of e (approximately 0.434)
.SQRT1_2	square root of 1/2 (approximately 0.707)
.SQRT2	square root of 2 (approximately 1.414)

The math object's methods are called like any other methods. For instance, the arc sine of a variable can be found by using the following:

```
Math.asin(your_num);
```

Table 9.3 shows the methods for the math object.

Table 9.3   Methods for the *Math* Object

Method	Result	Format
.abs	absolute value	Math.abs (*number*)
.acos	arc cosine (in radians)	Math.acos (*number*)
.asin	arc sine (in radians)	Math.asin (*number*)
.atan	arc tangent (in rads)	Math.atan (*number*)
.cos	cosine	Math.cos (*num_radians*)
.sin	sine	Math.sin (*num_radians*)
.tan	tangent	Math.tan (*num_radians*)
.ceil	least integer >= num	Math.ceil (*number*)

Method	Result	Format
.floor	greatest int <= number	Math.floor (*number*)
.exp	e to power of number	Math.exp (*number*)
.log	natural log of number	Math.log (*number*)
.pow	base to exponent power	Math.pow (*base, exponent*)
.max	greater of two numbers	Math.max (*num, num*)
.min	lesser of two numbers	Math.min (*num, num*)
.round	round to nearest integer	Math.round (*number*)
.sqrt	square root of number	Math.sqrt (*number*)

These methods should come in pretty handy in creating the functions for your scripts, especially if you'd like to do some heady scientific calculations on your Web pages.

In this lesson, you learned about creating and using JavaScript objects. In the next lesson, you'll learn how to apply what you know about JavaScript to HTML Forms.

Handling User Data and Forms

In this lesson, you learn from example how to check form data and submit HTML forms using JavaScript.

Event Handling and Alerts

The main reason for writing JavaScript programs is to handle events created by the user. In many cases, this isn't as tough as it seems. One way to respond to users is through an alert box, which is similar to a dialog box, except that it has only one button for a response. The point of an alert box is to say something directly to the user, then have him click OK to move on.

Listing 10.1 offers an example of handling an event by responding with an alert box.

Listing 10.1 A Simple Event

```
<HTML>
<HEAD>
<TITLE>Saying Goodbye</TITLE>
<SCRIPT>
<!--
   function goodbye () {
   alert("For more information about BigCorp products\nPlease call
1-800-BIG-CORP");
   return;
   }
// end hiding -->
</SCRIPT>
</HEAD>
<BODY>
<A HREF="http://www.netscape.com/" onClick="goodbye()">Click
here to leave.</A>
</BODY>
</HTML>
```

Notice the newline character \n which allows you to add a new line in the middle of a text string that's to be written to the browser, or another interface element.

It is possible to have eliminated the function goodbye with a simple line of script like the following:

```
onUnload="alert('For more information about our listings\nPlease call
1-800-WRITE-IT')"
```

Realize that this forces you to use the single quote character for the alert text. If you prefer to script this way, that's okay. However, this is generally considered poor programming technique, since it includes actual calculations in the interior of your HTML markup. For best results, you want to separate the calculations into functions, which should all be stored in the head of your document. Either way, it should look something like Figure 10.1.

Figure 10.1 Before the current link is followed, this alert will appear.

The alert box is a simple command, even though it's still in its own function. This example also offers us a few hints on JavaScript programming:

- Remember that putting even the simplest commands in a function is the best way to design JavaScripts—if you ever need to add to that function, you won't need to move too much around. You can just add more commands in the function declaration.
- Alert boxes are good for something else, too—error checking. If you're not sure what's going on at a particular point (or if a particular part of your JavaScript is being performed), drop in a quick alert command that tells you the current status. That way, when you test the JavaScript, you can make sure everything is working the way you expect it to.

Events for Form Checking

Now you'll use event handling for something a little more complex, and perhaps more useful. One of the best uses of JavaScript and event handling is to verify form data. You can use JavaScript to hand off your data object pointer to a function, which can then take a close look at what your user has entered and determine if it's correct.

Try it for a ZIP Code. You're simply going to make sure that the user has entered five numbers. Listing 10.2 is an example of an error-checking event handler.

Listing 10.2 Verifying Form Data with JavaScript

```
<HTML>
<HEAD>
<TITLE>Data Checking</TITLE>
<SCRIPT>
<!--
  function zip_check (form) {
  zip_str = form.Zip.value;
  if (zip_str == "") {
     alert("Please enter a five digit number for your Zip code");
     return;
     }
  if (zip_str.length != 5) {
     alert ("Your Zip code entry should be 5 digits");
     return;
     }
  return;
  }
// end hiding -->
</SCRIPT>
</HEAD>
<BODY>
<H3>Please fill out the following form:</H3>
<FORM ACTION="http://www.mycom.net/cgi-bin/address_form">
<PRE>
Name:    <INPUT TYPE="TEXT" SIZE="50" NAME="Name">
Address: <INPUT TYPE="TEXT" SIZE="60" NAME="Address">
City:    <INPUT TYPE="TEXT" SIZE="30" NAME="City">
State:   <INPUT TYPE="TEXT" SIZE="2" NAME="State">
Zip:     <INPUT TYPE="TEXT" SIZE="5" NAME="Zip"
           onChange = "zip_check(this.form)">
Email:   <INPUT TYPE="TEXT" SIZE="40" Name="Email">
<INPUT TYPE="SUBMIT" VALUE="Send it" onClick = "zip_check(this.form)">
</FORM>
</BODY>
</HTML>
```

This event-handling script discretely checks an entry in the Zip box, using the onChange handler to determine when the user has moved on from Zip's text box (either by pressing Tab or clicking in another text box with the mouse). It is a good idea to place the Zip text box before the E-mail box, since the user could just click the Submit button and skip past your error check.

Also, by adding the onClick event to the Submit button, you're able to catch users if they happen to skip the Zip Code box completely. Now we've double-checked their entry, as shown in Figure 10.2.

This script also brings up a method you've seen before, although you might not recognize it. Remember that String methods don't require the string object name to work correctly; they're simply attached to any string variable. In the function declarations, you may have noticed the following line:

```
if (zip_str.length != 5) {
```

variable.length is a method that allows you to determine the length of any variable in JavaScript. Since JavaScript does no variable typing (it doesn't explicitly require you to say "this is a number" or "this is text"), then any variable can be treated as a string. In this case, even though the ZIP Code could be interpreted as a number, zip_str.length tells you how many characters long it is.

The above snippet could be stated "if the length of zip_str does not equal 5, then…" Notice that != is the "does not equal" comparison. Similarly, == is the "does equal" comparison. Look at the following snippet from the function declaration:

```
if (zip_str == "") {
```

This could be read as "if zip_str equals nothing, then…" If the condition (zip_str == "") is true, then the code specified by the curly brackets is performed.

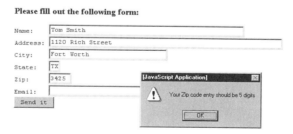

Figure 10.2 Error checking with JavaScript.

Client-Side JavaScript

Now you're ready to move up to the big time—create a customer service form that allows customers to send in data. Instead of using a CGI script to handle the data, though, you'll do the whole thing in JavaScript. After users have entered their preferences and values, you'll output them to the page for their perusal. If they like it, they can send it to you by mail.

Listing 10.3 is an example of a full-featured form handling JavaScript.

Listing 10.3   Customer Service Form Using JavaScript

```
<HTML>
<HEAD>
<TITLE>BigCorp Customer Service</TITLE>
<SCRIPT>
<!--
function processForm (doc) {
     if (doc.form1.os[0].checked)
         newline = "\r\n"
     else if (doc.form1.os[1].checked)
         newline = "\n"
     else
         newline = "\r";
     result_str = "";
     result_str += doc.form1.name.value + newline;
     result_str += doc.form1.address.value + newline;
     result_str += doc.form1.city.value + newline;
     result_str += doc.form1.state.value + newline;
     result_str += doc.form1.zip.value + newline;
     if (doc.form1.desktop.checked)
➥ result_str += "Desktop computers" + newline;
     if (doc.form1.notebook.checked)
➥ result_str += "Notebook computers" + newline;
     if (doc.form1.peripherals.checked)
➥ result_str += "Peripherals" + newline;
     if (doc.form1.software.checked)
➥ result_str += "Software" + newline;
     doc.form2.results.value = result_str;
     return;
     }
// -->
</SCRIPT>
</HEAD>
<BODY>
<DIV ALIGN="CENTER">
<IMG SRC="servlogo.html">
</DIV>
```

continues

Listing 10.3   Continued

```
<P>In order that we might better serve you we ask that you simply fill
➡out this
form. When you've submitted the form, the results will appear in the
➡text area
at the bottom of the screen. If everything looks all right, send it
➡away.</P>
<FORM NAME="form1">
<PRE>
Your Name:      <INPUT TYPE="Text" NAME="name" SIZE="40">
Your Address:   <INPUT TYPE="Text" NAME="address" SIZE="60">
Your City:      <INPUT TYPE="Text" NAME="city"
➡ SIZE="20"> State:<INPUT TYPE="Text"
NAME="state" SIZE="2">
Zip:<INPUT TYPE="Text" NAME="zip" SIZE="5">
<HR>
<H4>What products would you like more information about? (Check all
➡that apply)</H4>
<INPUT TYPE="Checkbox" NAME="desktop"> Desktop computers
<INPUT TYPE="Checkbox" NAME="notebook"> Notebook computers
<INPUT TYPE="Checkbox" NAME="peripherals"> Peripherals
<INPUT TYPE="Checkbox" NAME="software"> Software
<HR>
Please Choose Your Computer's OS:<BR>
<INPUT TYPE="Radio" NAME="os" VALUE="mac" CHECKED> Macintosh
<INPUT TYPE="Radio" NAME="os" NALUE="unix"> Unix
<INPUT TYPE="Radio" NAME="os" VALUE="win"> DOS/Windows/Win95<BR>
<HR>
<INPUT TYPE="Reset" VALUE="Clear Form">
<INPUT TYPE="Button" VALUE="Submit" onClick="processForm (document)">
</PRE>
</FORM>
<HR>
<FORM NAME="form2" METHOD="POST" ACTION="mailto:response@mycorp.net"
➡ENCTYPE="text/ascii">
<H4>Here's what your information will look like. If you'd like to
➡include a comment,
please type it below the other information. Then click below to mail
➡it to us:</H4>
<TEXTAREA NAME="results" COLS="60" ROWS="10" WRAP="soft"></TEXTAREA>
<INPUT TYPE="Submit" Value="Mail It Off">
</FORM>
</BODY>
</HTML>
```

Basically what this script does is:

1. Takes the information from the first form.
2. Translates it into some simple text values.

3. Assigns those values to the text area in the second form.

4. Allows the user to edit the data, as shown in Figure 10.3.

The script uses the result from the option buttons in the first form to determine which newline character to use for the text area, depending on the user's OS choice. Different OSes required different newline characters to format text correctly in a textarea. This script solves that problem.

Then, when users click the second **Submit** button (the "send it in" button), the data is sent via e-mail to the address of your choice. In that way, you've avoided using the Web server and CGI-BIN scripts for any of your form processing.

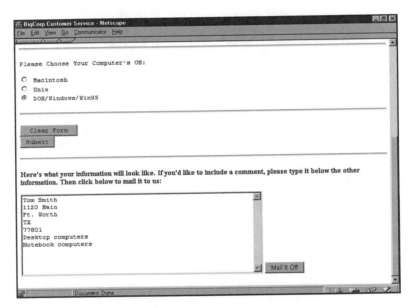

Figure. 10.3   Client-side form submissions.

The data is still going to come in like any other mailto: form submission, which means in the ugly POST format. But, you've created a wonderful JavaScript for displaying the data and getting approval from your users.

In this lesson, you saw a number of examples that cover event handling in JavaScript. In the next lesson, you'll see how to control links and use JavaScript with frames.

JavaScript for Frames

In this lesson, you learn how to change Web pages within frames using JavaScript.

Using JavaScript for Frames

Using forms, frames, and JavaScript, it's possible to create a page that allows the user to select from a menu of page descriptions, then load that page in a frame window. This might be useful for a help-style frameset that allows the user to go instantly to the topic that's important to her.

In fact, an interface such as this one would probably work well for any number of site types:

- A catalog of products, where each product has an image and description on a separate Web page
- A number of different images that can be selected by menu name
- A client list that takes users to the client's home page or "about" page
- Job listings that can be accessed by name, and then loaded into the viewer window of a frameset

Using scripts to manipulate pages gives you a great way to serve nearly any type of document from within a frames interface—product spec sheets, public relations material, software documentation, or just about anything else you can come up with.

In this example, you'll create a menu-based frames interface for job listings, as shown in Figure 11.1.

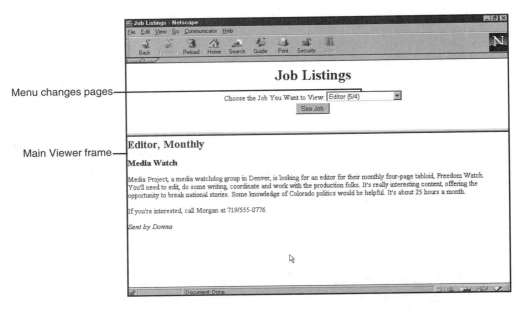

Figure 11.1   A JavaScript-enabled frames interface.

Creating this interface requires a number of different HTML documents, all designed to work together:

- A frameset that features two frames—a top frame for the menu control and a bottom frame for the main viewer.
- A JavaScript menu for the top frame.
- An initial page for the main viewer that explains a bit about what's going on.
- Document pages to be loaded in the main viewer by the menu.

Listing 11.1 shows you how to create the JavaScript-enabled menu.

Listing 11.1   Creating a JavaScript Menu—*jobform.html*

```
<HTML>
<HEAD>
<TITLE>Job Form</TITLE>
<SCRIPT>
<!--
 function changePage(form) {
    var choice=form.jobpage.selectedIndex;
    parent.main_viewer.location.href=form.jobpage[choice].value;
    }
```

```
// -->
</SCRIPT>
</HEAD>
<BODY>
<DIV ALIGN="CENTER">
<H1>Job Listings</H1>
<FORM>
Choose the Job You Want to View:
<SELECT NAME="jobpage">
<OPTION SELECTED VALUE="jobs.html"> About Job Listings
<OPTION VALUE="list1.html"> Editor (5/4)
<OPTION VALUE="list2.html"> Freelance Writer (5/6)
<OPTION VALUE="list3.html"> Copy Editor (5/7)
<OPTION VALUE="list4.html"> PR Specialist (5/8)
</SELECT><BR>
<INPUT TYPE="button" Value="See Job" onClick="changePage(this.form)">
</FORM>
</DIV>
</BODY>
</HTML>
```

The key to working with frames and JavaScript is the JavaScript object hierarchy parent.main_viewer. This is telling the script that the frame you want to change is the frame that you've named main_viewer within this same *parent* document. (The parent document is the one that is holding the frame.)

Another concept you need to understand here is the "array" in JavaScript, since this is how JavaScript stores the values for a SELECT form element. Here are the basics of an array:

1. Every time you create a new SELECT <OPTION> statement, that value is stored in a new variable. But notice that there's nothing to name the variable, since it would simply overwrite the last value that was assigned to jobpage.value.

2. Because each <OPTION> doesn't have its own NAME, your browser creates an "array" of jobpage values. The first one gets called jobpage[0] (the one with the value "jobs.html"). The next one gets called jobpage[1] and so on. The number is the "index" of the OPTION array—it's how you access each individual option.

3. Another variable is also created, called jobpage.selectedIndex. It holds a number that tells you which index has been chosen.

4. So, in the preceding script, you assign the value in selectedIndex to a variable called choice, and then you use choice to access the value of the OPTION that was chosen by your user.

5. Then the value (in this case, the URL of a job listing page) is passed to the frame's `location.href` variable, which causes a new page to be loaded.

Next, you need to create some filler pages. You'll create a "default" page that talks about the job's interface, and create one other example to test your frames interface.

Listing 11.2 is an example for the default `jobs.html` document.

Listing 11.2 A Default Page for Your Main Viewer—`jobs.html`

```
<HTML>
<HEAD>
<TITLE>Job Listings</TITLE>
</HEAD>
<BODY>
<DIV ALIGN="CENTER">
<H2>Write This! Job Listings</H2>
</DIV>
<P>Please choose the job listing you'd like to view from the menu at
➥the top of this page. If you've arrived here by clicking on the
➥graphic on our index page, read on.</P>
<HR>
<H3>About the Listings</H3>
<P>Our listings are free to anyone who'd like to post a job
➥opportunity, and we'll accept pretty much anything that can be
➥remotely shown to be of interest to our audience. While we welcome
➥submission from our members, we have no quarrel with headhunters,
➥placement agencies and corporate HR types who want to send along
➥some info. All we ask is that it arrive in the following form:</P>
<UL>
<LI>Position Title
<LI>Company Name
<LI>Hours/Commitment
<LI>Description
<LI>Qualifications
<LI>Salary
<LI>Contact Info
</UL>
<P>If you have a format that your organization follows and it's
➥remarkably different from ours, please write and let us know about
➥it -- we'll work something out.</P>
<DIV ALIGN="CENTER">
<H5><A HREF="index.html">Index</A> | <A HREF="tips.html">Tip Guide</A>
➥ |
```

```
<A HREF="bios.html">Member Bios</A> ¦ <A HREF="letter.html">
➥Letter From Editor</A> ¦
<A HREF="links.html">Other Interesting Sites</A></H5>
</DIV>
</BODY>
</HTML>
```

Since you probably don't plan to create a permanent job listing site for yourself, you might not want to get too mired in creating sample pages to link to with this interface. Here, however, is one sample listing that can be selected using the JavaScript-enabled menu.

Listing 11.3 offers an example listing, called list1.html.

Listing 11.3 Example—*list1.html*

```
<HTML>
<HEAD>
<TITLE>Editor, Monthly</TITLE>
</HEAD>
<BODY>
<H2>Editor, Monthly</H2>
<H3>Media Watch</H3>
<P>
Media Project, a media watchdog group in Denver, is looking for an
➥editor for their monthly four-page tabloid, <I>Media Watch</I>. You'll
➥need to edit, do some writing, coordinate and work with the production
➥folks. It's really interesting content, offering the opportunity to
➥break national stories. Some knowledge of Colorado politics would be
➥helpful. It's about 25 hours a month.
</P>
<P>
If you're interested, call Morgan at 719/555-0776.
</P>
<ADDRESS>Sent by Donna</ADDRESS>
</BODY>
</HTML>
```

Finally, you need to create the frame interface page. This one should be fairly simple, since it's just a two-frame frameset.

Listing 11.4 shows you how to create the frameset.

Listing 11.4 The Job Listing Frameset—*listings.html*

```
<HTML>
<HEAD>
<TITLE>Job Listings</TITLE>
</HEAD>
<FRAMESET ROWS="150, *">
   <FRAME SRC="jobform.html" MARGINHEIGHT="10">
   <FRAME SRC="jobs.html" NAME="main_viewer" MARGINHEIGHT="5">
</FRAMESET>
</HTML>
```

With all of this said and done, you're ready to test your new interface. When you load listings.html, you should see the logo and SELECT menu in the top frame and jobs.html (the default listings page) in the main_viewer frame. Selecting a new help page from the menu and clicking See Job should change the document in the lower frame. Figure 11.2 shows you the full interface.

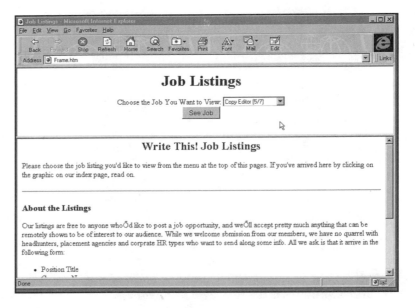

Figure 11.2 The final jobs interface using frames.

In this lesson, you learned how to use JavaScript with frames documents.

Dynamic HTML

Basics of
Dynamic HTML

In this lesson, you learn what Dynamic HTML is and how it can be applied to Web pages.

What Is Dynamic HTML?

For too long now, many Web authors and designers have lamented the fact that Web pages didn't allow them the freedom over placement, fonts, colors, and other aspects of the page that they'd grown used to controlling in the desktop publishing world. The fact that more attractive newsletters and documentation pages were possible in Windows WordPad or Mac's SimpleText, for instance, discouraged artists and cutting-edge authors from getting their hands dirty with HTML.

Then came HTML tables, frames, and style sheets. Now, designers have more control over the elements on the page, and the possibilities are almost endless. And, with scripting languages like JavaScript and VBScript, it's even possible to react to events created by the user, so that information a user enters can be altered, computed, and spit back to them—the scripting languages can even load new pages and create alert boxes to interface with the user.

But there was still one major problem with this system: Once a page was loaded in the user's browser, it was static. Aside from things like Java applets, animated GIFs, and Shockwave presentations, nothing could really move around on the page. That's why there's Dynamic HTML. Figure 1.1 shows an example of a Dynamic HTML page.

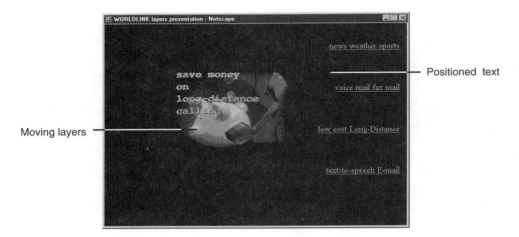

Positioned text

Moving layers

Figure 1.1   Dynamic HTML can significantly change the way people see your Web documents.

Dynamic HTML does the following:

- Begins scripting languages and style sheets together, so that the latest browser can change the style of HTML text and elements "on-the-fly." When a scripting element changes a style sheet property, that change is seen immediately in the browser.
- Works with new style sheet elements to position text on the page, and change that position if desired. Using Dynamic HTML, it's possible to move elements around on the page in a way that seems animated.
- Allows you to create layers of text on a document, meaning text can overlap or completely overlay other text (and other HTML elements) on the page. That way, you create interesting 3-D, watermark, and other effects for display on your pages. Figure 1.2 shows an example of this.

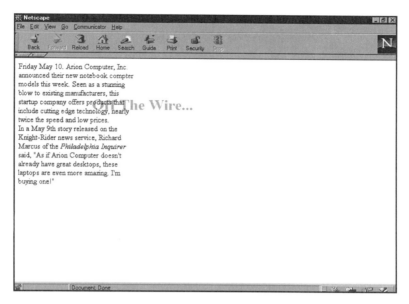

Friday May 10. Arion Computer, Inc.
announced their new notebook compter
models this week. Seen as a stunning
blow to existing manufacturers, this
startup company offers products that
include cutting edge technology, nearly
twice the speed and low prices.
In a May 9th story released on the
Knight-Rider news service, Richard
Marcus of the *Philadelphia Inquirer*
said, "As if Arion Computer doesn't
already have great desktops, these
laptops are even more amazing. I'm
buying one!"

Figure 1.2   One aspect of Dynamic HTML allows you to add layers of HTML elements to create a watermark effect.

Types of Dynamic HTML

Another phenomenon in the Web browser wars is the tendency for the two big players, Microsoft and Netscape, to define the same term in different ways—at least in the short term. While the World Wide Web Consortium is a standards body to which both belong, the standards tend to be ironed out after Netscape and Microsoft have already fought their way through the first version of a new concept.

In the case of Dynamic HTML, Netscape and Microsoft currently support some of the same ideas, but go off on other tangents that aren't necessarily supported by both—but are still called Dynamic HTML. Here's what their concepts of Dynamic HTML have in common:

Style Sheet Positioning   Using standard extensions to the Style Sheet specifications, you can determine exactly where elements will be placed on a page.

Layering   Text elements (and some others) can be placed behind other elements, creating a 3-D or watermark effect on a Web document.

Dynamic Font Characteristics   Netscape allows you to link directly to font definition files that allow you to specify the exact font family and point size of fonts.

Microsoft adds support for some other technologies that it lumps into the category of Dynamic HTML. These go beyond the Netscape standards, but match up with many of the World Wide Web Consortium's (the governing body of the HTML standard) early positions that may be included in later standards.

TIP   **Microsoft Only**   Using special Microsoft-specified Dynamic HTML commands will generally work only in Internet Explorer 4.0 and later. (Versions of Netscape Navigator beyond 4.0 may also support these.) If you decide to use them, you should warn your users that Internet Explorer is required for the full effect.

Here are some of the Microsoft additions to Dynamic HTML:

The Internet Explorer Object Model   Instead of a limited object model made available to JavaScript in Netscape's implementation, the IE model includes access to many more elements within a page, including making things like the CSS style sheet specification completely programmable.

Dynamic Text Attributes   When the user points the mouse to certain elements, you can change the font, color, size, and other elements to make the page act more dynamic. Users know immediately if they've placed their mouse in a "hot zone" for clicking.

Dynamic Content   The Microsoft Dynamic HTML implementation gives you the ability to have actual new content appear on the page within parts of a preexisting document. This doesn't require the page to be reloaded in the browser. It also readjusts the page to compensate for new content when necessary. An example is shown in Figure 1.3.

Data Binding   Internet Explorer supports the sending of data objects (using Java or ActiveX) to a client browser, where the data can then be manipulated by a Dynamic HTML Web page. For example, if the data objects hold information on a user's stock portfolio, then the dynamic page could access that data to display the portfolio sorted in different ways, focus on individual stocks, or similar manipulations, all without returning to the Web server to retrieve the same data over and over again.

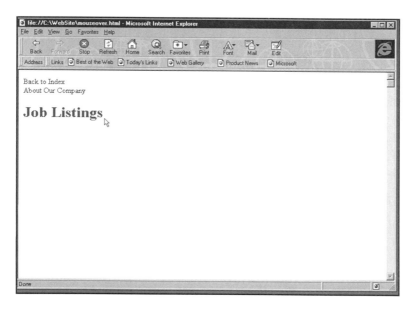

Figure 1.3   Text can change sizes and colors when your user passes their mouse pointer over the text to make it more clear that something has been selected.

How It All Works

In Part V of this book, you'll learn quite a bit about programming to manipulate your Web pages and the CSS style sheet specification, along with the different ways that Microsoft and Netscape implement Dynamic HTML. This part assumes, for the most part, that you're familiar with the programming and style sheet lessons that appear earlier in the text.

Because of the differences between the two browser manufacturers' standards, Part V is organized as follows:

- Lessons 2 and 3 begin with the standard HTML positioning and advanced positioning concepts.
- Lessons 4, 5, and 6 discuss Netscape-specific Dynamic HTML, including layers, animation, and the JavaScript Accessible Style Sheets.
- Lessons 7, 8, and 9 focus on the Microsoft version of Dynamic HTML, including active content, data awareness, and examples of dynamic pages.

TIP **Test Browser** For this part, you'll want copies of Netscape Navigator 4.0 or later or Internet Explorer 4.0 or later. These concepts do not work in browsers before the 4.0 level from the two companies.

In this lesson, you learned what Dynamic HTML is, the differences in Dynamic HTML between Netscape and Microsoft, and how the rest of this part will be organized. In the next lesson, you'll learn the basics of HTML positioning.

Style Sheet Positioning

In this lesson, you learn the basics of style sheet positioning in HTML and Cascading Style Sheets.

What Is Positioning?

Until now, there's been no way to absolutely position blocks of text and HTML elements on the Web page—the closest procedure was to use HTML tables to force elements into cells on the page. The new standard for positioning HTML elements, however, is better than HTML tables, because it establishes an actual coordinate system for laying out groups of HTML elements.

Here's what positioning is and what it does:

- Positioning is an extension of the existing Cascading Style Sheets (CSS) definition.
- Positioning allows you to create relative positions for groups of HTML tags, meaning the elements are positioned against other elements in the document, but flow naturally when the document changes.
- Positioning also allows absolute positioning, which fixes elements or groups of elements at specific coordinates on the page.

Using scripting languages, it's also possible to make positioning dynamic, so that the position of elements can change while the page is being viewed (ultimately creating an animation effect). In this lesson, however, you'll learn *static* positioning.

Positioning Elements

Before you begin to position elements on the screen, it's important to learn two new concepts that have been added to what you know of the CSS definition and HTML attributes:

ID definitions   In the <STYLE> section of your document, you'll define certain coordinate positions using the # symbol and a name of your choosing.

ID references   Within the document itself, elements can be assigned a certain ID using the id= attribute, followed by the name of the ID as defined in the <STYLE> section of your document.

An example of an ID definition would be:

```
<STYLE>
<!--
#layer1 {position:absolute; top: 50px; left:100px; width: 175px}
-->
</STYLE>
```

To reference that ID, then, you'd simply add the id= attribute to an HTML element, like:

```
<H1 id=layer1>Off The Wire...</H1>
```

TIP   **ID Attributes**   The id= attribute is used for nearly all block-level HTML tags, like <H1>, <P>, <BLOCKQUOTE>, and others. It's often used, however, with the special <SPAN> and <DIV> elements designed for style sheets.

Style Sheet Additions

There are also a number of properties that have been added to the CSS definition itself that are useful for static positioning. Table 2.1 shows these.

Table 2.1   CSS Additions for Positioning

Property	Possible Values	Example
position	absolute, relative	position:absolute
left	number+units	left:100px
top	number+units	top:50px

Property	Possible Values	Example
width	number+units	width:250px
height	number+units	height:5in

These properties are pretty straightforward in their definitions. Essentially, they each give you control over the *box* in which your positioned element will appear.

 Box In this lesson, box describes the dimensions created by using these positioning properties. It's useful to think of a position definition as creating a box into which the HTML elements are flowed. However, no box appears on-screen—it's just a useful metaphor for the purpose of positioning elements.

Here's what these properties do individually:

`position` This property is used to determine whether the positioning occurs relative to preceding elements or in absolute measurement against the dimensions of the Web document.

`left, top` These are the beginning coordinates for a given ID definition. They react to the position property. For example, if `position:absolute`, then `top:100px` places that particular ID definition at 100px below the beginning of the Web document. If `position:relative`, then the top of this element will appear 100 pixels below where it would normally appear in a regular HTML document.

`width, height` These two are used to determine the dimensions of the box in which elements with a particular positioning ID are flowed.

Here's a quick example of how two boxes can be created, filled with HTML elements, and positioned on the page.

```
<HTML>
<HEAD>
<TITLE>Basic Positioning</TITLE>
<STYLE TYPE="text/css">
<!--
#layer1 {position:absolute; top:50px; left:50px; width:250px}
#layer2 {position:absolute; top:100px; left:250px}
-->
</STYLE>
</HEAD>
```

```
<BODY>
<SPAN id=layer1>
<H1>Off the Wire...</H1>
</SPAN>
<P id=layer2>Text for body of docoument</P>
</BODY>
</HTML>
```

A lengthy bit of text has been cut out of the example (although it's pictured in Figure 2.1). Notice a couple of interesting things are going on in this example:

- id=? is used as an attribute to both the <P> and <SPAN> tags. Nearly any tag can accept an id style definition.
- In ID definitions, layer1 is defined as overlapping layer2 (in width) by 50 pixels. This would be difficult to do in table-based layout.

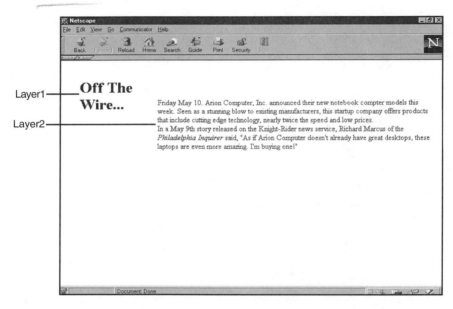

Figure 2.1 Using the positioning properties of the CSS definition, it's a simple matter to create more complex page layout.

Parents and Children

In absolute positioning, it's important to realize that an element is positioned relative to the coordinate system of its *parent*. In the case of this lesson's first example, both elements were children of the <BODY> element, which, in turn, was the parent for both the <SPAN> and <P> elements that were positioned.

Parent Element Any element that has some level of control over another element. If an <IMG> tag appears within a <P> container, for instance, then the paragraph is that image's parent. If an <H3> tag appears on its own within an HTML document, then the <BODY> tag is its parent.

But, if one of the elements contains the other, then the containing element becomes the parent element, essentially creating a new coordinate system for the child element. Here's an example:

```
<HTML>
<HEAD>
<TITLE>Basic Positioning</TITLE>
<STYLE TYPE="text/css">
<!--
#layer1 {position:absolute; top:50px; left:50px; width:250px}
#layer2 {position:absolute; top:10px}
-->
</STYLE>
</HEAD>
<BODY>
<SPAN id=layer1>
<H1>Off the Wire...</H1>
<P id=layer2>Text for body of document</P>
</SPAN>
</BODY>
</HTML>
```

Notice that the <SPAN> element actually contains the <P> container within it. Now, instead of having <BODY> as a parent, <P> has the <SPAN> element as a parent. That means that any positioning for the <P> element is based on a coordinate system that's created by the <SPAN> element, not <BODY>.

Figure 2.2 should hopefully make this more clear. Notice that the <P> content is formatted within the box created by <SPAN>. For instance, the paragraph text begins 10 pixels below the top of the <H1> element, not 10 pixels below the top of the Web page.

Relative Positioning

Relative position is useful for maintaining the "natural flow" of an HTML document, while allowing the element to participate in other positioning possibilities, like defining the top and left margins of the element relative to its parent. Again, relative positioning uses the coordinate system of its parent, but, unlike absolute positioning, the child element is not positioned at exact pixel coordinates.

337

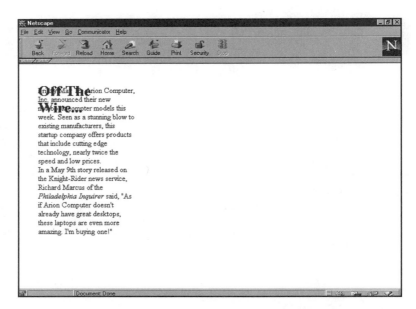

Figure 2.2   An absolutely positioned child element is positioned relative to its parent, not the page itself.

In the first example in this lesson, changing one or the other ID definitions to relative would have made no difference, since the <P id=layer1> and <SPAN id=layer2> elements both had <BODY> as their parent. But, if you change one to absolute in the second example:

```
<HTML>
<HEAD>
<TITLE>Basic Positioning</TITLE>
<STYLE TYPE="text/css">
<!--
#layer1 {position:absolute; top:50px; left:50px; width:250px}
#layer2 {position:relative; top:10px}
-->
</STYLE>
</HEAD>
<BODY>
<SPAN id=layer1>
<H1>Off the Wire...</H1>
<P id=layer2>Text for body of docoument</P>
</SPAN>
</BODY>
</HTML>
```

Because the paragraph is a child of the <SPAN>, it appears within <SPAN>'s box (or coordinate system). But, since it's not positioned absolutely to that coordinate system, the <P> text is actually offset from the <SPAN> text by 10 pixels, as shown in Figure 2.3.

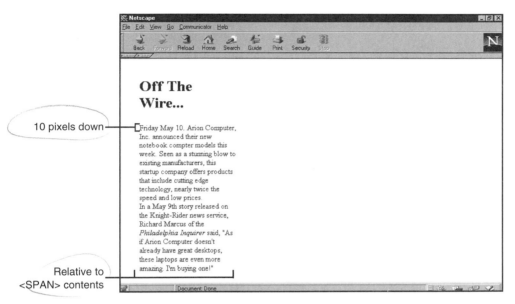

10 pixels down

Relative to
<SPAN> contents

Figure 2.3 Using relative positioning, an element takes on the characteristics of its parent, but isn't positioned absolutely to its coordinate system.

TIP   **Try Positioning**   Relative versus absolute can be difficult to grasp at first. Experiment with these examples until you get a feel for why elements are being positioned the way that they are. Try different values for the properties, too.

In this lesson, you learned how to position elements absolutely and relatively. In the next lesson, you'll learn advanced positioning.

Advanced Positioning

In this lesson, you learn advanced positioning concepts using additions to the Cascading Style Sheets specification.

Static Positioning

In the last lesson, you learned the `position` property that could accept values of `absolute` or `relative`. There is one other setting for `position` that isn't terribly difficult to grasp: the `static` value.

With `position: static`, the element in question acts exactly as it does when it's regular HTML. It cannot be positioned or repositioned, and it does not create a new coordinate system for any of its children. By way of example:

```
<HTML>
<HEAD>
<TITLE>Basic Positioning</TITLE>
<STYLE TYPE="text/css">
<!--
#layer1 {position:static}
#layer2 {position:absolute; top:10px}
-->
</STYLE>
</HEAD>
<BODY>
<SPAN id=layer1>
<H1>Off the Wire...</H1>
<P id=layer2>Text for body of docoument</P>
</SPAN>
</BODY>
</HTML>
```

This example is rendered by a browser as it appears in Figure 3.1. Notice that the paragraph text is positioned relative to the browser window (the <BODY> tag) and not a new coordinate system. (Note also that actual body text has been substituted for the purpose of illustration within the figure.)

Friday May 10, Arion Computer, Inc. announced their Repair Extension Program, implemented to address customer complaints **On the Wire** and further lamenting the decline of Arion. In a May 9th story released to the Knight-Rider wire service, Dan Stats of the Philadelphia Inquiring said, "As if Arion Computer doesn't have enough problems, the beleaguered firm issued Wednesday what amounts to a recall on a million or more of its PerfBook computers."

Figure 3.1 Static positioning renders elements the same as regular HTML, and also does not create a new parent coordinate system.

Floating Elements

The floating elements property actually already exists in the CSS specification, although it's generally assumed that this element is for creating floating images that have text wrapped around them. In fact, any element can be a "floating" element, allowing text to wrap around it—even other text.

Here's an example:

```
<HTML>
<HEAD>
<TITLE>Floating Elements</TITLE>
<STYLE TYPE="text/css">
<!--
#layer1 {position:absolute; top:50px; left:50px; width:600px}
#layer2 {float:right; top:10px; left: 10px; width 200px}
-->
</STYLE>
</HEAD>
<BODY>
<P id=layer1>Text for body of docoument
<SPAN id=layer2>
<H1>"Various news services reacted harshly"</H1>
</SPAN>
</P>
</BODY>
</HTML>
```

In this example, the layer1 definition creates a coordinate system (or box) for the floating element defined in layer2. The layer2 element is then positioned to the right of that box, with the paragraph's text flowing around it. Figure 3.2 shows how this would look in a browser.

Friday May 10. Arion Computer, Inc. announced their Repair Extension Program, implemented to address customer complaints concerning flaws in certain PerfBook models. Various news services have reacted harshly, however, calling the move a "recall" and further lamenting the decline of Arion. In a May 9th story released to the Knight-Rider wire service, Dan Stats of the Philadelphia Inquiring said, "As if Arion Computer doesn't have enough problems, the beleaguered firm issued Wednesday what amounts to a recall on a million or more of its PerfBook computers."

"Various News Services——Reacted Harshly"

Floating Element

Figure 3.2   The parent defines a coordinate system, which the floating element then aligns with on the right side.

Element Visibility

The visibility property determines whether or not an element is displayed. If the element is not displayed, then it still takes up the space that it normally would, but is invisible. This is especially useful in Dynamic HTML, because scripting languages are generally able to turn on and off visibility, making text and images appear or disappear in reaction to user-generated events.

An example of visibility might be Listing 3.1:

Listing 3.1   Basic Positioning of Layers

```
<HTML>
<HEAD>
<TITLE>Basic Positioning</TITLE>
<STYLE TYPE="text/css">
<!--
#layer1 {position:absolute; top:50px; left:50px;}
#layer2 {position:absolute; top:50px; left:50px; visibility:hidden}
-->
</STYLE>
</HEAD>
<BODY>
<IMG WIDTH=300 HEIGHT=300 SRC="image1.gif" ID=layer1>
<IMG WIDTH=300 HEIGHT=300 SRC="iamge2.gif" ID=layer2>
</BODY>
</HTML>
```

Because the layer2 definition includes the visibility:hidden property, the second image will not appear in the browser window, as shown in Figure 3.3. It is loaded but hidden.

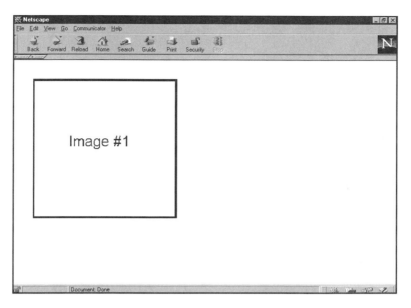

Figure 3.3 Only the image that wasn't specifically hidden appears in the browser window.

In fact, all you have to do is change the style definitions to get a completely different result in the browser window. Change the style code to:

```
<STYLE TYPE="text/css">
<!--
#layer1 {position:absolute; top:50px; left:50px;}
#layer2 {position:absolute; top:50px; left:50px; visibility:hidden}
-->
</STYLE>
```

With the rest of the example the same as Listing 3.1, the result is pictured in Figure 3.4.

Now, imagine changing visibility using JavaScript or a similar scripting language in response to the user clicking a button, moving the mouse over certain text, or something similar. That's Dynamic HTML at work.

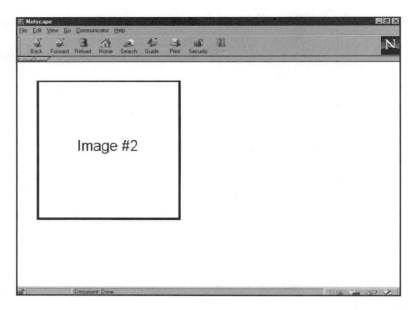

Figure 3.4   Once the visibility property is switched, the other image appears.

Layers and "Z Positioning"

If "x" moves left and right and "y" moves up and down, then the "z" direction is back-to-front, as in layering one element on top of another. If you've experimented at all with the positioning properties, then you may have already seen some elements overlapping. By default, elements are assigned a z-index number as they're created in the document—the higher the number, the closer the element is to the "top" layer.

There are three things to remember about layering:

- Elements are assigned default z-index numbers in the order that they're created, with each new element layered on top of the others.
- The z-index can be set for individual elements to change that order.
- All elements are transparent by default, so all layers before them can also be seen.

To change the order of certain elements, you simply add the z-index property and a number (see Figure 3.5), as in the following example:

```
<HTML>
<HEAD>
<TITLE>Layers</TITLE>
<STYLE TYPE="text/css">
<!--
#layer1 {position:absolute; top:50px; left:50px; width:600px;z-
➥index:2}
#layer2 {position:absolute; top:70px; left: 70px; width 200px;
➥color:gray;z-index:1}
-->
</STYLE>
</HEAD>
<BODY>
<P id=layer1>Text for body of document</P>
<SPAN id=layer2>
<H1>"Various news services reacted harshly"</H1>
</SPAN>
</BODY>
</HTML>
```

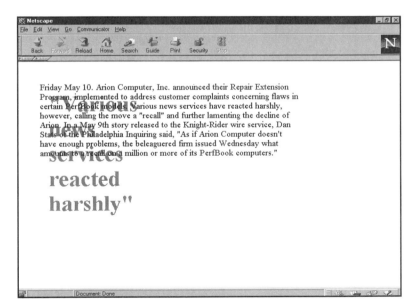

Figure 3.5 You can change the order of layers with the z-index.

Now, instead of the <H1> text overlaying the body text, it works the other way around. Note that with the addition of the basic CSS color property, this example is also able to approximate a "watermark" appearance.

TIP   **Background Transparency**   To change the transparency of an element, use the standard CSS background property to give the element's background some color.

In this lesson, you learned the advanced options for CSS positioning. In the next lesson, you'll learn how to use the Netscape layer tags.

Netscape Layers

In this lesson, you learn what layers are and how to use the Netscape layers tag.

What Are Netscape Layers?

In Lesson 3, you learned that the CSS positioning properties not only move HTML elements to exact parts of the screen, but they also place the elements in layers, so that the first element on the page is on the first layer, the second element is placed on top of the first, and so on. You also learned that it's possible the use the attribute z-index to change the order of the layers.

Netscape, however, opts to include a second way to accomplish this—the <LAYER> tag. The <LAYER> tag is Netscape-only, completely duplicates the functionality of the CSS tags, and requires a bit of effort to enter over and over again. It is, however, okay to use if you plan to have only Netscape users—especially in a controlled environment like an intranet. The Netscape tags do offer simplified syntax and a few extra layout features, so you may choose to use them over CSS anyway.

There are a few key differences between the <LAYER> tag and its CSS counterparts:

- The <LAYER> tag doesn't require any definition before it is used. While it does include an ID, it doesn't require a style definition or anything similar.
- Because <LAYER> is a tag, its attributes (like ID, TOP and LEFT) work like tag attributes, not style sheet properties. That means they accept values after an equal sign and don't require semicolons between them.
- <LAYER> has an optional SRC attribute that can be used to load an HTML document into that layer.
- <LAYER> also has the attributes PAGEX and PAGEY that have no equivalent in the CSS definition.

Adding Netscape Layers

Aside from a few differences, the <LAYER> tag works pretty much the same way that the CSS positioning elements work. Here's an example:

```
<HTML>
<HEAD>
<TITLE>Basic Positioning</TITLE>
</HEAD>
<BODY>
<LAYER ID=layer1 TOP=10 LEFT=50>
<SPAN>
<H1>Off the Wire...</H1>
</SPAN>
</LAYER>
<LAYER ID=layer2 TOP=60 LEFT=250>
<P>Text for body of document</P>
</LAYER>
</BODY>
</HTML>
```

The <LAYER> tag is used as a container that holds all of the elements in its particular layer. The ID tag is used to give the layer a name (primarily for JavaScript access) while the TOP and LEFT attributes are used to position the layer against the origin created by its parent layer or the <BODY> tag if there are no other parents.

This example displays exactly like the basic CSS style sheet examples you saw in the last two lessons. In this case, it is displayed in Netscape Navigator as shown in Figure 4.1.

Positioned versus Inline

As with the CSS positioning properties, the <LAYER> tag allows you to position elements in an absolute fashion, using TOP and LEFT values to position the contents relative to the coordinate system created by the layer's parent. In layer-parlance, these are considered "positioned" layers.

The <ILAYER> tag, conversely, is used to specify a layer that is intended to act as an inline or "in-flow" layer—that is, a layer that appears in its "natural" position in the flow of the HTML document. Because the <ILAYER> tag can accept the same attributes that the <LAYER> tag does, it's actually simply designed to use its "natural" coordinates as an origin—TOP and LEFT attributes can be used to move it from that origin.

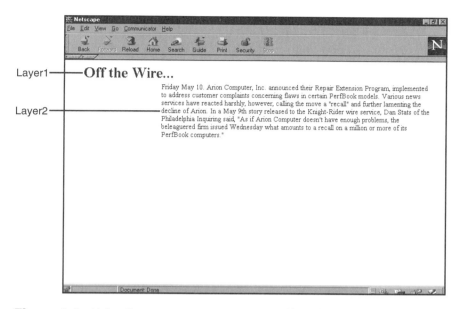

Figure 4.1 Using the <LAYER> tag to create positioned text.

Here's an example:

```
<BODY>
<P>This is the first paragraph.</P>
<ILAYER LEFT=10>
<P>This paragraph began at its natural origin, then moved ten
➥pixels to the right.</P>
</ILAYER>
<P>This paragraph is another natural paragraph.</P>
</BODY>
```

In this case, the example looks like Figure 4.2 in a copy of Netscape Navigator.

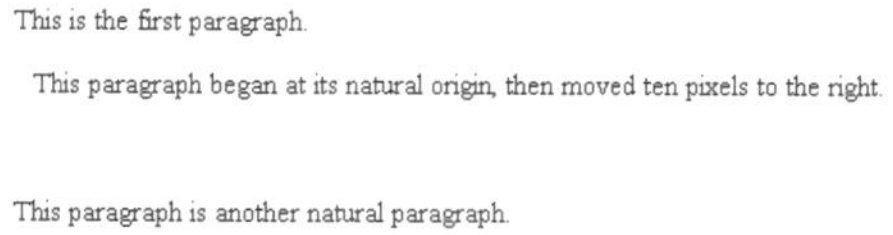

This is the first paragraph.

This paragraph began at its natural origin, then moved ten pixels to the right.

This paragraph is another natural paragraph.

Figure 4.2 The <ILAYER> tag works much the same way that relative positioning does in CSS.

Layer Attributes

<LAYER>'s attributes tend to be fairly similar to the CSS positioning properties, but some of them vary a bit from the standard. All are designed specifically to work well with JavaScript, the Netscape-preferred scripting language for page positioning.

Here are the attributes for <LAYER> (and <ILAYER>):

ID   The ID attribute was previously called NAME, but was changed to reflect the property used in CSS. ID simply gives the layer a label for accessing via JavaScript. Example: ID=layer1.

LEFT and **TOP**   The attributes specify how far from the origin of the layer's parent the new layer begins. Pixels are assumed to be the units for the number used. Example: LEFT=10.

PAGEX and **PAGEY**   These attributes can be used with the <LAYER> tag to specify the number of pixels away from the top-left corner of the enclosing document the layer should begin. Using these attributes overrules the parent's control over origin coordinates. Example: PAGEX=50.

SRC   The SRC attribute points to an HTML document that is to be included in this layer. Example: SRC="about.html".

WIDTH   This attribute accepts either a number (for pixels) or a percentage of the width of the containing layer (parent). Example: WIDTH=65%.

HEIGHT   The main purpose of this attribute is to act as a reference for child layers that use this attribute with a percentage; it's a reference only. If a frame needs to grow past the height specified in this attribute, it will simply grow the layer. Example: HEIGHT=400.

CLIP   This attribute is used to determine the boundaries of the visible area of a layer. The value is a set of four numbers that represent the left, top, right, and bottom values, respectively. Example: CLIP=10,10,50,50.

Z-INDEX   Accepts a number that places overlapping layers in order from back-to-front. Example: Z-INDEX=3.

ABOVE and **BELOW**   These attributes cannot be used with the Z-INDEX attribute, but they can be used to specify the layers that should appear above and below the current layer. The layers' ID attributes are used to identify them. Example: ABOVE=layer1.

VISIBILITY   The visibility attribute can accept three values: SHOW, HIDDEN, and INHERIT. The INHERIT value is used to tell Netscape Navigator that the current layer should have the same visibility as its parent. Example: VISIBILITY=SHOW.

BGCOLOR and **BACKGROUND**   These two attributes are used to change the layer's background from transparent to something else. BGCOLOR accepts a color name or 3 hex-pairs for red, green, and blue values. BACKGROUND accepts an URL to an image file. Example: BGCOLOR=#010101.

OnMouseOver, OnMouseOut, OnFocus, OnBlur, OnLoad   These attributes are all event handlers that accept a function name or inline JavaScript coding. Example: OnBlur="change_color()".

In addition to all these attributes, there is also the <NOLAYER> container tag, which displays its contents in browsers that don't recognize the <LAYER> tags. An example would be:

```
<NOLAYER>
Netscape Navigator 4.0 or above is required to view these pages,
➥since they use the Netscape Layer tags.
</NOLAYER>
```

Applets, Plug-Ins, and Forms

In Netscape's implementation of layers, any element that's considered a *windowed* element automatically floats to the top of all layers and is always visible. Even if the layer that contains them is obscured, windowed elements always come to the top and remain visible.

 Windowed Element   Any element that requires its own screen-area within a typical HTML document. This includes elements like plug-ins, applets, and HTML form buttons or menus.

In this lesson, you learned the basics of Netscape Layers. In the next lesson, you'll learn how to access Netscape layers with JavaScript.

Advanced Netscape Layers

In this lesson, you learn how to use JavaScript to access layers.
You also learn how to animate layers.

The Layer Object Model

Like most other elements in HTML, the <LAYER> element generates correspond-ing objects that can be accessed by JavaScript or a similar scripting language. Associated with each instance of a layer are a number of properties (that correspond to the attributes for the <LAYER> tag) and methods, or built-in functions.

For instance, a particular property of a layer can be accessed and changed using a JavaScript assignment like:

```
layer1.left=10
```

These follow the general format of:

```
layerName.methodName (parameters)
layerName.propertyName
```

Through JavaScript statements in the layers themselves or through functions created to handle events that affect each layer, these properties and methods can be changed so that layers themselves seem to change dynamically on the page.

Layer Object Properties

Most of the layer object properties will be familiar to you because they're the same as attributes you used in the last lesson to change the properties of indi-vidual layers. Table 5.1 shows many of the layer object properties that you can access and change.

Table 5.1 Layer Object Properties and Corresponding Attributes

Property	Attribute	Description
name	ID	name of the layer
left	LEFT	horizontal position of layer's left edge
top	TOP	vertical position of layer's top edge
pageX	PAGEX	horizontal position of layer relative to page (not CSS)
pageY	PAGEY	vertical position of layer relative to page (not CSS)
zIndex	ZINDEX	z-order of this layer relative to other layers
visibility	VISIBILITY	whether layer is visible, hidden, or inherits parent's visibility
clip.left	CLIP	First value of CLIP attribute (left boundary)
clip.top	CLIP	Second value of CLIP attribute (top boundary)
clip.right	CLIP	Third value of CLIP attribute (right boundary)
clip.bottom	CLIP	Fourth value of CLIP attribute (bottom boundary)
clip.width	WIDTH	Pixel value or percentage of parent's width for a layer
clip.height	HEIGHT	Pixel value or percentage of parent's height for a layer
background	BACKGROUND	Image for layer background; use background. src to access URL
bgcolor	BGCOLOR	Background color; layerName.bgcolor = null for transparent
src	SRC	URL to HTML document for layer's content

 TIP **Use JavaScript** These properties can be accessed using JavaScript regardless of whether they were created on the page using CSS positioning or the <LAYER> tag syntax.

The layers themselves are actually held in an *array* of layers that are part of the document object. To access a particular layer, you can use the name of the layer as the value for the array, as in:

```
document.layers["mylayer"]
```

Array A method by which the same variable can hold more than one value at a time. In order to do that, it must have an index, which is generally a number. In the case of layers, that index can be the name of the layer in question, since JavaScript stores a number that corresponds to that ID name.

In many cases, you'll want to set the layer in question to a new variable that can be accessed as a stand-alone object, such as:

```
theLayer = document.layers["mylayer"]
```

The properties and methods of that particular layer can then be accessed using the new layer variable, as in:

```
theLayer.top = 5
```

Layer Object Methods

Along with the layer object properties come a number of layer object methods that can be accessed in the same way that other methods are accessed in JavaScript. Notice that many of these methods are designed to help you animate and manipulate layers.

Table 5.2 shows many of the methods available for use with layers.

Table 5.2 Layer Object Methods

Methods	Description
moveBy (x,y)	Changes the layer position by the number of pixels specified
moveTo (x,y)	Changes the layer position to the specific pixel coordinates
moveToAbsolute (x,y)	Changes layer position to specific coordinates on the page
resizeBy (width, height)	Resizes layer by specified values; does not reflow HTML
resizeTo (width, height)	Changes layer size to specified values
moveAbove (layer)	Stacks this layer above specified layer
moveBelow (layer)	Stacks this layer below specified layer
load (src, width)	Changes the source of a layer to the contents of a file

In general, it's important to note that resizing layers generally doesn't cause the HTML to be reflowed to fit the new size; if the layer is made smaller, the contents of the layer will be clipped. This can be useful for creating visual transitions between layers, for instance.

The layer-moving methods will not only change the position of a layer to a new z-index, but they'll also change layer parents for the moved layer. A moved layer takes on the same parent as the layer it is placed above or below.

Methods are accessed in the same way that they are in any JavaScript programming situation:

```
mylayer.resizeTo (50, 100)
```

Manipulating Layers

You may already see the possibilities with layers. Using the various methods and properties of layers, it's possible to programmatically move, hide, and resize layers, making it possible to have them seem to animate, wipe, appear, and disappear or any other number of actions.

To do this, you'll need to create the layers, then use JavaScript to manipulate them. Listing 5.4 is a simple example of using two different layers to change the view of information on a page.

TIP **CSS Syntax** Remember that these scripting examples work just as well with layers that are defined using CSS syntax.

Listing 5.4 Hiding and Revealing Layers

```
<HTML>
<HEAD>
<TITLE>Layers Example</TITLE>
<SCRIPT>
<!--
function hideAllLayers() {
        document.layers["job0"].visibility = "hide";
        document.layers["job1"].visibility = "hide";
        }

function changeJob(n) {
        hideAllLayers();
        document.layers["job" + n].visibility = "show";
```

```
}
// -->
</SCRIPT>
</HEAD>

<BODY>
<H1>Job Listing Page</H1>

<P>Each job is listed separately. To view a job that interests you,
➡select it from the pull-down menu.</P>

<H3>Please select a job:</H3>

<FORM>
<SELECT name=menu onChange="changeJob(this.selectedIndex);">
<OPTION>Editor
<OPTION>Publication Specialist
</SELECT>
</FORM>

<LAYER name="job0" LEFT=50 width=400 TOP=200 LEFT=50
➡BGCOLOR="#FFFFDD">
<H3>Media Watch</H3>
<P>
Media Project, a media watchdog group here, is looking for an
➡editor for their monthly four-page tabloid, Media Watch. It's
➡about 25 hours a month. You'll need to edit, do some writing,
➡coordinate and work with the production folks. It's really interesting
➡content, offering the opportunity to break national stories. Some
➡knowledge of Colorado politics would be helpful.
</P>
</LAYER>

<LAYER name="job1" LEFT=50 width=400 TOP=200 LEFT=50
➡VISIBILITY="HIDE" BGCOLOR="#DDFFFF">
<H3>Children's Hospital</H3>
<P>
Children's Hospital is looking for a publications specialist.
➡This writer/editor position requires 3 - 5 years writing/editing
➡experience, knowledge of the health care industry, database management
➡and Web site development experience. Fax resumes. Attn: HR.
</P>
</LAYER>

</BODY>
</HTML>
```

Here's a step-by-step account of what this page and script does:

1. The page itself begins by declaring two functions, hideAllLayers and changeJob. It then goes on to add the static HTML, including form controls and headings. It then creates two different layers, each positioned at the same absolute coordinates on the page. The first layer is shown, but the second layer is hidden.

2. The form menu is designed to handle the event of the menu being changed (using the inching event handler) by calling the function changeJob and sending the value of the selectedIndex associated with the <SELECT> menu.

3. The changeJob function accepts the selected value, then calls the hideAllLayers function, which simply hides both of the job listing layers (this is easier than selectively hiding those that don't correspond to the selected index).

4. Back in the changeJob function, the visibility property of the selected layer is changed to **show**. Now, only the layer that corresponds to the selected index for the <SELECT> menu is visible.

This example (which was borrowed from a more lengthy example posted by Netscape) offers one flash of brilliance—notice that the possible values for selectedIndex correspond exactly to the number in the job layer names. If Editor is selected in the menu, then the selectedIndex is 0; if Publication Specialist is chosen, the selectedIndex is 1.

This is interesting, because it allows you to use string concatenation (or "text addition") to add the selected index value to the word "job," thus making the array index equal to either job0 or job1 in the statement:

```
document.layers["job" +n].visibility = "show";
```

Notice that the concatenation takes place because the term "job" is in quotes; otherwise, JavaScript would try to interpret job as a variable to be added to n.

Animation in Layers

Here's another quick and fun example. In this one, you'll create two layers that move in from different sides of the page in a way that's somewhat like a multimedia presentation. To do this, you'll need to know a special built-in JavaScript function called setTimeOut ().

The setTimeOut () function is designed to insert a delay in other functions so that action can be perceptible to humans. Here's an example:

```
setTimeOut ("function", 5, "arg")
```

The first argument setTimeOut accepts is the function it is supposed to call after waiting the allotted time; the second is the time in milliseconds it should wait; and the third is any argument it should send to the function it calls.

Now, you're ready to create the animating layer example. Listing 5.2 includes the entire document.

Listing 5.2 Animating Layers

```
<HTML>
<HEAD>
<TITLE>Simple Move Example</TITLE>
</HEAD>

<BODY>

<LAYER NAME="words0" LEFT=700 TOP=50 WIDTH=250>
<H2>Welcome To</H2>
</LAYER>

<LAYER NAME="words1" LEFT=-200 TOP=75 WIDTH=250>
<H3>The Writer's Page</H3>
</LAYER>

<SCRIPT>
<!--
function moveLeft() {
    var leftlayer = document.layers["words0"];
    if (leftlayer.left > 165) {
       leftlayer.moveBy(-20, 0);
       setTimeout("moveRight()", 1);
       }
      return;
    }

function moveRight() {
    var layer1 = document.layers["words1"];

        if (layer1.left < 235) {
        layer1.moveBy(20, 0);
        setTimeout("moveLeft()", 1);
        }
      return;
    }
```

```
// -->
</SCRIPT>

<SCRIPT>
moveLeft ();
</SCRIPT>

</BODY>
</HTML>
```

Notice that the function call appears at the very end of the script, while the function definition occurs in the middle of the script—this is actually the only way this script will work, due to what might be seen as a deficiency of its design:

- Because the function uses the `document.layer[]` object directly (instead of being passed a pointer to that object), the layers must be defined before the function is declared.

- At the same time, the function call must appear after the function declaration; otherwise, JavaScript sees nothing to call. That's because it's a direct function call instead of an event handler. If it were an event handler, the function declaration could appear at the end of the script; it would have the time to load before being called.

 TIP **Dynamic Changes**   Remember that images can be added to layers as well, which can then be animated. Also, nearly any property of the layer can be changed on-the-fly, so try changing colors, visibility, and so on.

In this lesson, you learned to work with layer objects and animate layers. In the next lesson, you'll learn how to dynamically alter Netscape fonts.

Netscape's Dynamic Fonts

In this lesson, you learn about the abilities Netscape has added for supporting fonts and how to add new fonts to your Web pages.

In earlier HTML implementations, one of the problems with incorporating tags like the <FONT> tag or CSS properties like {font:} has been the fact that, as a Web author, it's almost impossible to know what fonts the user has on his or her system. So, font family control has been limited to a few, very standard options: Arial, Helvetica, Times, and similar basic fonts.

But what if you have a special symbol font, script style, or another sort of font family that you'd like to incorporate into your pages? Netscape's Dynamic Fonts specification deals with this problem.

With dynamic fonts, you can:

- Specify a particular font definition to be used in your Web page or site.
- Assign a particular font or font family to nearly any HTML element.
- Link entire font definitions to your pages using special <LINK> tags in the head of your document.

Figure 6.1 offers examples of fonts included in a Netscape Web document.

 TIP **Netscape Only** At the time of writing, Netscape was the only browser to support this technology. Don't forget that not everyone who reads your pages will see these dynamic fonts. If you're worried about the universal appeal of your pages, you might choose to stick with basic HTML style sheets.

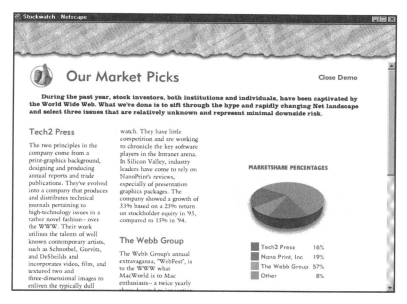

Figure. 6.1 For seasoned Web surfers, the fonts on this page make it look like a large graphic image, but it's just dynamic fonts at work.

Font Definitions

When you specify a particular font definition within your document, that font is actually downloaded to the user's browser along with the font commands that place it within the document. That makes it possible for any of your users to see the fonts the way you designed the page, since you're not relying on their computer system to have the right fonts available.

It also means you need to know where to get the fonts and how to place them in your document so that they're properly downloaded. This is done using a new style sheet definition, as follows:

```
<STYLE TYPE="text/css">
<!--
@fontdef url(http://home.netscape.com/fonts/sample.pfr)
-->
</STYLE>
```

Font definition files are stored in files with a .PFR extension, and must be accessible by the URL in the @fontdef statement in order to work correctly.

PFR stands for Portable Font Resource, a new file type created by Bitstream and Netscape as part of their TrueDoc font technology. Each PFR file is a highly compressed font resource not unlike the TrueType fonts installed on Mac and Windows systems.

TIP   **Buy the Fonts**   There is a catch, though—you have to buy these font definition files to include them on your Web page. Check out **http://www.bitstream.com/world/** for more info.

It's also perfectly reasonable to download the font definition file to your Web server directory, then access it using a relative URL, like:

```
@fontdef url(sample.pfr)
```

The font definition will then be sent along with your Web document without requiring an extra download from across the Web.

Linking Fonts

Netscape also makes it possible to link fonts using the tag <LINK> instead of a style sheet definition. Linking accomplishes much the same thing as the style sheet procedure, causing the font to be downloaded to the user's system if necessary for displaying it.

The <LINK> tag uses two attributes:

- The REL attribute specifies that you're linking to a font definition file.
- The SRC attribute accepts a complete or a relative URL to the .PFR file.

The <LINK> tag is placed in the head of your document and requires a new instance of the tag for every font that you include in your page. Here's an example:

```
<LINK REL="fontdef" SRC="http://www.netscape.com/font/fontname.pfr">
```

Or, you can use a relative URL:

```
<LINK REL="fontdef" SRC="fonts/fontname.pfr">
```

Either of these works fine, although it's generally recommended that you link to font definition files stored on your own Web server so they're always accessible to users of your Web pages.

Adding Fonts to Pages

Once you've linked your page to the new font definition, adding the font to your page is simple. Using the existing <FONT> tag along with some new attributes—POINT-SIZE and WEIGHT—it's just a matter of wrapping some text in the <FONT> container to change its appearance.

Here are the new attributes:

POINT-SIZE   This attribute accepts a number that sets the exact size of the font, in points. Example: POINT-SIZE=16.

WEIGHT   This attribute allows you to specify the "boldness" of a font. Values range from 100 to 900, in steps of 100, where 100 is least bold and 900 is maximum bold. Example: WEIGHT=800.

Entire paragraphs, headings and other sections of text can easily be changed using the <FONT> command and the new font definition. An example of an entire page using new fonts might be:

```
<HTML>
<HEAD>
<TITLE>New Fonts</TITLE>
<LINK REL="fontdef" SRC="http://www.netscape.com/font/monospace.pfr">
➥<LINK REL="fontdef" SRC="http://www.netscape.com/font/fancy12.pfr">
</HEAD>
<BODY>
<H3><FONT FACE="monospace" POINT-SIZE=24> Children's Hospital</
FONT></H3>
<P>
<FONT FACE="fancy" WEIGHT=400>
Children's Hospital is looking for a publications specialist.
➥This writer/editor position requires 3 - 5 years writing/editing
➥experience, knowledge of the health care industry, database
➥management and Web site development experience. Fax resumes.
➥Attn: HR.
</FONT>
</P>
</BODY>
</HTML>
```

The page is rendered first as Web pages usually are (using default fonts) until the font definition files are loaded by the user's browser. Then the new fonts are displayed.

CAUTION

Watch Speed Early implementations of dynamic fonts (in Netscape Communicator 4.01) slow down the browser considerably, even on reasonably fast computers. This will probably improve, but don't forget to test your pages to make sure they're scrolling smoothly.

In this lesson, you learned how to add dynamic fonts to your Web pages. In the next lesson, you'll learn how to create pages using Microsoft's Dynamic HTML.

Microsoft's Dynamic HTML

In this lesson, you learn how to animate your Web pages with Microsoft's version of Dynamic HTML.

Microsoft's Dynamic Philosophy

Microsoft easily goes beyond the Dynamic HTML championed by Netscape, offering a slew of options that aren't provided with the 4.0 level of Netscape Navigator. While Microsoft's Internet Explorer supports CSS positioning and layers (within the CSS syntax), it also supports dynamic styles and dynamic content, allowing you to change the appearance of a Web page without reloading the page—and without the sleight-of-hand of positioning layers.

For the most part, IE manages to support these dynamic HTML concepts by revamping the Document Object Model. In doing so, Microsoft essentially allows almost any CSS style sheet property to change, and then be displayed in the browser without reloading the page. This gives the impression of immediate feedback, while allowing Web pages to look and act more like multimedia presentations.

Dynamic Styles

Using a scripting language, nearly any CSS style property can be changed in a Dynamic HTML document. That change will be rendered instantly in the browser window, giving the appearance of a dynamic page. This is especially useful as a device for responding to events generated by the user, like mouse movements.

In fact, one of the more popular early uses of Dynamic HTML use onMouseOver and onMouseOut event handlers to change the appearance of anchor text. Using these events makes the text style of an anchor change as the user moves the mouse pointer over that anchor. When the user moves the pointer away from the anchor, the text changes back to a normal style. This makes for a more exciting page that responds directly to user input.

Listing 7.1 is an example of using these events to change style properties dynamically.

Listing 7.1   VBScript and CSS Properties for Dynamic HTML

```
<HTML>
<HEAD>
<TITLE>Dynamic Style Demo</TITLE>
</HEAD>

<SCRIPT LANGUAGE= "VBSCRIPT">
<!--
    sub Job1_onMouseOver
            Job1.style.color="red"
    End Sub

    sub Job1_onMouseOut
            Job1.style.color="blue"
    End Sub

    sub Job2_onMouseOver
            Job2.style.color="red"
    End Sub

    sub Job2_onMouseOut
            Job2.style.color="blue"
    End Sub

-->
</script>

<BODY>
<FONT FACE="Arial,Helvetica"SIZE="2">
<P>
<B>Job Listings</B>
<UL>
<LI><A HREF="/jobs/job1.html" id="Job1">Editor</A>
<LI><A HREF="/jobs/job2.html" id="Job2">Document Specialist</A>
</UL>
</FONT>
</BODY>
</HTML>
```

For such a simple effect, this actually requires a bit of scripting. Here's what happens with this page:

1. Starting with the body of the document, typical hyperlink anchors are defined, along with a name for each. This allows VBScript to react to user events.

2. When one of these anchors is touched by the mouse pointer, the `onMouseOver` event for that hyperlink is called. The color of the hyperlink is then changed by accessing the hyperlink color object property (for example, `document.anchors("Job1").style.color="red"`).

3. When the user moves the mouse away from the anchor text, the event handler `onMouseOut` is called on to change the color of the text back to its default `blue`.

Dynamic Style IDs

You can give nearly any HTML element an ID, and it can be referenced using object terminology that ultimately allows you access to nearly any of its properties. Not only could you change the color of a link, for instance, you could also change the size of its text:

```
sub Job1_onMouseOver
        Job1.style.color="red"
        Job1.style.font="24pt"
End Sub

sub Job1_onMouseOut
        Job1.style.color="blue"
        Job1.style.color="12pt"
End Sub
```

And, you don't necessarily have to use hyperlinks, either. You could just as easily make paragraph text change colors and sizes, as in the following example:

```
<H2>Job Listings</H2>
<P id="Job1">Editor</P>
<P id="Job2">Document Specialist</P>
```

Figure 7.1 gives you some idea of how this looks in a browser.

Job Listings

Editor

Document₁Specialist

Figure 7.1 Dynamic styles are rendered in the browser window without forcing a reload. The moment an event (like `MouseOver`) is recognized, the style changes.

What you're taking advantage of to change these properties is Microsoft's Element Model, allowing you to programmatically (that is, using scripting language) access and change nearly anything conceivable about that element. For instance, you could change the CLASS associated with a particular element so that, without doing much programming at all, you could change many things about a single element with a simple command.

For instance, assume you've created two scripting classes something like:

```
<STYLE>
.notPicked {color:Black; font:small; font-family:Arial,Sans Serif}
.isPicked {color:Red; font-size:big; font-family:Times, Serif}
</STYLE>
```

Now, with those styles defined, it takes only a few simple commands added on to a particular element to change many different properties at once. For example:

```
<H1 onMouseOver="this.className=isPicked"
➥onMouseOut="this.className="notPicked">
```

And, as a bonus, you don't even have to specify an ID in this instance. If you like, just use the this keyword to refer to the current object.

Styles and JavaScript

The possibilities begin to approach endless with the dynamic styles capability built into Internet Explorer 4.0 and later. In fact, all of these events and changes can be programmed just as easily in JavaScript (JScript in Microsoft's implementation).

Listing 7.2 is a JavaScript example.

Listing 7.2   JavaScript for Dynamic Styles

```
<HTML>
<HEAD>
<TITLE>Dynamic Style Demo</TITLE>
</HEAD>

<SCRIPT LANGUAGE= "JavaScript">
<!--

function changeColor (job) {
    job.style.color="red";
    job.style.font="24pt"
    }
```

```
function changeBack (job) {
    job.style.color="black";
    job.style.font="12pt"
    }

-->
</script>

<BODY>
<FONT FACE="Arial,Helvetica"SIZE="2">
<P>
<B>Job Listings</B>
<UL>
<SPAN id="Job1" onMouseOver="changeColor(Job1)";
➥onMouseOut="changeBack(Job1)">
<P>Editor</P></SPAN>
<P id="Job2" onMouseOver="changeColor(Job2)"
➥onMouseOut="changeBack(Job2)">Document Specialist</P>
</UL>
</FONT>
</BODY>
</HTML>
```

This example is very similar to the VBScript examples except that the event handlers need to be spelled out more explicitly while, at the same time, each function can be reused by passing it a different value. Notice that this example is using the exact same object process to access the various style sheet properties:

1. The page assigns each element an ID name.

2. Each event handler passes that ID name to its respective function.

3. The function stores the ID name in a variable (for example, job) then uses it to reference the properties stored in that particular element's properties.

 TIP   **More Style Sheets**   To get a good idea about the possible properties that can be affected by scripting in Dynamic HTML, check out the lessons on Style Sheets in Part III of this book. If you'd like to see every single attribute you can change, see **http://www.microsoft.com/workshop/author/dynhtml/** on the Web.

In this lesson, you learned how to dynamically change style sheet elements by using Microsoft's object model. In the next lesson, you'll learn how to add multimedia controls and access data in ActiveX objects.

Web Publishing Tools

Microsoft FrontPage Express

In this lesson, you learn how to create and edit Web pages using Microsoft FrontPage Express (formerly FrontPad).

What Is FrontPage Express?

Available for a free download (and included with Microsoft Internet Explorer 4.0), FrontPage Express is quickly becoming a very popular way to create and edit Web pages—especially if you're a fan of Microsoft's HTML extensions and ActiveX.

 Any Other Name... During the writing of this book, Microsoft changed the name of FrontPad to FrontPage Express, although only, apparently, in the Internet Explorer 4.0 distribution. Available for download under both names, realize that FrontPad and FrontPage Express refer to the same program, albeit perhaps different versions.

FrontPage Express is a basic, WYSIWYG (What You See Is What You Get) Web editor that allows you to create fairly advanced layouts, using menu commands and icons in the toolbar. In fact, FrontPage Express is especially useful when it comes to Microsoft-specific commands, which aren't always built in to third-party Web editors.

The following are some of the major advantages of FrontPage Express:

- Free for download and distributed with Microsoft Internet Explorer 4.0
- Works with the Web publishing wizard to make uploaded files to your Web server much more automatic
- Has strong support for Microsoft's HTML additions like <MARQUEE> or ActiveX controls
- Allows you to view and edit the HTML codes directly

If you don't already have FrontPage Express, you can download it directly from **http://microsoft.com/** or as part of the Internet Explorer 4.0 distribution. Realize that FrontPage Express is different from Microsoft FrontPage, which is Microsoft's flagship (and somewhat expensive) retail Web editing application.

Starting a Web Page

After starting up FrontPage Express, you're presented with a blank, untitled document. To begin, you can set the page properties for your document:

1. Click the right mouse button and choose **Page Properties** from the pop-up menu, or choose **File**, **Page Properties** from the menu.

2. In the Page Properties dialog box, edit the Title, Base location (if desired) and other options under the General settings tab.

TIP   **Background Sound**   The background sound option in this dialog box uses the Microsoft-specific <BGSOUND> tag to create the background sound. This tag may not work in other browsers.

3. Click the **Background** tab to change the background or colors for the background and the different states of hyperlinks. The Watermark option can be used to force the background not to scroll behind text.

4. Click the **Margin** and **Custom** tabs to change those settings if desired. Click **OK** when you're done with page settings.

It's a good idea at this point to save your page to a directory or folder on your hard drive that's specifically designed for your Web testing. To save your document as a file (instead of on the Internet), choose **File**, **Save**, then click the **As File** button in the Save As dialog box.

Entering Text and Images

FrontPage Express offers a convenient Styles pull-down menu in its toolbar that makes creating a basic Web page move along very quickly. For instance:

1. To begin your page with a heading, pull down the styles menu and choose **Heading 1**. Now, type your heading.

2. When you hit return at the end of your heading, the style turns back to normal. This is the basic setting for paragraph text. Now, type a paragraph of text for the first heading on your page. When you're done with the paragraph, hit **Enter**.

 TIP **Many Returns** FrontPage Express automatically inserts the appropriate <P> tags when you hit the **Enter** key, and it compensates for extra spaces or hitting the tab key while you type. If you'd like to enter a <BR> tag, hit **Shift+Enter**.

3. Next, you'll enter a list. To begin your list, choose **Bulleted List** from the pull-down **Style** menu. Now, type your first bullet point. To move on to the next bullet point, hit **Enter**.

4. Once you're finished with your bulleted list, choose **Normal** from the menu to erase a blank bulleted line and return to paragraph text.

Figure 1.1 shows how things look so far.

Now, you'll add an image to the page. If you want to place the image back toward the top of the document, use the mouse to place the cursor where you want the image to appear. Then, do the following:

1. Choose the **Insert Image** button from the toolbar or choose **Insert**, **Image** from the menu.

2. In the Image dialog box, click the option button that corresponds to the type of URL you want to use (local file or Internet location).

3. In the associated text box, enter the name (or full URL) of the file. You can also click the **Browse** button to browse your hard drive for an image file.

4. Once you've located an image, click the **OK** button to add it to your document. It will appear in the document text.

5. To edit the image's properties (like alignment, HEIGHT, WIDTH, and so on) either double-click the image or right-click and choose **Image Properties** from the shortcut menu. The Image Properties Dialog box appears, as shown in Figure 1.2.

Style menu

Paragraph text

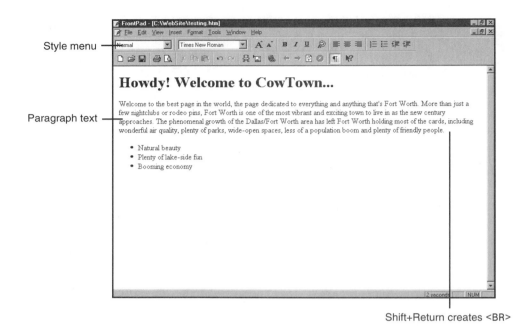

Shift+Return creates

Figure 1.1   With common HTML tags available from a quick menu, creating a page is pretty easy.

For source, ALT and hyperlinks

(Microsoft-only) For alignment, dimensions

For DyMSRC

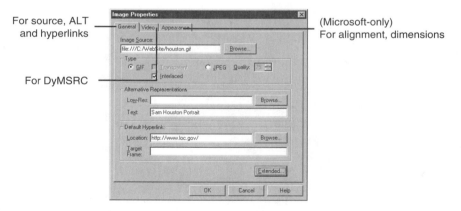

Figure 1.2   FrontPage Express offers a number of different properties for a simple image file.

6. The Image Properties dialog box includes General, Video, and Appearance tabs that allow you to change nearly any conceivable property for an image. When you're done, choose **OK**.

TIP   **Floating Image**   If you choose to align your image to the left or right, you've created a floating image. To place it where you want it to appear on the page, click and drag the image into the document. Actually, the image doesn't come with you—instead, you'll see a faint insertion point. That's where the <IMG> tag will go in the document, since the image must, by definition, stay aligned to the left or right. Placing the <IMG> tag elsewhere in the document will change the image's relative position.

Special Features

FrontPage Express offers support for a number of special Microsoft tags. To use them, simply select them from the Insert menu.

Marquee   To add a marquee, choose **Insert**, **Marquee** from the menu. In the Marquee Properties dialog box, enter the text for your marquee and specify any properties for it. Click **OK** when finished.

ActiveX   To enter an ActiveX control, choose **Insert**, **ActiveX Control** from the menu. In the ActiveX Control Properties menu, pull down the **Pick a Control** menu and choose the control you want to include. Enter any other applicable settings and click **OK**.

WebBots   Microsoft includes a few simple *WebBots* that you can add to your page by selecting **Insert**, **WebBot Component**. You'll then see the Insert WebBot Component dialog box, from which you can choose the **Include** (for time and date), **Search**, and **Timestamp**.

TERM   **WebBots**   These Microsoft-created objects are a combination of scripting and ActiveX components that work behind the scenes to allow you to add special features to your Web page. For example, the Include object automatically enters the date and time the page was last edited.

TIP   **Web Publishing Wizard**   When you're done creating your page, you're ready to save it to the Web. Choose **File**, **Save As** from the menu. Now enter a Page Location—the URL at which this page will be stored. Choose **OK** and the Web Publishing Wizard will be started up by FrontPage Express. Follow the on-screen instructions to publish your page.

In this lesson, you learned how to use FrontPage Express to create Web pages. In the next lesson, you'll learn to use Netscape Composer.

Netscape Composer

In this lesson, you learn how to use Netscape Composer to create Web pages.

What Is Composer?

Part of the Netscape Communicator Suite, Composer is the Web development tool of many folks who like the Netscape bundle, and those who use Netscape exclusively for corporate intranets. Composer is a WYSIWYG Web editor that supports standard HTML and makes adding elements fairly easy.

Some of the advantages of Composer include:

- Browser-like representation and the ability to instantly preview work in Netscape Navigator
- Word processor-like controls make font, text styles, and emphasis (such as bold and italic) work as they do in more familiar text programs
- Publish button in toolbar makes uploading simple
- Integrated spell checking

So how does Composer stack up? It's quite a bit more user-friendly than FrontPage Express, although the two are designed with different purposes in mind. FrontPage Express was created as a tool for managing Microsoft-oriented Web sites that include features like ActiveX support. Composer, on the other hand, is a lot more Netscape-centric.

If you're already a fan of the Netscape Communicator package, go ahead and take Composer for a spin. If you already understand HTML, Composer is a great, visual way to quickly build Web pages.

Creating a Web Page

Composer works like many Web-editing programs, relying on a pull-down style menu for many block-level tags (like paragraphs and headings). To add text to the page:

1. Begin by loading Composer (or switching to Composer in Communicator), then choose **Format**, **Page Colors and Properties**.

2. In the Page Properties dialog box, choose the **General** tab and edit the Title, Author, Description and Keywords, if desired. To add background colors or a background image, choose the **Colors and Background** tab. You can add other <META> tags using the **META Tags** tab. Click **OK** for settings to take effect.

TIP <META> **Again** Many of the General tab's settings, such as Keywords and Description, are actually using popular <META> tags that are often used by Web search robots to catalog your page.

3. Now, save the page by choosing **File**, **Save** from the menu and choosing a location. As with most Web editing, it's best to choose a special folder on your hard drive designed to be a mirror image of your online Web site.

4. To add a heading to the page, place the cursor in the document window and choose **Heading 1** from the pull-down **Style** menu in the toolbar. Enter text for the heading, then hit **Enter** (or **Return**).

5. Now you're back to the Normal style, which represents regular paragraph text. Type a paragraph, but don't hit Enter until you've finished the entire paragraph. That inserts the <P> tag. (To insert the <BR> tag instead, hit **Shift**+**Enter**.)

6. Now, try a list. You can create a list in Composer a number of ways. Try choosing **List Item** from the pull-down **Style** menu, then enter some text for each item, hitting **Enter** and the end of each.

7. Next, change it from a bulleted list (the default setting) to a numbered list. To do this, highlight the list, and then click the **Numbered List** icon in the toolbar, as shown in Figure 2.1.

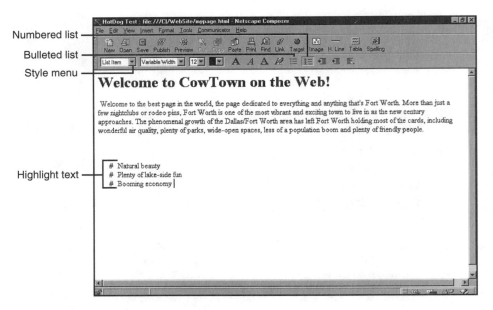

Figure 2.1 Changing list types in Netscape Composer is little more than a mouse click.

Adding an Image

Composer gives you access to most of the <IMG> tag attributes through a Preferences dialog box, allowing you to customize how your images appear in a browser without manually editing the settings. To add an image:

1. Place the cursor in your document where you'd like the image to appear.

2. Choose the **Image** button in the toolbar or select **Insert, Image** from the menu.

3. Enter the URL for the image in the Image Location text box or click the **Choose File** button to search for the image on your hard drive.

TIP **Edit Image** You can use the Edit Image button to open the image in an image-editing program of your choosing. The first time you select the button, Netscape asks you to specify the image-editing program; after that, images can be edited directly by clicking this button.

4. With the Image tab selected in the Image Properties dialog box, you can choose to edit a number of other options. Click the **Leave Image at Original Location** check box if you don't want Netscape to automatically copy the image to the same directory as your Web page; click **Use as Background** to use the image as your page's background image.

5. Other options include aligning the image, changing its dimensions, and adding space around the image. When you're done, you can choose the **Link** tag to specify a hyperlink for this image, and then click **OK** to add the image. To return to the Image Properties dialog box shown in Figure 2.2, you can double-click the image in the document window.

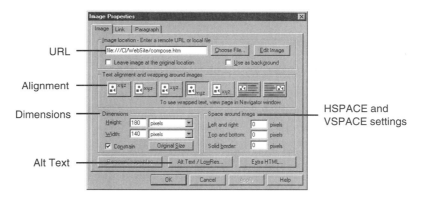

Figure 2.2 Adding an image (or changing attributes) is accomplished through this Image Properties dialog box.

Adding a Hyperlink

With Composer, you can simply highlight text that has already been typed in the document window; then apply a text style, alignment attribute, HTML list command, or even a new font. In this same way, you can add a hyperlink:

1. Highlight the text you'd like to turn into a hyperlink.

2. Choose the **Link** button in the toolbar or **Insert**, **Link** from the menu.

3. In the **Link to a Page Location or Local File** text box, enter the URL for this link.

4. If you'd like, edit the Character and Paragraph properties for this link by clicking the respective dialog tabs.

5. Click **OK** to add the hyperlink.

Unique to Composer

Some other features of Composer are worth mentioning, because they are unique and tend to be useful to Netscape-oriented Web authors:

Publish button   In Composer's toolbar, click the **Publish** icon to quickly publish your page on the Web. (You can also choose **File**, **Publish** from the menu.) The Publish dialog box can also include a user name, password and the option to include all pages in a particular HTML document's folder.

Preview button   Click the **Preview** button in the toolbar and you'll be asked to save your document. Then, your page is immediately displayed in the full version of Netscape Navigator, allowing you to see exactly how the page will look when it's published on the Web.

Check Spelling   Begin by clicking at the beginning of your document and make sure no text is highlighted. Then choose the **Spelling** icon from the toolbar or choose **Tools**, **Check Spelling** from the menu. The Check Spelling dialog box appears, allowing you to check your document's spelling like you would a typical word processing document.

In this lesson, you learned to use Netscape Composer to create Web pages. In the next lesson, you'll see how to use HotDog to create Web pages.

HotDog

In this lesson, you learn how to use the HotDog Web editor to create a page.

Create a Page with HotDog

HotDog is a professional-level editing program that is semi-WYSIWYG, allowing you to preview a document in one part of its window while you type HTML codes into the other side of the interface. This lets you get deep into the HTML codes (like this book does), while not requiring you to constantly load the page in a Web browser to preview the page.

If you don't have a copy of HotDog, you can download it from **http://www.sausage.com/** on the Web. The Professional version is currently priced around $100, but a free trial period is available if you download the program.

 TIP   **Free HotDog**   Sausage Software also offers HotDog Express, a small, simple Web page creator that's available as freeware. It's not as fully functioned as HotDog Pro, and it lacks strong editing tools.

Adding Text and Markup

There are a number of ways you can use HotDog, including as a straight text editor—as long as you're typing in your own codes, there's no reason to use the menu commands. They can make life a little easier, though.

To start a page:

> **1.** Launch HotDog and choose **File**, **New** in the menu (you may have to maneuver through some splash screens and animations first).

2. Choose the **Normal** template in the **New** dialog box (actually, there isn't much difference between the Default and Normal templates) and click **OK**.

3. An HTML template appears. You can highlight the **Title** text and enter your own title for the page.

4. To add a heading, just type the heading tag in the editing window, and then type the text for your heading.

5. Then, enter a <P> tag and type your document text. End the text with a </P>.

6. To add a list after your paragraph, place the mouse cursor in the editing window and choose **Insert**, **List**. In the Create List dialog box, enter your list items, choose the type of list, and then click **OK**.

Figure 3.1 shows your progress so far.

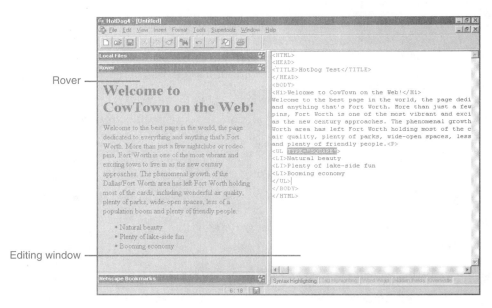

Figure 3.1 Rover, HotDog's WYSIWYG preview technology, makes it possible to edit HTML codes and preview your work at the same time.

Adding an Image

HotDog also includes automated tools for adding images to your pages:

1. Place the cursor where you'd like the image to appear in your document.

2. From the menu, choose **Insert**, **Image**. The Insert Image dialog box appears, shown in Figure 3.2.

3. Enter a file name for the image you want to add or click the **Folder** icon to browse for a file on your hard drive. You can also click the **Wizard** icon to use the Image Wizard built into HotDog.

4. Once you've chosen a file, enter values for the Height and Width (if desired), then enter a text description for the image.

5. Click **OK** to add the image.

After entering the image tag, you'll notice the Rover is sophisticated enough to display images along with the WYSIWYG text.

Figure 3.2   The Insert Image dialog box allows you to easily enter common image properties.

Adding Hyperlinks

HotDog also makes it easy to change text you've typed in the editing window into hypertext:

1. Highlight text for the hyperlink in the editing window.

2. Choose **Insert**, **Hyperlink** from the menu. The Insert Link dialog box appears.

3. In the URL text box, enter an URL for this hyperlink or click the **Folder** icon to browse your hard drive. You can also click the **Wizard** icon to use the Insert Link Wizard.

4. The Description is the hyperlinked text—there's no need to edit it unless you want text added or deleted from the browser window (or, if you didn't highlight any text to start).

5. You can also enter a target name (for example, **main_viewer**) if this link is intended for loading a page in another frame.

6. Click **OK** to enter the link.

The <A> tag appears in the browsing window and the hyperlink itself appears in Rover—it looks good, but you can't test the link itself without using an external browser.

In this lesson, you learned to create a basic page in HotDog. In the next lesson, you'll create a page in Adobe PageMill.

PageMill

In this lesson, you learn how to use Adobe PageMill to create Web pages.

What Is Adobe PageMill?

Available for Windows and Macintosh, Adobe PageMill is a full-featured, professional WYSIWYG editing environment that includes a special Preview mode, the ability to directly edit the HTML codes, and a drag-and-drop interface for creating HTML framesets.

PageMill has a number of interesting advantages and features:

- Edit pages using familiar word processor-like tools
- Create framesets by dragging the edges of the browser window
- Add transparency effects and client-side image map features directly to images from within the program
- Add properties for the page, forms, images, and framesets easily by using menus and text boxes in the Page Inspector

Starting Your Page

To begin editing your page in PageMill, you'll want to launch the program, then familiarize yourself with Editing and Preview mode. The icon in the top-right corner:

- Looks like paper dolls and a planet when you're in Preview mode
- Changes to a pen and paper when in editing mode

To change modes, just click the icon. Once you're in editing mode, you should change the page's basic properties. To do that, make sure the **Page** tab is selected in the Inspector:

1. While in Editing mode, click the **Page** icon in the Inspector.

2. Now, you can choose the base font, base target, body text, link text, and background colors. You can also add a background to the page by clicking the small page icon at the bottom of the Inspector, which opens a File Open dialog box that allows you to search for the background image. (The small trash icon deletes the background image from your page.) Figure 4.1 demonstrates the Inspector.

3. Now, save the page using the **File**, **Save** command. If possible, choose a new folder on your hard drive that will be a mirror image of the site you plan to upload to your Web server computer.

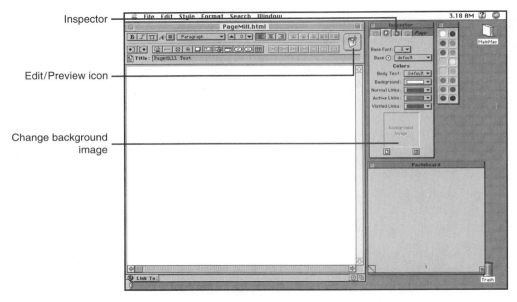

Figure 4.1   Originally developed for the Macintosh, PageMill has a graphical approach to creating Web pages and setting preferences.

Adding Text and Images

PageMill takes basically the same approach to Web editing that most other WYSIWYG editors do, allowing you to enter different types of HTML text and markup in one of two ways:

- Begin by selecting the type of text you'll type from the menu or toolbar, then type the text. For instance, you can select **Largest Heading** from the **Style** pull-down menu in the PageMill toolbar, then type a heading. To change to paragraph text, choose **Paragraph** from the Style menu.

- Type the text first, then highlight it with the mouse. Now, select the formatting you'd like applied to the highlighted text. This can include both styles from the Style menu or formatting commands from the toolbar or menu (like bold, italic, and font sizes).

Adding images to your page, however, offers up some differences from most other Web editors. To add an image and change its properties:

1. Place the cursor in your document where you want the image to appear.

2. Click the **Place Object** icon in the toolbar. In the **File Open** dialog box, highlight the image you want to include, and click the **Place** button.

 TIP **Copy Images** PageMill doesn't automatically copy images to the current directory, so make sure you've stored the image in the folder or subfolder that you'll want it in once it reaches the Web server.

3. Click the image once to select it. This changes the Inspector to reflect <IMG>-related attributes such as Height, Width, and ALT text. You can also choose what sort of image this is, including options like Button and Map.

4. Double-click the image, and you can edit it to create a client-side image map. Using the highlighted shape tools in the toolbar, draw shapes on the image. Then, highlight each image and enter an URL for that hot zone in the Link To: text bar at the bottom of the page. Enter an URL for each shape, and then click somewhere else in the document to make the image map take effect. The mapping tools are shown in Figure 4.2.

Creating a Frameset

PageMill also allows you to quickly create a frameset document, using nothing but the mouse. For instance, if you wanted to add a frame for menu controls at the top of your page, you'd do the following:

1. Place your mouse cursor close to the top of the document window (below the Title bar).

2. While holding down the **Option** (or **Alt**) key, drag down with the mouse. This should create a new frame in the top of your document.

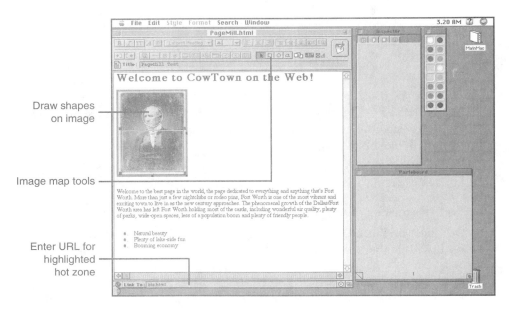

Draw shapes
on image

Image map tools

Enter URL for
highlighted
hot zone

Figure 4.2 PageMill rolls in unique tools for creating image maps.

TIP **Deleting Frames** To delete a frame, drag it back to the very edge of the document.

3. Click in the frame and the Inspector changes to frame-related options. Give the frame a name (like you would do for the NAME attribute to a <FRAME> tag) then resize it, choose **Scrollbars** or **None,** and change the margin height.

4. Now, to add a page to the frame, choose **File**, **Insert Page** from the menu. Or, you can simply begin to add the page yourself.

5. To make the main window a target, begin by clicking in the main window, then edit its frame properties. Now, highlight text in the top frame that you'd like to make a hyperlink.

6. With the text highlighted, enter an URL in the Link To: text box, hitting **Return** or **Enter** after completing the URL. Then, click the **Target** icon in the bottom-right corner of the page and choose the frame that this link should load in (see Figure 4.3).

TIP **Just Save All** You now have many options in the File menu for saving framesets, files, and other elements. Choose **File**, **Save All** from the menu if you just want to make sure everything is secure.

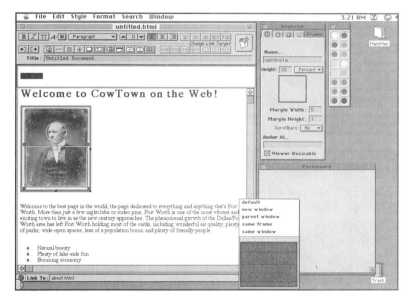

Figure 4.3 The target menu is a convenient way to point your frame links in the right direction.

PageMill's Unique Features

PageMill offers some other unique abilities to make your Web editing experience a little less painful. These include:

Edit Source Mode Choose **Edit**, **HTML Source** from the menu to not only view the raw HTML codes, but edit them directly in PageMill. It's a great way to add scripting elements or other special tags. It works for individual frames, too.

Check Spelling Place the cursor at the beginning of your document, then choose **Search**, **Check Spelling** from the menu. Like a good word processor, PageMill lets you check the spelling of your pages, including headings, lists, and other elements.

In this lesson, you learned how to use PageMill to create Web pages. In the next lesson, you'll see the special features in PageSpinner for Macintosh.

PageSpinner

In this lesson, you learn how to use PageSpinner for Macintosh to create Web pages.

What Is PageSpinner?

PageSpinner, a shareware HTML editor designed exclusively for Macintosh, may seem like an odd choice. It's neither written by one of the major browser companies, nor does it (like many other professional-level programs) sell for $100 or more. Instead, it's a $25 shareware program that may be the most advanced HTML editor to date—especially because it supports some of the very latest HTML tags in a very intelligent way.

PageSpinner isn't a WYSIWYG editor—it's only "semi-WYSIWYG," meaning it displays certain tagged text in different styles and sizes. To really get a sense of what the page looks like, though, you need to preview it in a browser.

This shouldn't stop Mac users from trying PageSpinner; check out some of its advantages:

- HTML Assistant technology walks you through creating nearly any HTML tag.
- PageSpinner extension programs can be written to support new tags. For instance, the Style Assistant allows you to create HTML style sheets for your pages.
- The Tag menu includes tags for common JavaScript constructs, Java applets, and an area for custom tags.
- AppleScript support features scripts that reformat mailed HTML form data, back up your files, or send files to the Web server.

If you've learned HTML from the other parts of this book, you'll appreciate this tagged-text approach to Web design. PageSpinner is like using a text editor for Web authoring, but with an entire HTML reference built in.

Adding Text and Images

When you first launch PageSpinner, you'll be greeted with the splash screen that forces you to wait a few seconds if you haven't registered the program. Then, a blank document appears with nothing but the main document tags: <HTML>, <HEAD>, <TITLE>, <BODY>, and so on. To begin:

1. Start by highlighting the text **Untitled** that appears between the <TITLE> tags, then edit the text by typing a new title for your document.

2. Pull down the **File** menu and select **Save** to save this document to the folder that you use to mirror your Web server. (Now when you save the document, any relative addresses are correctly created.)

3. To create a heading, select a heading tag from the Size menu (such as Heading 1), then type the text for the heading between the <H1> tags that appear.

TIP   **Deleting Tags**   Sometimes it seems that PageSpinner won't allow you to delete certain tags by highlighting them and hitting the delete key. Usually, this is because PageSpinner thinks the tag is necessary for your HTML to be correct. Double-check and make sure you aren't breaking any HTML containers or something similar. If you then decide you still want to delete, use ⌘+Delete to get rid of the tag.

4. Click outside of the header tags and you can begin typing your text. Once you've finished a paragraph, you can either select the entire block of text and hit the **Paragraph** icon in the toolbar, choose **Tags**, **Paragraph** from the menu, or hit ⌘+**Return** to insert a <P> tag.

Adding an Image

Here's how you add an image to your Web document in PageSpinner:

1. To add an image, place the cursor in the document where you want the image to appear and click the **Image** tag in the toolbar or choose **Image** from the **HTML Assistant** menu. Now the HTML Assistant changes to offer you help in creating an <IMG> tag, as shown in Figure 5.1.

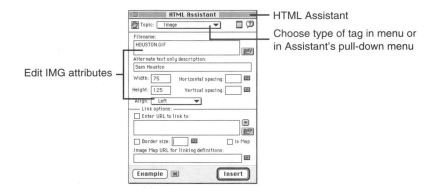

Figure 5.1 labels (left to right):
- HTML Assistant
- Choose type of tag in menu or in Assistant's pull-down menu
- Edit IMG attributes

Figure 5.1 PageSpinner gives you access to a full set of options for nearly any type of tag using the HTML Assistant.

2. Enter a filename or URL for the image (or choose it by clicking the **Open File** button).

TIP **Save Before Images** If you haven't already saved your document, you may want to do so before adding images, so PageSpinner can calculate relative paths. If you haven't saved your document, PageSpinner will warn you that paths may not work correctly.

3. You can also enter ALT text, HEIGHT, and WIDTH numbers, change the alignment and spacing, and enter an URL to create this image as a hyperlink. Notice that the Assistant uses a little "3.2" icon to let you know what elements are part of the HTML 3.2 standard.

4. When you're finished entering data for your image, click the **Insert** button.

Preview Your Work

Because PageSpinner is only semi-WYSIWYG, you'll need to preview your work often in a Web browser so you can see how things are shaping up. Here's how you preview the first time:

1. Choose **File**, **Preview** or click the **Preview** button in the toolbar.

2. In the Select Helper Applications dialog box, click the **Select Application** button.

3. Use the Open dialog box to find your Web browser. When you find the program, highlight it and click the **Open** button.

4. Click **OK** in the Select Helper Applications dialog box. Now, choose to **Preview** your document again. The document should appear in the browser you chose.

PageSpinner's Features

PageSpinner offers a number of very exciting extras for the intermediate Web author, as well as the opportunity for new authors to have access to a number of helpful features and assistants. In particular, check out these features:

Style Sheet Assistant   The Assistant is an add-on program that allows you to use the CSS style sheet definition to set many options for your page. From the **Tags** menu, choose the **Style Sheet** item, and then choose the **Style Sheet Assistant**.

Robot Tags   Place the cursor in the head of your document, then pull down the **Tags** menu, select **Robot Tags**, and choose the <META> tag you'd like to add to your page. (META tags are tags used to talk to Web robots, like those used by Web search engines. Using the "keyword" and "description" robot tag commands, you can tell Search engines what sort of site you have and how it should be described to others. META tags are discussed in greater detail in Part I, Lesson 5.)

JavaScript Examples   Again, from the **Tag** menu, choose **JavaScript**, **Example**. A dialog box appears with sample JavaScript routines that you can copy to your Web page. The Examples dialog box can be used for other features such as Netscape HTML and regular commands.

AppleScripts   Pull down the **AppleScript** menu (it looks like the AppleScript icon at the top of the page) and see what's possible using outside AppleScripts.

In this lesson, you learned how to use PageSpinner for Mac to create Web pages. In the next lesson, you'll use LView Pro to view and manipulate images.

LView Pro

In this lesson, you learn to resize images and add transparency using LView Pro.

6

Resizing with LView Pro

Another must-have program for most Windows-based Web designers is LView Pro, a shareware graphics-manipulation program. Although the program has some of the same features as Paint Shop Pro (discussed in the next lesson), LView is designed less for creating images and more for changing them from one size to another or from one file format to another.

You can download LView from **http://www.lview.com** on the Web.

To resize an image to create a thumbnail, launch Lview, then follow these steps:

1. Choose **File**, **Open**. The Open dialog box appears.
2. In the Open dialog box, find the image that you want to resize.
3. With the image in a window on the desktop, choose **Image**, **Resize**. The Resize Image dialog box appears (see Figure 6.1).
4. Now you can use the slider controls or enter a new size for your thumbnails. A good rule is somewhere around 75 pixels wide (width is the first field after "New Size:" in the dialog box). Changing the width also changes the height, in order to preserve the aspect ratio of your images.
5. When you have finished resizing, click **OK**.

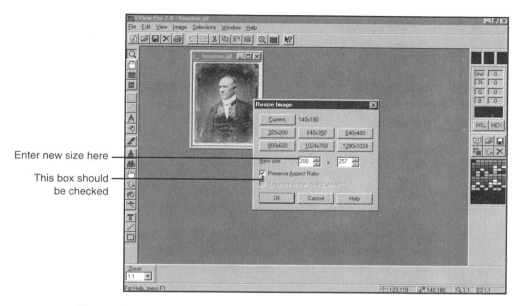

Enter new size here ———

This box should ———
be checked

Figure 6.1 Resizing graphics in LView Pro for Windows.

TIP **Thumbnail Dimensions** If you plan to offer many thumbnails on one page, it's a good idea to make them a uniform width (or height) to keep the page orderly.

When you create thumbnails, you'll probably want to maintain the *aspect ratio* of the current graphic in resizing, so that LView keeps the height and width of the new graphic at the same ratio as the original graphic, making the thumbnail smaller but similarly proportioned. Don't forget to save the new file with a slightly different name, using the appropriate file extension (.GIF or .JPG).

Aspect Ratio The percentage of an image's height to its width. If you choose to preserve aspect ratio, you can only set either the height or the width—the other value is calculated by LView so that the shape of the image is maintained.

Creating Transparent GIFs

You can also create transparent GIFs in LView Pro. To do so, follow these steps:

1. Load the program, and choose **File**, **Open** to open a graphics file.

2. If the file isn't already a .GIF image, choose **Image**, **Color Depth**, and make sure the image is palette-based.

3. Click **OK**.

4. You can now use the dropper (click the **Dropper** button shown in Figure 6.2) to select the color that should be transparent. If you click the **Mask** button before selecting the color, the image will change colors so that transparent parts are white and other parts are black.

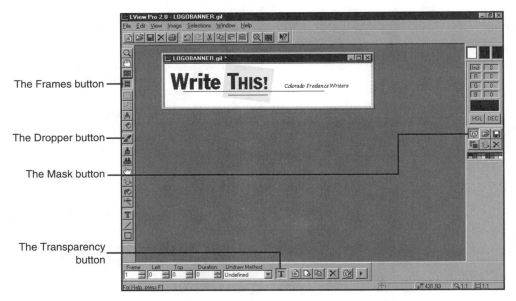

Figure 6.2 Click the Dropper to choose the transparent color.

5. Choose the **Frame** button. In the toolbar that appears at the bottom of the screen, make sure the **Transparency** button is selected.

6. Choose **File**, **Save As**, and save the graphic as a .GIF file. Click the **File Type Options** box and ensure that **GIF89a** and **Save Transparent Color Information (GIF89a Only)** are checked.

7. Click **OK** to close the File Format Options dialog box, then click **Save**. The background color will appear transparent in a Web browser's window.

In this lesson, you learned to use some of the features of LView Pro. In the next lesson, you'll learn how to use Paint Shop Pro.

Paint Shop Pro

7

In this lesson, you learn how to create and manipulate images in Paint Shop Pro for Windows.

Creating Graphics

A popular program for creating Web graphics in Windows and Windows 95 is Paint Shop Pro, which has the added advantage of being try-before-you-buy shareware. To download Paint Shop Pro, access the URL **http://www.jasc.com/ pspdl.html** with your Web browser, and find the hypermedia link for downloading the program for your particular version of Windows.

 TIP **Register Shareware** As with any shareware program, you should register Paint Shop Pro (by sending in the requested fee) if you find it useful.

To start Paint Shop Pro:

1. Paint Shop Pro arrives as a PKZip-compressed file archive, so you also need a program on your hard drive to unzip it when the download is complete. (WinZip is available from **http://www.winzip.com/**.)

2. Then install the program in Windows and start it. You should see a window like the one shown in Figure 7.1.

Simple Graphics

You can use Paint Shop Pro to create a simple graphic, such as a logo or title, for your Web pages. Using the fill-color tool, for example, allows you to select a color and "pour" it into the window, creating a background color for the rest of your graphic.

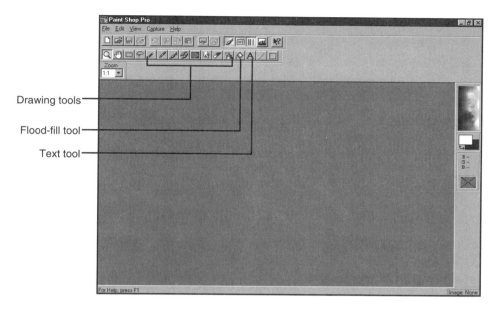

Drawing tools

Flood-fill tool

Text tool

Figure 7.1   The Paint Shop Pro interface.

Here's how you create a new image and background:

1. Choose **File**, **New** from the menu.

2. In the New Image dialog box, enter a Width and Height for your image. In the Image type menu, choose the number of colors this image will use. (The fewer the colors, the smaller the images.) Click **OK**.

3. Click the **Fill** icon and then choose a color from the color palette on the right side of the window.

 TIP   **Foreground Color**   Notice that selecting a color changes the color of the foreground indicator on your tool bar (the first of the two overlapping rectangles toward the bottom). The other rectangle represents the background color—not the color of the background you're creating, but rather the color you'd get if you used the eraser tool.

4. To apply that color to your graphic, click in the graphic window.

5. Now select the text tool, choose another color from the palette, and click the graphic window. Type your text (your company name, for example) in the dialog box; then click **OK**.

401

6. Now you should be able to drag the text around the window. When you have the text arranged correctly, right-click anywhere in the window to place the text permanently (see Figure 7.2).

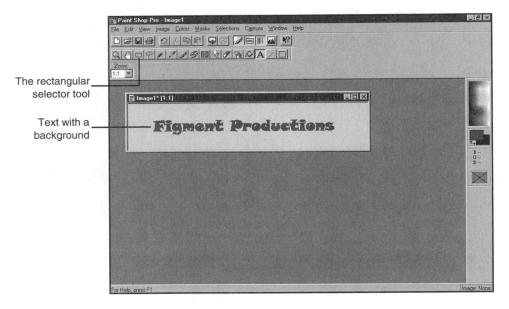

Figure 7.2   Creating a simple graphic.

Resize Image

Before you save this graphic, you should make it *physically* as small as possible so that it works well on your Web page:

1. To cut the image down a bit, select Paint Shop Pro's rectangular selector tool (shown in Figure 7.2).

2. Click somewhere near the top-left corner of the graphic (at the point you want to make the new top-left corner of your cropped image), and drag the mouse pointer to the other side (bottom right corner) of the image. When you release the mouse pointer, a thin box should appear around this slightly smaller portion of your graphic.

3. Now choose the **Image**, **Crop** command, and the graphic is cropped to that size. If everything went well, you have a smaller graphic that is just as useful for your Web site.

Save File

Your last step is to save the graphic in a file format that's useful for the Web. To do this, follow these steps:

1. Choose **File**, **Save As**.

2. In the Save As dialog box, you can select the file type from a drop-down list. Select either **GIF** or **JPEG**, type a file name, and click **Save**.

Now you've created a graphic for use on your Web page. Use the Windows Explorer to check the file size. You want the file to be somewhere around 20K— an ideal size for a Web-page graphic.

In this lesson, you learned to create a simple graphic with Paint Shop Pro. In the next lesson, you'll learn how to use Graphic Converter for Mac.

Graphic Converter

In this lesson, you learn how to use Graphic Converter to convert and edit images for your Web pages.

What Is Graphic Converter?

Sometimes called the "Poor Mac's PhotoShop," Graphic Converter does quite a bit more than its name implies. Although it's primarily a program designed to convert files between different graphic file formats (like PICT to GIF), it also has a number of built-in image editing tools as well.

With Graphic Converter, you can:

- Convert files from one graphic format to another.
- Edit files, adding shapes, text, or changing pixels.
- Resize, rotate, and crop images.

Graphic Converter can be downloaded from most Macintosh file archives on the Internet. Its Web site is **http://members.aol.com/lemkesoft** on the Web. Graphic Converter is $35 shareware.

Converting Images

Because the Mac's native picture format is PICT, there are a lot of programs and helpers that support PICT, but don't save to GIF or JPEG. In fact, some programs support other file formats as well, but don't have the programming built in to save images for the Web. (Mac's built-in screenshot keystroke, ⌘+Shift+3, saves screen images in PICT format.)

Graphic Converter is designed to make converting files simple. In fact, the program has a special interface designed especially for converting more than one image file.

Here's how to convert a single file in Graphic Converter:

1. Launch Graphic Converter, then chose **File**, **Open** from the menu (you can also drag and drop most image files onto the Graphic Converter icon).

2. Once the file is loaded, simply choose **Save As** from the **File** menu.

3. In the Save As dialog box, choose the format for this image from the **Format** pull-down menu, then choose the **Options** button to set options for that file format. When you're ready to save the converted file, click the **Save** button.

Of course, you can also use Graphic Converter to convert multiple files:

1. From the **File** menu, choose **Convert More**. The Convert More dialog box appears, as shown in Figure 8.1.

2. In the source window of the dialog box, use the pull-down menu to select the folder that contains the images you plan to convert. In the target window, use the pull-down menu to choose the folder you want the converted files saved to.

3. Select one or more files for converting. You can select more than one file by holding down the ⌘ key while clicking file names.

4. Under the target window, use the **Format** pull-down menu to select the type of file you want to convert to.

5. Click the **Convert** button.

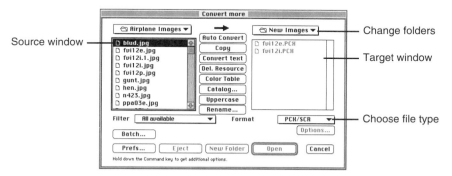

Figure 8.1   Successfully converted files appear in the target window with a new file name extension.

Image Manipulation

One of the conveniences of Graphic Converter is the fact that it's a quick, convenient, and cheap way to crop (or trim) and resize images—one of the most important steps in making images small enough for transmission over the Internet. Fortunately, the process is pretty simple.

TIP   **Information**   In the Information window that appears below the image in Graphic Converter, you can learn a lot about the image, including the images resolution (72×72 is fine for Web sites) and the amount of colors being used (the fewer, the smaller the file). You can also keep track of the image's file length and the amount of memory it takes up—both of which are signs of how long it will take to download. The smaller, the better.

To trim an image:

1. Load the image in Graphic Converter using the **File**, **Open** command.
2. In the toolbar next to the image, choose the **Selector** tool (square with broken lines).
3. On top of the image itself, drag to create a box that encloses the portion of the image you'd like to keep.
4. Choose **Edit**, **Trim Selection** from the menu. Graphic Converter trims the image so that only the selected area is part of the resulting image.

To resize an image:

1. From the **Picture** menu, choose **Size**, **Scale**.
2. In the Scale dialog box, click the option button that corresponds to the type of resizing you'd like to do (factor or actual pixels).
3. Now, click the option button next to the attribute that you'd like to change (if Proportional is selected).
4. Enter a new value for any attributes you want to change and click **OK** to resize the image.

Other Graphic Converter Features

Aside from cropping and resizing, Graphic Converter is capable of many of the same tricks that more advanced programs like Adobe PhotoShop can perform on images. If you've ever used PhotoShop, you'll probably even recognize some common interface elements, as shown in Figure 8.2.

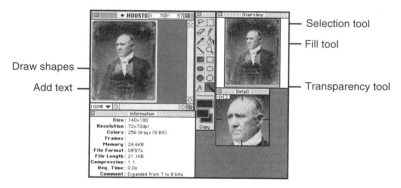

Figure 8.2 Although not quite as feature-heavy, Graphic Converter has some features in common with PhotoShop.

Other features include:

Dithering Tools The first four options on the Effects menu allow you to change the method used to dither the colors in your image.

Digital Effects The rest of the Effects menu gives options for touching up and transforming your images. Aside from standards like Gamma Correction and Sharpen Edges, Graphic Converter can also use certain PhotoShop-compatible plug-ins.

Transparency Using the special transparency tool, you can click a particular color in an image (like the background color) to turn the color transparent. This is especially popular with Web designers.

In this lesson, you learned to manipulate Web graphics using Graphic Converter. In the next lesson, you'll see how to use the GifBuilder to animate a GIF.

GifBuilder

In this lesson, you learn how to animate GIFs using GifBuilder for Macintosh.

Animating GIFs

If you're a Macintosh user, you can use an image creation or manipulation program (even Graphic Converter) to create a series of images that you'd like to animate. Using GifBuilder, you can piece together the animation frames, add delays and other features between each frame, and then save it as a GIF89a for display as an animated GIF on the Web.

To begin an animated GIF, you'll need a series of images in either GIF or PICT format that will look good as an animation (or an images sideshow) when played one after the other. If you don't already have a copy of GifBuilder, you can download it from most Mac archives, like MacWorld Software **http://www.macworld.com/software/** on the Web.

TIP **Keep It Small** Although an animated GIF tends to compress to a fairly small file, it's important to keep animated GIFs reasonably small (screen-size wise) so they don't take too long to transfer over the Internet.

With your images ready, you can begin to piece them together for animation. Here's how you add images in GifBuilder:

1. Launch GifBuilder. You'll see an empty Frames window (where individual frame images will be listed) and a blank window that represents the current state of your animated GIF.

2. To add images to your animation, choose **File**, **Add Frame**. In the Open dialog box, find the frame image you want to add and click **Open**.

3. Repeat this process for every image you want to add to the animation.

 TIP   **Drag and Drop**   GifBuilder supports drag and drop, so you can select all your frame images at once and drag them to the Frame window to add them quickly.

Animation Settings

Once you have the frame images loaded in GifBuilder, you can test the animation by choosing **Animation**, **Start** from the menu. (Choose **Animation**, **Stop** to stop the animation.) You may find that the animation takes place too quickly. If that's the case, you'll want to add a delay between each frame.

To add a delay between each frame (and slow down the display of the animation), do the following:

1. Hold down the **Shift** key while dragging in the **Frames** window to select all the frames in your animation.

2. Pull down the **Options** menu and choose **Interframe Delay**.

3. In the Interframe delay dialog box, click the option button for **/100** seconds and enter a value. Each multiple of 100 represents a second of delay (for example, 600 = 6 seconds). Figure 9.1 shows the Delay dialog box.

If you'd like one particular frame to have a different delay, you can set it for each individual frame. To set a frame's delay, double-click the **Delay** column for that particular frame in the Frame window. The same Interframe Delay dialog box appears, allowing you to enter a special value.

Other settings you might consider include:

Loop   Regardless of what's selected in the Frames window, you can select the **Options**, **Loop** menu item and choose whether the animation should loop once, indefinitely, or a certain number of times.

Transparency   Select all the frames in the Frame menu, then choose **Options**, **Transparent Background** and choose the color that should be transparent. (**Based On First Pixel** will often work.)

Background Color   Choose a background color for your animation, especially if you plan to use a transparent image (although it's not necessary). Choose **Option**, **Background Color** from the menu.

Disposal Method   If you choose transparency, you'll definitely have to change the disposal method or each frame. Choose **Options**, **Disposal Method** and the method you'd like to use.

Saving   Saving the GIF couldn't be easier. Choose **File**, **Save**, then give the file a name in the Save dialog box. No special settings or manipulations are necessary for naming your image.

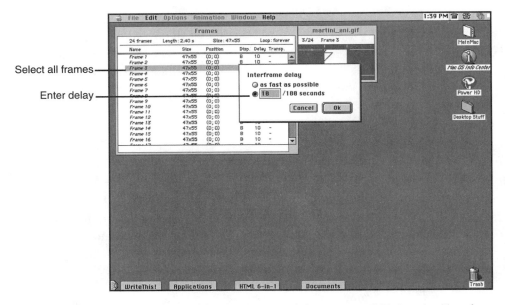

Figure 9.1   Placing a delay between each frame, even if it's hundredths of a second, makes the animation seem considerably slower.

Destroying Animation   Don't load an animated GIF in another program to manipulate it once you've created the animation. Other image manipulation programs tend to destroy the animation data, turning your animated GIF back into a regular, static image.

CAUTION

In this lesson, you learned how to build an animated GIF using GifBuilder for Macintosh.

Index

Check out Que® Books on the World Wide Web
http://www.quecorp.com

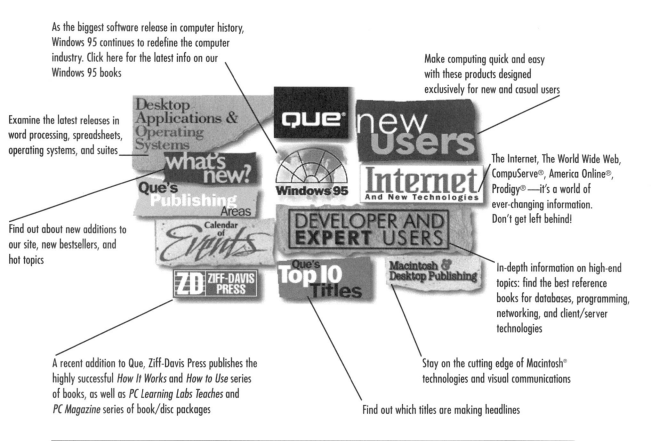

As the biggest software release in computer history, Windows 95 continues to redefine the computer industry. Click here for the latest info on our Windows 95 books

Make computing quick and easy with these products designed exclusively for new and casual users

Examine the latest releases in word processing, spreadsheets, operating systems, and suites

The Internet, The World Wide Web, CompuServe®, America Online®, Prodigy® —it's a world of ever-changing information. Don't get left behind!

Find out about new additions to our site, new bestsellers, and hot topics

In-depth information on high-end topics: find the best reference books for databases, programming, networking, and client/server technologies

A recent addition to Que, Ziff-Davis Press publishes the highly successful *How It Works* and *How to Use* series of books, as well as *PC Learning Labs Teaches* and *PC Magazine* series of book/disc packages

Stay on the cutting edge of Macintosh® technologies and visual communications

Find out which titles are making headlines

With six separate publishing groups, Que develops products for many specific market segments and areas of computer technology. Explore our Web Site and you'll find information on best-selling titles, newly published titles, upcoming products, authors, and much more.

- Stay informed on the latest industry trends and products available
- Visit our online bookstore for the latest information and editions
- Download software from Que's library of the best shareware and freeware

Complete and Return This Card
for a *FREE* Computer Book Catalog

Thank you for purchasing this book! You have purchased a superior computer book written expressly for your needs. To continue to provide the kind of up-to-date, pertinent coverage you've come to expect from us, we need to hear from you. Please take a minute to complete and return this self-addressed, postage-paid form. In return, we'll send you a free catalog of all our computer books on topics ranging from word processing to programming and the Internet.

☐   Mrs. ☐   Ms. ☐   Dr. ☐

Name (first) ☐☐☐☐☐☐☐☐☐☐☐ (M.I.) ☐   (last) ☐☐☐☐☐☐☐☐☐☐☐☐☐☐

Address ☐☐☐☐☐☐☐☐☐☐☐☐☐☐☐☐☐☐☐☐☐☐☐☐☐☐☐☐☐☐☐☐

☐☐☐☐☐☐☐☐☐☐☐☐☐☐☐☐☐☐☐☐☐☐☐☐☐☐☐☐☐☐☐☐

City ☐☐☐☐☐☐☐☐☐☐☐☐☐☐   State ☐☐   Zip ☐☐☐☐☐ ☐☐☐☐

Phone ☐☐☐ ☐☐☐ ☐☐☐☐   Fax ☐☐☐ ☐☐☐ ☐☐☐☐

Company Name ☐☐☐☐☐☐☐☐☐☐☐☐☐☐☐☐☐☐☐☐☐☐☐☐☐☐☐☐☐☐

E-mail address ☐☐☐☐☐☐☐☐☐☐☐☐☐☐☐☐☐☐☐☐☐☐☐☐☐☐☐☐☐☐

1. Please check at least three (3) influencing factors for purchasing this book.

Front or back cover information on book .... ☐
Special approach to the content .... ☐
Completeness of content .... ☐
Author's reputation .... ☐
Publisher's reputation .... ☐
Book cover design or layout .... ☐
Index or table of contents of book .... ☐
Price of book .... ☐
Special effects, graphics, illustrations .... ☐
Other (Please specify): _____ ☐

2. How did you first learn about this book?

Saw in Macmillan Computer Publishing catalog .... ☐
Recommended by store personnel .... ☐
Saw the book on bookshelf at store .... ☐
Recommended by a friend .... ☐
Received advertisement in the mail .... ☐
Saw an advertisement in: _____ ☐
Read book review in: _____ ☐
Other (Please specify): _____ ☐

3. How many computer books have you purchased in the last six months?

This book only .... ☐   3 to 5 books .... ☐
2 books .... ☐   More than 5 .... ☐

4. Where did you purchase this book?

Bookstore .... ☐
Computer Store .... ☐
Consumer Electronics Store .... ☐
Department Store .... ☐
Office Club .... ☐
Warehouse Club .... ☐
Mail Order .... ☐
Direct from Publisher .... ☐
Internet site .... ☐
Other (Please specify): _____ ☐

5. How long have you been using a computer?

☐ Less than 6 months   ☐ 1 to 3 years
☐ 6 months to a year   ☐ More than 3 years

6. What is your level of experience with personal computers and with the subject of this book?

	With PCs		With subject of book	
New	☐		....	☐
Casual	☐		....	☐
Accomplished	☐		....	☐
Expert	☐		....	☐

Source Code ISBN: 0-7897-1407-8

7. Which of the following best describes your job title?

Administrative Assistant .... ☐
Coordinator .... ☐
Manager/Supervisor .... ☐
Director .... ☐
Vice President .... ☐
President/CEO/COO .... ☐
Lawyer/Doctor/Medical Professional .... ☐
Teacher/Educator/Trainer .... ☐
Engineer/Technician .... ☐
Consultant .... ☐
Not employed/Student/Retired .... ☐
Other (Please specify): _____ ☐

8. Which of the following best describes the area of the company your job title falls under?

Accounting .... ☐
Engineering .... ☐
Manufacturing .... ☐
Operations .... ☐
Marketing .... ☐
Sales .... ☐
Other (Please specify): _____ ☐

9. What is your age?

Under 20 ....
21-29 ....
30-39 ....
40-49 ....
50-59 ....
60-over ....

10. Are you:

Male ....
Female ....

11. Which computer publications do you read regularly? (Please list)

_____
_____
_____
_____
_____
_____
_____
_____
_____
_____

Comments: _____
_____
_____

Fold here and scotch-tape to